# the Facts of My Life

## By Charlotte Rae
## and Larry Strauss

Published in the USA by:
BearManor Media
P O Box 71426
Albany, Georgia 31708
www.bearmanormedia.com

ISBN: 978-1-59393-852-9

BearManor Media, Albany, Georgia
Printed in the United States of America
Book design by Robbie Adkins, www.adkinsconsult.com

To my wonderful parents, Esther and Meyer,
who gave me everything.

# CAN YOU TELL ME HOW TO GET, HOW TO GET TO… BELLEVUE?

I was living in a nightmare come true. My older boy, Andy, was locked in the juvenile psycho ward at Bellevue because he had been deemed a "danger to himself and others." He had dislodged the bathroom sink in a sudden and unexplainable rage and thrown a heavy glass ashtray out the window, just missing the head of a maintenance man sweeping the sidewalk. I felt as unhinged as that sink Andy had pulled from the wall. I had to be back on Sesame Street in the morning delivering the mail to Oscar the Grouch and Big Bird and those bright-eyed children who would sit on my lap. They were so adorable and precocious and I was in such pain. I couldn't sleep and I didn't think I could do another scene with those beautiful children. I tried to talk myself into it: Come on, Charlotte. You're an actress. You can love them and admire and marvel at them. In truth, I envied them and their parents— for being normal and seeming happy.

I didn't know any more if Andy would ever be happy or what would become of him. All night to numb my pain and catch a few winks of sleep, I drank Four Roses or vodka and swallowed the occasional Milltown.

Somehow I slept and, in the morning, somehow, I woke up, and somehow got through the morning on Sesame Street. I never drank before or during work but probably smelled at least a little of it from the night before. I didn't want to be there. It was an honor to be part of that wonderful cast and the noble mission of the show but my son needed me and I was beginning to think I should step away from acting altogether.

As soon as the director said the words, "That's a wrap for today," I was through the exit, rushing across town to visit Andy. It was his sixteenth birthday so I stopped at a grocery store to buy a cake and his favorite cran-apple juice. I carried it all down First Avenue and up to PQ-5, Bellevue's juvenile ward. I saw Andy inside that place through the glass window of a locked door. His hands clutched his ears. A mob of teenagers formed around him. They were raging mad at Andy and he cowered from them, hitting and scratching and biting himself. I rang the doorbell and pounded on the metal door. I was terrified.

Finally, someone opened it up and I rushed inside. The cran-apple juice slipped out of my hands and smashed on the floor. I stood in the puddle of reddish liquid and chips of broken glass. I was beside myself. I felt defeated, humiliated, and still terrified for Andy. The exploding bottle distracted the boys who had been attacking Andy but they were still surrounding him and now he was even more agitated.

"Please, don't hurt my son!" I pleaded, and burst into tears.

They looked at me and one of them said, "Hey, I know you. You was on Car 54 Where are You? Sure… Sylvia Schnauser. Car 54 where are you," he sang and some of the others laughed. They kept laughing and I kept crying.

"What's a matter, Sylvia?" one asked.

"My son," I said, and then got to Andy and hugged him. He trembled in my arms.

"We ain't gonna hurt him. We was just mad 'cause he broke the TV set."

"He didn't mean it," I said and a few of the boys got down on the floor to pick up the shards of broken glass. A staff member showed up with a mop but then stood there watching the boys pick out pieces of glass.

I knelt down with them to pick up the broken glass. To me these teenage boys looked so normal, so cognizant—not like Andy.

We cleaned the floor and then I put candles on Andy's birthday cake. A staff member lit them with his Bic and we all sang Happy Birthday and everyone helped Andy blow out his candles and as we shared pieces of the cake, I told these boys, "You have a chance in life. We don't know how much of a chance Andy has—we're hoping but we just don't know." It was the first time I'd ever said that to anyone. Maybe it was the first time I'd allowed myself to think it. It wasn't easy. "Pull yourselves together," I told those young men. I suppose I had no business saying it. What did I know about why they were locked up at Bellevue—only that they seemed so much more capable than my son, so I told them, "Get it together and get out of here and move on to a better life. You have a chance."

I hugged my son again and then each of the other boys came to me for a hug, and I hugged them all too.

The young men nodded their heads. A few made pledges to me about their futures. One said he was going to be president one day. After that night they were kind to Andy and even protected him from other residents until my husband John and I were able to get him out of there.

I have often thought of those boys and how nice they were to me that afternoon and to Andy after that. I hope they did get themselves out of PQ-5. I hope they accomplished things and found love in their lives and peace, beauty and meaning beyond the walls of an institution.

# SECOND SISTER

My mother was less than a year old when her parents brought her to this country. I never learned much about why they left Russia but I have heard stories of terror and violence—pogroms that plagued the Jewish peasants and the threat of young men being drafted into the Russian Army never to return. I've been told that they lived near the border of Poland in a town called Yashehnovekeh though no town by that name exists anymore.

My mother was the baby of the family. She had six older brothers and an older sister. There had been other siblings who had died young, before Mother was born. Her older brothers had gone to America first. They'd landed on Ellis Island and took the last name of their Russian village: Ottenstein. Like many immigrants, they found New York City overcrowded and menacing. Somehow they made their way to Chicago and then Milwaukee where they eked out a living as pushcart peddlers and sent money home to the rest of the family, who eventually made the journey across Europe and across the Atlantic in steerage. My grandparents, Rose and Verke, brought the younger children (they had eleven altogether) to Milwaukee where my mother attended grammar school with Golda Meir, who grew up to become the Prime Minister of Israel.

Verke went by the name Boris and, like his older sons, became a peddler. He worked long hours in often harsh weather for pennies. In 1914 he developed what he thought was a rash on his arm. He couldn't afford to park his cart for a day and didn't want to "waste" money on a visit to the doctor. His arm turned red, then black and when he did see a doctor it was too late. He died of a blood infection when my mother was fifteen. My mother never talked about what it was like for her to lose her father but it must have been devastating. I think it made her a little extra cautious with my sisters and me when it came to our health. The slightest concern and we were off to the doctor.

Boris's sudden death sank the Ottensteins deeper into a kind of poverty they hadn't believed possible in America. So when Mother's older brother, Sam, showed a photograph of his sister to a fellow soldier, encouraging him to court her after the war, it might well have been with a slight desperation about the fate of his younger siblings—or maybe just a hunch about that young soldier's talents for business and his good character and generosity.

My father, Meyer, had come to America in 1911 with his older brothers Samuel and Abraham. Like my mother's family and millions of others they fled poverty and religious oppression. My father was only thirteen when he came across the Atlantic. He and his brothers convinced immigration officers that he was sixteen.

The brothers all went to Milwaukee and got work as car mechanics. There were no workplace safety rules back then and immigrants like Meyer Lubotsky were given risky jobs. When he refused to work on a car that was leaking gasoline fumes, he was fired. When the car he refused to work on exploded and killed another mechanic, he was re-hired—but only stayed until he could find another job. Eventually, he and his two brothers started a business selling tires. Then, just after his sixteenth birthday, based on the false age he had given at Ellis Island, he was drafted into the United States Army and sent back to Europe as a soldier in the Great War.

He was proud to serve his new country as an ambulance driver for the Army Medical Corps—and that pride never diminished. He belonged to the American Legion and one of my favorite photographs of him is one he posed for in full uniform. Often under fire during the war, he drove a motorcycle through the battlefields, transporting wounded soldiers in a sidecar. He never said much to my sisters or me about those experiences but we all figured he'd seen and heard things he spent the rest of his life trying to forget. What he did tell us all was that when Sam Ottenstein showed him a photograph of his younger sister, Esther, it was love at first sight.

My father returned from the war and began courting her. Things quickly got serious. One evening when Meyer came to call on Esther, she was asleep. Meyer asked her mother—my bubbe—if he could come in and just look at her while she was sleeping. Bubbe liked Meyer and said fine. It sounded romantic anyway—he just wanted to see her face a moment. Actually, he later admitted that what he really wanted was to make sure there would be no surprises if she became his wife—no wig, no false teeth.

A year or so later they were married in an orthodox Jewish wedding. They didn't have much money so for their honeymoon they rode a streetcar downtown and saw a movie. At the time, Meyer made his living fixing flat tires. Roadside assistance we call it now. He was just a guy with a motorcycle you sent for. Day or night he'd get on that bike and zoom out to wherever a stranded driver and his car were. Eventually he saved enough for a small storefront and opened his own tire store and for a while times were hard. He and his new wife made great sacrifices to invest in the business and build a nest egg on which they might one day raise a family.

Neither of my parents ever said much about the past—in the old country or their early struggles in America—but in their silence was a dark sadness, a profound hunger my sisters and I could sense. These were people who had gone for weeks at a time with scarcely anything to eat. They seemed always in wonder at the abundance of food in America—even during the austerity of the Great Depression—and they always savored whatever food they were blessed to have.

They lived together above Meyer Lubotsky Tires in downtown Milwaukee on 12th Street between Vliet and Galena, renting out part of the upstairs to make ends meet. The Sterns stayed for many years. Even after Lubotsky Tires became successful enough that we no longer needed the rental income, my father let them remain as tenants. By then they were our friends and nothing was more important to my father than family and friends. My father quickly became a part of my mother's family. He had a regular pinochle game with his brothers-in-law. They had nicknames for each other. Bennie Weber had dark hair so they called him Mr. Black. Morris Ottenstein, a fruit and vegetable peddler by trade, was Mr. Green. Rudolph, also a produce peddler, was Mr. Brown. My father, who had blond hair, was Mr. White.

When weather permitted they convened their game at a table under a shady tree in the park. Their wives would sit nearby and gossip and knit. Sometimes they would hear from my mother's older brother Peter Ottenstein. He was the intellectual in the family. He didn't play cards. He talked about philosophy and his passionate commitment to Zionism. My mother was also a Zionist. She'd heard the horror stories from the old country—the mistreatment of Jews by Russians and Poles—and believed the Jewish destiny ought to include a Jewish state. She belonged to the Pioneer Women. She always kept a collection box for the Jewish National Fund in our home and my father always had one on the front counter of his store.

In 1922, my parents were blessed with the arrival of their first child, my big sister Beverly. Four years later I was born. Beverly didn't think much of me—and let me know it as soon as I was old enough to understand her contempt. She became my absolute authority on pretty much everything, towering over my life with expertise and absolute confidence. I think she was a more powerful influence on me than our mother. I'm sure it was her own insecurity that made her boss me around and put me down all the time. She managed to convince me that I was hopelessly incompetent at pretty much anything worthwhile. People of our parents' generation knew little about the psychology of children. To them we were empty containers waiting to be filled. Feed us and love us and keep us warm and send us to school and teach us about God and the traditions of our ancestors, and the rest would fall into place.

Our parents were good people. They were regarded highly in their community. My father was a very generous man. He extended credit to virtually anyone who needed it or said he did. He excused debts. He trusted people and I don't think he ever regretted it. He seemed to understand the value of trust—even if it sometimes cost him a few dollars. From as far back as I can remember I loved to spend Saturdays with him in his store. It was a way to get out from under the judgmental eyes of Beverly and watch my Daddy charm his customers and run his operation. I loved crawling through the long tunnels of tires stacked on their metal racks. To this day I still get a little sentimental when I get a whiff of a new set of radials. Another smell that lingers in my memory is the smoke from my Daddy's cigars. On Sunday afternoons, after a big lunch, Daddy would lie on the couch and smoke. He'd listen to a ball game or a fight on the radio for a while, then put out his cigar and fall asleep and I'd sit there with him, drawing or just close my eyes and smell the smoke and listen to him snore. I felt peaceful. I felt safe. Those were perfect moments.

When I was four, my baby sister Miriam was born. Mimi was adorable with her dimples and Shirley Temple curls, a real life doll. We were all very excited to have a new member of the family. Of course, I would have been happier if she'd been a little less adorable and if our parents and everyone else had been a little less smitten with her. Having a baby sister helped me begin to understand why Beverly was so mean to me though it would be years before any of it would make sense.

Meanwhile, Mimi's arrival only intensified Beverly's disapproval of me—which continued for years. When she wasn't judging me she was trying to control me or my life. In high school I got asked out by a really nice guy. The night before our first date when he called the house, Beverly answered and gave him the third degree. "You better get Charlotte home early. She's never been on a date before," she told the guy. Yeah, just what I wanted him to hear from my big sister. But mostly it was just her intense disapproval which never entirely stopped until I became the star of a television series in the late 1970s and we were both middle aged. Then she would proudly claim me as her sister and actually offer people *her* autograph. She even, begrudgingly, admitted her jealousy to me. "You always had those googly eyes," she remembered. "Grown-ups would stand around and make such a fuss over all your little facial expressions." She said that one time she got so jealous she threw the lid of a tin can at another girl and sent her to the hospital. It was a stunning revelation. I guess it shouldn't have been, but I'd never imagined Beverly had paid so much attention to me or that anything I'd ever done could have made her jealous. Her confession all those years later brought us closer and it also taught me a hard lesson—I realized how much time I had wasted worrying about her opinion of me.

We were all competitive with each other and maybe we all felt somehow overlooked in the family. I still remember my Uncle Eddie (who was actually just one of my father's employees) telling my parents that I was the prettiest of the three sisters. I'll never forget it because it was the only time anyone ever said anything like that. I was pretty young and I looked up and said back to him, "Uncle Eddie, why is your nose so wide?" I wish I'd been a little more appreciative.

Over time, of course, I've realized a lot of things about my childhood and about our family. Being the middle child wasn't easy but I think it was a gift. I had so many feelings, deep feelings, and I used them as an actress.

I watched my mother struggle with migraine headaches and frustration with my father who loved all of us but had a second family—his business, and everything that went with it, including his buddies and their card games. He stayed late in the shop downstairs and organized card games with his workers. They'd drink schnapps and smoke cigars and deal and bet amidst the Firestones and Goodyears and Daytons and sometimes, to show her frustration, my mother would get in the car and burn some rubber peeling out of the driveway.

When Daddy was around, we three sisters competed fiercely for his attention. Beverly would plop down in his lap, her arm around him. Mimi would hop up on his knee and climb up on his shoulders. I couldn't ever quite figure out how to get in there. But he was my hero. I had a picture of him in his army uniform taken just after he'd returned from overseas. He was lean with blondish hair. He looked just like

Gary Cooper—at least to me he did. He was my Prince Charming. I used to dream about him all the time.

There were lots of good times. Fun times. Our mother's mother, Bobeh Ottenstein—lived with us, and other relatives were always over at the house. Chanukah was a truly joyous time, a great celebration with parents and grandparents passing out shiny silver dollars and feeling the freedom and prosperity they had earned in their new world.

On Friday nights, even in a summer heat wave, we'd have chicken soup with matzo balls, and wipe the sweat from our brows while we ate. Summer nights turned into extended family get-togethers. These were the days before air-conditioning and in the scorching heat and suffocating humidity, we'd flee our homes and take refuge at Lake Park. Late night picnics in the cool breezes that blew in off Lake Michigan rescued us from our hot sticky misery. We'd splash in the water and play games and sing songs. Daddy would, of course, bring his cards. He'd play with his brother-in-laws, except one. Uncle Sam didn't play cards. He would sit with the women and be part of their conversation. Meanwhile all the kids would fall asleep to the sound of card shuffling and gossip in English and Yiddish and sometime later, when the cool air would finally descend onto the city behind us, our parents carried us home and tucked us in, leaving us to sleep until the morning heat woke us.

It seemed my sisters and cousins and I were always traveling in a great mass. Just before my sixth birthday, my sisters and I and our cousins Jeannie and Bernard were taken to Mount Sinai Hospital on Wisconsin Ave to have our tonsils and adenoids taken out, a common medical practice back in the 1930s. Can you believe it? Even if there was nothing wrong with them! Our parents told us we'd get to eat ice cream after the surgery but it was a lie. We were all so sore we couldn't swallow anything.

Some of my cousins attended the Folkshul, the nearby Yiddish school. My parents enrolled me there too but I didn't want to go. I loved the traditions of our family, of our people, and I understood how special they were and how difficult it had been for our ancestors to preserve them for so long. But the passionate shrieking of the teacher, Chaver Melrod, frightened me. Don't get me wrong, I was proud to be Jewish, but I just didn't like that place. Now, I regret not learning Yiddish. It is such a rich language. So much great literature, like the plays of Sholem Aleichem, and you always lose something in the translation. I kind of wish my parents had made me go to that Jewish school but they never wanted to force anything on any of us.

Mother and Father wanted us to fit in, to be American, though they did want us to be aware of and maybe to carry on the Jewish traditions. Mother kept kosher and lit the Sabbath candles every Friday. For Rosh Hashanah and Yom Kippur, we dressed in our best clothes and went to temple. The music was incredibly beautiful. Our synagogue had Richard Tucker, Metropolitan Opera singers who would come from New York to be our cantors for the high holidays at Temple Beth Israel.

It was an orthodox synagogue with the mothers all upstairs and the fathers downstairs but nothing about it felt separate. There was such warmth and everyone seemed to belong to everyone, all the children nestled in our nest, so cozy with our parents and aunts, uncles, cousins, and neighbors, and that beautiful music resonating. It always made me cry with joy—which was, of course, a cue for Beverly to sneer at me and say, "There goes Charlotte, she's crying again."

But I didn't care. For me the music was a spiritual experience. It was God. Exquisite. It made Beverly and her insults seem so unimportant—at least for the moment.

Our parents, like other Russian and Polish Jews of their generation, practiced the superstitions of the old country. I remember Mother finding a small hole in my sleeve and making me take off the blouse so she could stitch it. When I asked why she couldn't just fix it while I was wearing it she said, "Oh, dear, no. I might stitch up your mind." I remember Daddy and his cronies playing cards at night in the shop. Daddy sneezed while his friend, Morris, was talking, and someone said, "*Emes genossen.*" Later, I asked what those words meant and Daddy laughed and said, "It meant I proved what Morris had just said was true. *Emes genossen*—I sneezed so it's the truth." I asked if that was really true. Daddy said it was—except if you sneeze when someone is talking about the dead. That put a hex on the sneezer. But the hex could be removed by yanking on his earlobe.

The one superstition they never explained to me was the *Kenahora*. That's the evil eye that could strike any time our parents dared to praise us. I never heard of it until many years later, not until both my parents had passed away—from a friend who also had parents from the old country. The *Kenahora* tied the tongues of millions of Jewish immigrant parents. They were proud of their children but kept it secret for their well-being. Of course, my sisters and I knew that our parents never seemed to have anything particularly good to say about anything we accomplished and sometimes it hurt like hell—like when Mother would come backstage after a performance and tell me that her seat wasn't very good and her neck hurt or there was a wrinkle in my costume and how great everyone else in the show was. It still hurts sometimes to think about it. Not just because of how lousy it felt to pour my heart out on stage and think my parents still weren't proud of me, but also now to know how proud they probably were and how crazy it was for them to be so enslaved to those fears.

Downtown Milwaukee was a diverse community, a real melting pot, and so was the Seifert Elementary School where I went from Kindergarten until we moved out of Downtown. I loved getting to know all the children who weren't Jewish. I had friends whose families were from Greece and Romania and Russia and Germany and elsewhere. In first grade, a Norwegian boy named Keith died of consumption and we all went to his funeral. At the cemetery I stood next to Thelma Patrick who was African-American and we held onto each other. I remember when she and I became friends on the school yard. She asked me, "Are you really my friend?" When I said yes, she said, "Then give me a hug." So we hugged. When FDR won the 1932 election, we hugged again. My friend Betty Boyer told everyone in our class to sing "Happy Days are Here Again." Pretty much all of us did. Betty's father owned the neighborhood filling station down the street from my father's store and had an FDR banner strung across the awning above his pumps. My parents and everyone we knew had supported FDR and now everyone believed he would make things better. And he did.

I felt the same kind of optimism for myself, realizing that not everyone looked down on me the way my big sister did. Maybe I wasn't such an idiot after all. The four year gap that separated Beverly and me had made me vulnerable to her influence and her little cruelties but as we got older those four years gave me a little breathing room. Still, the inferiority she instilled in me never entirely receded. In my most frightened moments I always seemed to hear her voice assuring me that I would fail, that I wasn't up to snuff.

But having Beverly also helped me to always strive to be my best, especially when it came to the performing arts. Beverly and I took tap dancing and acrobatics at Gelman's Dance School in downtown

Milwaukee. Every Tuesday and Saturday, Mother would bring us there and then sit watching us from a cushioned seat along the wall. Sometimes I'd hear one of the other mothers telling Mom how talented they thought Beverly and I were. They'd say something like, "Mine is like a lump on a log! No umph! Your girls have umph!" One time Beverly and I got to dance together. We were a Dutch boy and girl. Bev was taller so she was the boy and I was the girl and at the end I got to slap her. That was my favorite part.

Our parents not only bought us dance lessons. They made sure we had piano lessons as well. We had great music teachers, passionate, knowledgeable, patient, and inspiring.

Mimi started piano when she was only six years old and took right to it. Miss Mazur was her teacher. Beverly's too. Miss Mazur also taught our cousins—Marcella, Nanette, Louis, Bernadine, and Austin. I studied with her for a while but I didn't want to play classical music. I think a lot of parents would have said too bad, you can't always get what you want, but Mother never said that when it came to the performing arts. She wanted us to love what we did and thrive in it. She took me to the Schaum School of Music where they taught me how to play popular music.

Father's business thrived despite the most severe economic hard times. He had always been fair to his customers—never once overcharged, even when he could have gotten away with it, so his customers were loyal and he could still make money when people didn't have much. He was also loyal and fair to his workers. He paid them well and they worked hard for him. Sometimes I felt so sorry for them, though, especially in the summer when their shirts were soaked through with perspiration. I'd go down to our cellar where we seemed to have an endless supply of Coke and Pepsi—"pop" as we called it—in the ice box. I'd carry up as many as I could and toss them to the workers.

Business was so good that Daddy even expanded the business and started selling appliances, electric refrigerators and freezers. Household freezers were a new thing and he had a hunch they would be popular and, of course, he was right. He managed to keep all his employees working and kept all of us well fed—overfed, actually—and even had enough money to buy us all a piano and fill our apartment with music.

With the store's expansion came our saddest days as workers dug up the grass and flowers and even the cherry tree behind the shop and cemented it over to make it easier and faster to roll the tires from the racks to the installation area to keep up with demand. The blossoms on that cherry tree had marked springtime for us every year. Behind those flower beds my sisters and friends and I had played hide-and-seek and had been "safe" in a game of tag. We'd played doctor in the back of the curtain of hedges.

Still, there were fun times ahead—and soon our outdoor interests took a backseat to our performing aspirations. We were the three musical sisters. Beverly was the opera singer. The diva. Mimi was the piano prodigy—it wasn't until she got older that she started singing and let the world hear her beautiful voice. I sang the popular songs of the day and my family and friends in the neighborhood labeled me the blues singer. I didn't like that label. I was a performer and wanted to sing everything. When one of my father's friends from the B'nai Brith asked me to perform at one of their meetings, I agreed without hesitation. I chose Cole Porter's "My Heart Belongs to Daddy." The lyrics, of course, are meant to be ironic—a girl's tribute to her sugar daddy—but I rendered them as a sincere statement to my Daddy and poured my heart out to him.

I don't know if he didn't get my interpretation and was embarrassed, or if he was worried that he would show favoritism toward me and hurt his other daughters, or if it was fear of the *Kenahora*, but he tensed as I sang it, he seemed unable to open up to my public affection for him. When I finished the song, I hugged him and he barely hugged me back. It hurt—but it shouldn't have surprised me. Neither of our parents were very affectionate with any of us. Neither of them had received much affection growing up. I used to notice the parents of my friend, Marilyn Clark, who lived across the alley from us. They'd kiss and hug every morning before Mr. Clark went off to work and Marilyn got a big hug from her father—and from her mother too. One morning I told my mother and father about the Clarks and how affectionate they were and I told them they needed to do the same thing. They did—they put their arms around each other and kissed—but it didn't become a regular thing. It just wasn't their nature.

Some years later, when our parents got separate beds, I cried. I had read in the Reader's Digest that getting separate beds was the first step toward divorce. I don't know what evidence the Reader's Digest had based that upon but my parents defied it.

My first experience under the hot lights came early—I couldn't have been more than six years old. Our family was watching a Vaudeville show at the Riverside Theater when singer Ted Lewis asked for a volunteer from the audience, Beverly pushed me out of my seat and toward the stage. Lewis saw me and pulled me up onto his lap.

He sang, "Me and My Shadow" and got me to sing with him. From the audience he had looked unassuming and funny. But up close, he was a horrifying sight—his face was caked in white powder with sweat filling the cracks. His hair glistened black with shoe polish. The spotlights hurt my eyes. The heat and odor of his body almost made me faint. I didn't think I could keep singing and smiling with him but something in that moment, the electricity of being on stage and having all those eyes on me, kept me going.

But I didn't go home thinking that's what I want to do with the rest of my life. I wasn't even thinking about the rest of my life. Just enjoying life as the lucky child of hard-working parents eager to give my sisters and me all the things they'd never had.

In 1936, we moved to a house in the suburb of Shorewood—4431 North Murray Avenue. Daddy needed a larger office and wanted to convert our apartment for that purpose. We were thrilled to get out of those blistering summers in downtown Milwaukee and looked forward to the cool breeze from the lake just a few blocks away from our new house.

We rented for a few years until Daddy had saved enough money for a down payment. The house cost $12,000. That was no small sum in those days, but Daddy was still doing well despite the depression and Mr. Baum counted the rent money we'd paid for two years toward the down payment. Imagine that. You don't see too many home sellers offer that kind of arrangement these days!

Shorewood was a peaceful community on Lake Michigan just outside Milwaukee. Our new house was on a quiet street and I'm sure Mother and Father thought it would be a better place for my sisters and me to grow up. Maybe it was, but I was sad to leave our apartment, our neighbors, the kids and their parents in our vibrant community where we'd lived. I would miss the diversity of our old neighborhood until, after college, I found it again in New York City (and even though I haven't lived there full-time for more than thirty years, NYC is my real home).

Sadly, my sisters and I said goodbye to all of our friends. We might see them again—Daddy's store would still be where it had always been and we still sometimes spent Saturdays there with him—but we knew things would never be the same. Still, it was an exciting time—a new house, new friends, and a new school to look forward to.

I remember packing my things up in boxes and a suitcase, deciding what to bring—and realizing this was a chance to reinvent myself and maybe get out from under Beverly's scrutiny and judgment and stop feeling like a jerk. I was a blues singer, a jokester, an Anglophile, a young woman of mystery (at ten years old, mind you). I had secretly seen two people making love, or starting to, through the window of an apartment across the alley. A waitress I knew from the corner delicatessen appeared in a man's apartment. She held two bags of food and set them down on a table. The man was in his pajamas. He paid her for the food and then as she reached for the door to leave he put his hand on her shoulder. She stopped in the doorway and for a moment they seemed like statues. Light from a car on the street shone on the window and in the glare I lost track of them. When the view was clear again they were kissing and he was starting to take off her blouse. I was so excited and terrified and thrilled and watched, spellbound, as the man removed the blouse and then her large white pale breasts fell out of her brassiere. Oh, this was SO exciting! Then some children somewhere in the alley made noise below and the man went to his window and looked out. I hid behind the wall of our living room so he wouldn't see me and when I peeked back out he had pulled the shade. I couldn't even see their shadows and was left to try to imagine what they were doing. I'd got to sleep that night imagining I was the woman who had delivered that corned beef sandwich (or whatever it was) and got seduced by that man.

I told all my new friends about it when I hosted my first slumber party at our new house in Shorewood. We were talking about sexual intercourse and what it was and what we knew about it—which wasn't very much. We ended up talking about how our parents must have done it with each other—at least once!—and how unbelievable the idea of that was.

The schools were really good in Shorewood and I know that was very important to our parents. I never asked either of them but I'm guessing that they'd heard about the schools there and that was a big reason why they moved us there. We still lived close enough to school to walk each day, and Beverly quickly figured out the route that would take us past the grocery store on the way to school and Heineman's Bakery on the way home.

At the grocery store you could get candy bars—Baby Ruth, Mounds, Hershey's milk chocolate, whatever—three for a dime! So that's what Beverly and I did on the way to school. And on the way home we'd stop at Heineman's Bakery and get some sweet rolls (in NY they call them Danish) and we'd eat them on the way home.

One time, some years later—after Beverly had graduated high school and gone to a conservatory in Cincinnati—I walked up our driveway still finishing a Heineman's sweet roll. I was coming home for lunch and Mother leaned out of the upstairs window and caught me wiping the crumbs on my chin before I walked in. She came downstairs and gave me a smack across my sugar-powdered face. Mother cooked lunch for us every day. She didn't appreciate me spoiling my appetite.

Mother didn't hit us a lot but she did it enough that sometimes while I was eating lunch, I would duck suddenly thinking maybe she was about to crack me one across the face. Mother was a perfectionist. I think she worried about us. Little things. I felt sorry for her. She didn't seem to be able to relax. One time while we were having lunch she said, "Why do you move your face so much? You always have such expressions on your face." I was annoyed and a little hurt and said, "You want me to be like Heddy Lamar who never moves a muscle in her face? I guess she'll never get wrinkles. I guess that's what you want me to be." And then I did it. Froze my face. Didn't move a muscle. Mother laughed. She was a perfectionist but she had a sense of humor about it.

She was a lovely lady. Stunningly beautiful—at least to me—and always very well put together. I don't think she'd ever received much nurturing herself. I often felt like she needed me to show her love and affection and nurturing and I always tried to. I think we all needed a little more TLC but no one really knew how to ask for it.

I think we all sought emotional refuge in performing—Bev and Mimi and I performing, Mother watching us with her silent pride. I liked to sing show tunes from the great American songbook of Cole Porter, Irving Berlin, Gershwin, Rogers and Hart, Jerome Kern, and Johnnie Mercer. Mimi would accompany me on those tunes and then she'd play while Beverly sang something from Puccini or Verdi. Bev had a brilliant voice. Absolutely beautiful and technically astounding. Truly exciting. And powerful. She could break crystal with a high note.

I loved being one of the sisters. I never felt the need to stand out. Until one night something changed. I was baby-sitting for our neighbors and found myself singing their young children to sleep on the living room couch. Mr. and Mrs. Paulson returned home before I finished "Blue Moon" and applauded after the last note. I was stunned. They said they couldn't believe how beautiful my voice was, that I sounded like a singer on the radio or on a record. Mrs. Paulson gave me an extra dime (quite a sum in those days) and said it was for my terrific voice and for giving them a show. That dime was worth much more than ten cents. Somehow the small coin made my whole life seem worthwhile. Suddenly, I thought, this is my future—become famous and people won't notice how inferior I really am. Hide it all behind my talent!

I didn't tell Beverly or my parents about it but I kept that little dime as a reminder of who I was and who I could, one day, be. I had it in my pocket the night I snuck out of the house and entered a talent contest at the Riverside Theater. I wore a navy blue dress with a white sailor collar and sang, "As Time Goes By" and I wasn't crazy about what the accompanist was doing on the piano but I could see on the faces in the audience that I was doing something right with that song, that the audience and I were feeling something together. They were really listening. I felt so comfortable. I felt at home. The spot-light was on me and I could feel the warm approval of the audience. I loved it.

I thought I had a good chance to win but then, right after me, a man hobbled out on stage with crutches, tossed them aside and stood on his hands, and with wooden blocks tap-danced with his hands while his legs and their metal braces dangled above him. His shirt rode up and everyone could see his emaciated torso. He won, poor darling, by a landslide.

The next time I went to get my teeth cleaned the dental hygienist told me she had seen my performance. "You were very good," she said, rinsing off my molars, then whispered, "but your slip was showing."

# GEOMETRY AND BOURBON

I wasn't the only member of our family who found a new identity in the suburbs. My mother, who was born in a Russian shtetl and raised in Milwaukee by Orthodox Jews from the old country, found herself a new persona in the suburbs. She joined the Shorewood High School Opportunity School—for parental involvement and adult education. She studied ceramics and joined the mixed chorus. Surrounded by mostly gentile women (and a few men) she assumed the speech and gestures of her new companions. It was shocking—to see my mother suppressing her usual Yiddish curses for the sake of "Golly gee," and such.

I used to see them at my school sometimes, my mother and her new chums. They barely moved their mouths when they spoke, tight lips and that lilting upper-midwest twang. Years later, in NY, my mother and her cultural schizophrenia became part of my comedy act. I invented a fictitious garden club that Mother belonged to with "Gert" standing before the rest of the garden club ladies, her hands clasped together while she reported on her recent trip to France. "France was just lovely. Like a city a thousand miles away. The natives there are very very colorful. They all speaks French—the children too… From there it was on to Italy. Lots of things to see in Italy. They've got that leaning tower of Pisa. Of course Jim took a picture at an angle so the tower appears to be standing straight. Looks good as new. In closing, Gert said she wouldn't leave me go if I didn't sing a little song I learned while I was in Germany. The German Translation into English is by F. Von Holstein. English version is by Henry G. Chapman. Then I'd sing Ich Liebe dich (Ick-lee-ba-dick, I pronounced it), German for 'I love you.' I sang it with that Midwest garden club lady twang, and said, 'Then we all took a boat and came home…' Next up was the church-singing contralto who sang almost mooing like a cow and clucking like a chicken. I got that character partly from being part of the chorus at our synagogue. I sang every Saturday morning until I was in high school. One time it was so hot in the temple that my ears started to ring and I fainted."

I finished grammar school at Lake Bluff School with wonderful teachers who made my transition from the Seifert School easy. I sang in the 5th grade chorus, and in the Snow White song, "Hi Ho," was asked by Miss Knight to take a solo. I refused vehemently out of blind fear. Funny that I could get up in front of a theater full of strangers but if I could see the audience and if they were people who knew me, it was so overwhelming. Miss Knight didn't push.

That choir was a rambunctious group though probably nothing by today's standards. The naughtiest remark I remember any of us making was when David Davidoff somehow made a pun out of "menstruate" and the sewing term "mend straight." Everyone blushed and we all laughed our heads off.

When I think back on those years they sometimes seem agonizingly long and at the same time blindingly short, my childhood starting to slip away when, at nine-and-a-half years old, I got my first period. It happened while I was home sick with the mumps. Mother seemed as unprepared for it as I was. When I showed her the stain and described to her what I was feeling she uttered long and sadly, "Oy!" I thought that I had contracted a fatal illness. "Now, you're a woman," she said. "I'd hoped it wouldn't happen so soon." She told me that when she had gotten her period her mother had slapped her—a superstition. An older niece, Beatrice, who was a nurse, was informed about my milestone (*mill*stone, as it was treated) and she brought me a pamphlet about the pollination of flowers. Stamens and pistols.

Well into my teens I still wasn't entirely comfortable in my body— or anywhere else. There were moments when I was having the time of my life and other moments when I felt utterly lost and alone. For months at a time I craved solitude—the total escape from the world's observations and judgments. I'd stay home on Saturday night for a few fleeting hours alone in the house.

One Saturday night, when I was fourteen, I wandered down to the rec room Daddy had built in the basement. He and some of his workers had laid down asphalt tiles and put together a ping pong table and a portable bar, a plain old thing that held my father's schnapps and all the rest of our liquor. Couple of bar stools and next to them a small card table with four folding chairs around it.

I sat on a folding chair and read the Milwaukee Journal and listened to a record on the Victrola which sat on a wooden shelf mounted to the wall. I forget what the record was. Probably "Deep Purple." Or maybe it was "Stardust." I pulled the Green Sheet out of the paper. That was all I was really interested in. It was all about Judy Garland and Deanna Durben and what wonderful lives they had. I started feeling sorry for myself. Drama queen—that would be me soaking up all the gossip about Judy and Deanna, girls my age basking in the brilliant spotlight of stardom while I sat there in the dim glow of a lamp that leaned slightly, its bulb humming and whining and every now and then flickering. Judy and Diana seemed so happy in their glamorous lives. The more I read the worse I felt but I couldn't stop reading. I was dying to know every detail, and desperately impatient with my own sorry life. I thought about Judy Garland at the opening of her latest movie and got up and walked to the bar. I thought about what she was drinking—a glass of milk, maybe, or a ginger ale. I was feeling so unfulfilled and depressed with my life, I pulled a bottle of bourbon from under the bar and poured it into a tumbler and drank it. I did it almost in one long motion—the pull, the pour, the sudden sip. It was horrible. Like fire going down my throat. Then my whole body felt warm, a lush cozy comfort. I took another shot. It went down easier and I collapsed on the folding chair with that feeling. By the time my parents came home, I was drunk. The warmth had worn off and they found me crying over the Green Sheet, unable to endure the misery of not being Judy Garland.

If my parents were upset with my behavior, they didn't show it. Daddy put away the bourbon and Mother straightened the room, then Daddy helped me to my room and put me in bed. The next morning, no one said a word about my being drunk. And no one ever did. I guess they could have scolded me or punished me but I really don't think that's what I needed and maybe they understood that. I don't know what I needed really. A little perspective on my life maybe. What I didn't need was to get yelled at. My parents were very understanding and I guess sometimes a little indulgent. Like when my Mom drove me all the way to Madison Wisconsin to an endocrinologist who specialized in growth hormone therapy. I really really wanted to be taller. Even just an inch or two would have made such a difference. I was such a shrimp with my short legs. But the doctor told us that my bones had already fused and that nothing could be done. Perhaps if I'd come there a few years before. Would my life really have been different? Would it really have been better? I doubt it. And who knows what the side-effects might have been.

During the war, I became Anglophile. I wore Oxfords with flaps and loved all the British movies with John Mills and Charles Laughton. Mother bought me a beautiful sea-foam green Worumbo coat. I don't even know if it was from England but to me it was as English as anything. I couldn't get over the fact that my mother spent fifty dollars on that coat. For me! I was overwhelmed that she thought I was worth it.

My interest in all things English was surpassed only by my passion for the theater. It was the very air I breathed. Every week I'd wait for the latest issue of *Theatre Arts* magazine to come in the mail. I read about what was happening on Broadway and in theaters across the country and studied the ads for all the playhouses and theater schools and felt like I was part of something grand and wonderful. Those glossy pages were, for me, a religious text. The local theaters of Milwaukee were my church—The Davidson, The Pabst.

I went to work in my father's store doing accounts receivable and filing and answering the phones, and saved my money so that I could go see Helen Hayes and Maurice Evans in *Twelfth Night* and a matinee of Gertrude Lawrence in *Skylark*. Toward the end of the first act of Skylark, someone on stage called someone else a bitch and all the blue haired ladies in the audience blushed and went, "Oooooo!" and covered their mouths.

I saw *The Philadelphia Story* with Kate Hepburn and Shirley Booth. I saw Ethel Barrymore in *The Corn is Green* and Ethel Waters in *Mamba's Daughters* and Canada Lee in *Native Son*.

There seemed to be no show one couldn't see in Milwaukee—or at least Chicago. Stars loved to tour in those days. They'd get their own private car on the train. Luncheons and teas were held in their honor at every stop. Lots of special attention—and who wouldn't love that? And they were all—or at least the ones I got to say hello to—exceedingly gracious.

The more I saw those great shows, the more I wanted to be a serious actress, though I still loved to sing. Beverly and I harmonized together at home with Mimi accompanying on the piano. Bev and I were pretty competitive. She'd hit the high note and then I'd try to top her and then she'd top me. But I was really very proud of her. We were all proud of our diva (though our parents, of course, never showed it, *Kenahora!*).

Beverly finished high school and went off to the Cincinnati School of Music with renowned vocal coach, Professor Korst.

A year later Professor Korst moved to New York and Beverly followed him there. She continued her opera vocal studies and also took up acting at Julliard. I envied her and used to dream about being in the fantastic glare of New York City. I was more than a little star struck. My friend Margie and I were autograph hounds. We'd go downtown and wait outside the stage door of the Riverside Theater with our autograph books, during rehearsals, hoping someone important would step out for a smoke or to go get lunch. Our first afternoon, we got an autograph from Benny Goodman's singer, Martha Tilton. She signed her name high up on the page. Then Benny Goodman himself came out and—I guess he felt the need to maintain top billing—found a way to sign even higher than she had. And then so many other great performers signed on other afternoons—too many to remember.

One I will always remember was Red Skelton. I was standing inside the stage door on a cold day during one of the Vaudeville shows at the Riverside. I saw him hurrying from the wing toward the metal spiral staircase that led to the dressing rooms. I was too shy to say anything but he noticed me from the top of the stairs, and yelled down, "Hey, little girl, you want an autograph?" I nodded my head and he came all the way back down to sign my book. It was a small gesture that loomed so large in the eyes of a star-struck teenage girl—a lesson for me about graciousness and the idea that appreciation between a star and a fan can go both ways. Years later—1965, to be exact—I was touring in the musical *Pickwick* (an adaptation of Dickens' *The Pickwick Papers*) and happened to see Red on the sidewalk in San Francisco. By then we were peers in show business but I let him know how much I appreciated his kindness toward me all those years ago.

Shorewood High School had a terrific theater department and I took full advantage of it, acting in plays every year. More than that, Shorewood prepared me with a quality education in beautiful surroundings. It looked like a college and the teachers were very dedicated—though not very well paid. My science teacher drove a cab at night to make ends meet for his family. My social studies teacher, Ms. Bubeck, brought in an orange one day and asked us if we'd rather pay twice as much for that orange if it meant that the people who picked our fruit, the men, women, and children who had to stoop in the fields from dawn till dusk, could be paid a decent wage and live in reasonable conditions. She inspired me to write a research paper about the Conservation Corps and other youth volunteer organizations and all that they were accomplishing and she made me rethink many of my assumptions about the world and about the way things ought to be. One night at dinner I told my father that I sided with Ethiopia in its war against colonial Italy. My father thought I'd become a Communist. Years later, when I decided to leave the Facts of Life, the writers and I discussed the story line to explain Mrs. Garrett's departure from the show and I asked if she could leave to join the Peace Corps. They wanted me to marry a doctor. We compromised and she married a doctor who was going to Africa with the Peace Corps.

The summer after my freshman year of high school I apprenticed with the Port Players in Shorewood. It cost $150 and I had to work in my father's office filing and organizing the accounts receivable. I loved putting in those hours at the tire store, working for quirky office manager, Mr. Goerkie. He was so funny. Reminded me of Hardy from Laurel and Hardy. Daddy still kept sodas in an ice box in the cellar so I could still toss a few to the workers in the hot sun.

As for the internship, I took classes in makeup and acting technique from Hazel Strayer. I worked with some of the best young actors and actresses in the region, including June Wetzel, who came all the way from Dayton, Ohio. She later changed her name to June Dayton and had a successful career on Broadway and television, acting in everything from *The Green Ivy* and *Lovely Me* to *Gunsmoke* and *The Streets of San Francisco*. We had a lot of fun together doing play readings and breaking down scenes and playing small parts in the Port Players' productions. I played a corpse in one show, a chamber maid in another. The other teachers were actor/director Morton DaCosta who went on to direct The Music Man on Broadway, and Eileen Heckart who starred on Broadway in *Picnic, The Dark at the Top of the Stairs*, and *Butterflies are Free*. She also had a long and very successful film and television career.

I was so thrilled to be an apprentice with all those wonderful people. Jim McKenzie who ended up running the famous Westport Playhouse. Jean Dixon, a white-haired character lady who did dozens of films. Morton DaCosta, a really really good director. I had a crush on one of the young actors. Everyone said the guy was a "homosexual" but I didn't even understand what that meant. One afternoon I ended up cuing one of the actresses in the company. I wish I could remember her name. She had a lot of lines to learn and she was having trouble with one scene and she got frustrated with herself and said, "Oh, shit." I couldn't believe it. I'd never heard a woman say that kind of thing. It just wasn't done in the world in which I'd lived and it actually took my breath away. I just couldn't believe it. This lovely petite young lady saying *that* word. Funny now to recall how shocked—and appalled—I was at her profanity. Of course, I've done it myself many many times—often for the same reason. I remember the first time I ever said it on-stage, years later, in the first play of the *Morning, Noon, and Night* one-act trilogy, I played a black woman who found magic pills and turned the skin of her and her family white. At one point I affectionately told my husband, "I love you, you li'l shit."

During my sophomore year in high school I joined the North Shore Children's Theater. I didn't have a car yet but my friend Hank McKin-sey lived nearby and would pick me up. We both had big dreams and weren't shy about discussing them. If, however, the conversation got at all personal, I became torturously shy. Hank was very good looking and I was sure he would be a movie star and I wouldn't have minded being his leading lady. A few years later he changed his name to Jeffrey Hunter and went out to Hollywood. He played alongside John Wayne in *The Searchers* and played Jesus in *King of Kings*. He died too young, in 1969, after a very successful film career.

The children's theater was a great experience. It taught us all how to work fast. We put plays together in a matter of weeks and everyone played a variety of roles. I still remember the rehearsal in which I got screamed at by one of our directors for moving on someone else's line and learned the most important actor's lesson: No matter who you are, never upstage another actor. Your job is to serve the play by serving your character, period! Sacrificing either of those for the sake of an individual performance is a sell-out. It still shocks me when I see an actor try something like that. They'll come up with some clever little piece of business right in the middle of another actor's most important speech and then act surprised if someone tells them to knock it off.

Doing all those plays, one after the other, also helped me get over my stage-fright—well, actually, it helped me get used to it. I was always more than slightly terrified before a performance (still am!) One time, during a Shorewood High School play, my friend Gwendolyn Montz insisted that I relax. She said, "You always get so nervous and then everything always ends up just fine." It's been nearly seventy years since she said that and I still remember it every time I'm about to perform. It doesn't really help me with my butterflies but I remember it anyway.

When my friends and I weren't busy rehearsing for our next play we loved to go to the movies. We saw *The Little Foxes* and *The Maltese Falcon* and *Sullivan's Travels* by Preston Sturges, which showed us all how the movies could give laughter and fulfillment to ordinary people struggling in hard times. When *Higher and Higher* opened we all read about how girls were swooning and fainting over its young star, Frank Sinatra. He was just a skinny little guy then but the press agents did a great sales job and had us all hysterical for him. I didn't want to be left out so when he came on screen I concentrated really hard and started breathing a little extra and went, "Oooo! Oh, my!" I worked myself up into what I thought was a swoon.

On some weekends during high school I performed on local NBC radio affiliate WTMJ. They had a public service program that raised thousands of dollars for Milwaukee's Community Fund by performing skits and plays to raise public awareness about the challenges people were facing as the depression dragged on. I had a good ear for accents and they were always looking for someone to portray the members of our city's many immigrant groups. I played a Viennese seamstress, a Russian mother, and a Polish widow.

During my junior year of high school, at an audition for a community theater, I met a girl named Mary Widrig who told me about a theater camp at Northwestern University. She had studied acting and directing and raved about it. I applied and got in and she was right—it was a great experience. I got to know young people from all over the region who shared my passion for theater and also started to realize how many really talented people there were. Our student theater group was called Cherubs and we built sets and did scene work and mounted productions: *Cherry Orchard*, *Once in a Lifetime*, *Arms and the Man*, *Measure for Measure*. I returned home with an even greater enthusiasm for acting.

By the end of that summer I had decided where I wanted to go to college. The University of Wisconsin would have given me—and my hard-working father—a virtually free education. But my summer at Northwestern had convinced me that I wanted to go there. I felt a little guilty for wanting my parents to spend all that money but I knew it was worth it and was willing to assert myself. Beverly had always managed to get what she wanted and needed. I sent in my application to Northwestern University and prayed to God they would take me and then set out to overcome what would be my greatest obstacle to a college education: geometry.

Beverly had flunked that class her senior year of high school and if she couldn't succeed at something how could I? My teacher, Mrs. Miller, was a tall woman with icy blue eyes and steel gray hair. Other students were afraid of her but I think that I was so pitiful with my math-phobia and my terror that her heart seemed to melt. She tried so hard to explain it all to me that I felt bad when things still didn't make sense and pretended that I did understand so she wouldn't think she was wasting her time on me.

I did admit to my parents that I was lost and they found me a tutor. My cousin David was a whiz at math. Twice a week he'd come over to our house and try to feel me up while he showed me how to measure angles and prove congruent triangles. He didn't grope me or do anything overt but he always managed to rub against some part of my body while I tried to pay attention to what he was saying. It was disgusting and I loathed it but I was so desperate to go to Northwestern—and David was otherwise a really good tutor—that I put up with the abuse.

Passing geometry became an overwhelming preoccupation—I believed that my entire future depended on it, and maybe it did. Still, I managed to accomplish some other things during that senior year. I wrote the best paper of my school career—a paper I was more proud of than any stage performance. The paper was about ways our country could help those less fortunate throughout the world. I researched such efforts and the difference they were making in Africa and elsewhere. I don't have many regrets about my life and the choices I've made but sometimes I do wish I'd devoted at least a few years to that work.

I wound up with a D in geometry—a minor miracle, given my confusion and complete lack of confidence—and I was elated. I mean I was so thrilled, so relieved. Just to pass! It might seem strange to be celebrating a D but I really had thought I was doomed and now it was as if I'd gotten a new lease on life. That D was good enough for admission to Northwestern. Still, because the university had a Jewish quota, I had to take an entrance exam. Fortunately, I passed.

# LUBOTSKY AND LYNDE

Northwestern University was only one-hundred miles from home but for me it was another world. Saying goodbye to my parents and my little sister, I downplayed the giant step I was taking but I knew—I hoped anyway—that I was never going back. I loved my family but for years already I'd been living with the pent up longings to be on stage, to be where the action is.

The freshman dorm at Northwestern was a melting pot, a global community. At least that's how it seemed to me after four years in the suburbs. I think most of us were Midwesterners but one of my roommates had come all the way from Atlanta. Her name was Lorraine and she was Jewish. I wondered if they had put us together for that reason or whether our common heritage was coincidence.

I think that question was answered when we encountered a girl from down the hall. Donna was from Kentucky and couldn't get over the fact that she might have encountered two actual Jews! "Hot damn," she said. "You're a Jew? You ain't just pullin' my leg?"

Lorraine stared back at her. "Yes," she replied. "Jewish and proud of it."

I didn't think Donna meant anything malicious by it. She seemed just genuinely flustered to be encountering such exotic people. I can only imagine what crazy notions she might have had about us. I tried to assure her that we were pretty much like everyone else.

One group of people not well-represented at the Northwestern School of Speech was African-Americans. There was one. His name was Bill Branch and he was one of the best orators of our class. He was also a patient and tolerant man. He had to be. College President Snyder's favorite song was "Shortnin' Bread." I once found myself on a stage performing it for President Snyder to his absolute delight—and my delight at pleasing the head of the school, until I saw Bill Branch among the sea of white faces watching and listening. Bill was stone-faced—and

I was mortified. I promised myself that from then on I would think deeply about implications of anything before performing it. Looking back I kind of wished I stopped mid-song to make a statement and to make amends with Billy, but I was young and lacked the courage of my convictions.

Mother was relieved that I had a Jewish roommate. I think she assumed my other roommate, Dorthy "Dottie" Davison was also Jewish. She probably thought her name was DAVIDson. Funny how important something like that was to parents of my parents' generation. Anyway, Dottie wasn't Jewish and Mother was very upset about that but what could Mother do? I certainly didn't care—I loved Dottie; we became friends for life—and anyway I had real things to worry about. Like whether I might crush a finger in my stagecraft class.

All the freshmen were required to take stagecraft before we could study acting, so we all swung our hammers and stroked our paint brushes and anxiously awaited scene study with Alvina Krause, Northwestern's legendary acting teacher.

The first day in her class the tension was so thick you could cut it with a knife—the same knife she liked to plunge into the hearts of all of us wide-eyed theatrical dreamers. She walked among us that first day and said, "Less than one percent of you will be successful actors." Then she pointed at me—and I thought she was going to make me an example of the delusional 99%. Standing on her stage, I realized suddenly that I lacked any perspective about my abilities and potential as an actor. For all I knew, everything I'd ever done on a stage up to that moment had been amateurish make-believe and I was about to be exposed. I felt dizzy with my anticipated mortification, and through her long silent stare at me, I felt angry at myself for being such a hopeless dreamer. Then, still pointing at me, she said, "You. You will be an actress." I wasn't sure what to make of her strange attention. I was relieved she didn't condemn me but I didn't exactly believe what she was telling me. Perhaps she sensed that I was about to crumble and burst into tears and felt pity for me. Or maybe she was playing mind games with me—and everyone else in the room. She told one of my classmates he would never be a big star and I think that always affected him. I won't say his name but I will tell you he is a very fine actor, works all the time, and to this day remembers what she said to him. What right did she have? Why should any acting teacher wield that kind of power?

I never liked her—especially her method with new students—but I did as she told me, as an act of faith, and I learned a lot. I was never one of the many students whose acting attempts she chose to humiliate, ridicule, mock, and often reduce to tears. I was very fortunate.

Alvina made everyone sit in alphabetical order by last name so she could keep track of us. That is how Paul Lynde and I found ourselves

next to each other and became friends. He used to mutter things under his breath about how awful someone's performance was or make
cracks about Alvina's hair, which was sometimes disheveled or mis-
colored. On written tests, Paul always made crib notes to cheat but
then he'd hide them so far up his sleeve that he couldn't retrieve them
during the test. Later, we'd laugh our heads off. Everyone associated
Paul and me with each other. "Lubotsky and Lynde," they called us, all
over campus—especially when, as upper-classmen, we performed in
the famous Northwestern Waa-Mu show.

Claudia Webster, one of our most beloved and talented acting
teachers, cast me as Maria in *Twelfth Night*, with sophomore Patricia
Neal as Olivia. Paul played Sir Toby Belch. Claudia also directed Eric
Bentley's translation of *Threepenny Opera*. I was Mrs. Peachum. Mr.
Peachum was Joe Bova, Paul played Police Commissioner Brown. We
put on a hell of a production, but Evanston, Illinois was a very con-
servative community—home of the Women's Christian Temperance
Union (WCTU)—and I guess they weren't quite ready for Brecht.
During the first act on opening night, as soon as the play's political
perspective became clear, a large group of WCTU members got up
and walked out of the theater. The show was ultimately a success—but
pretty much the entire audience came from places far away.

Evanston was a dry city but within walking (sometimes stumbling)
distance was the Chicago city line and the liquor stores and bars on
Howard Street. Boilermakers were the preferred beverage of Northwestern theater students.

My father had warned me about drinking too much at college. He'd
advised me to drink scotch and water because it "flushed the system."
A few weeks into my first term, an older guy named Don Wolin asked
me to a formal school dance. There was a cocktail party earlier, which
I attended with my dorm-mates. I forgot my father's advice and had a
Manhattan. It went down so smoothly and I felt so lighthearted that I
decided to have a martini too. An hour later I was crouched before the
dorm toilet puking my guts out. My roommate Dorothy had to hold
me up in the shower and help me into my gown. When Don arrived
in his tux to pick me up, I thought I was doing a pretty good job of
concealing my queasiness but then Don put his hand under my chin
and said, sympathetically, as if it was the cutest thing he'd ever seen:
"Aw, so you tossed your cookies?"

I hadn't really considered pledging a sorority. Not until I was asked, just before my sophomore year, to pledge the Jewish sorority on campus. I guess I'd become popular around the school for my performances and they thought I would add a little status. I'm glad I did. The sorority house was right on the quad. Close to class and the theater. It kept me in the thick of things, helped me get places on time with my busy schedule, and avoided long walks in the dark after rehearsals. More important, my new roommate, Barbara Shamansky, has been a lifelong friend. I couldn't have asked for a nicer, better roommate. Sham was like me—Jewish and Midwestern all the way. She was from the same small town as Paul. Mount Vernon in Southern Ohio. She and her family were the only Jews in town. Her parents didn't try to hide it. They fit in and showed neighbors they were no different. They talked like everyone else. When their clothes were dirty, they "warshed" them. Her father was the town doctor and much beloved.

Casting for Northwestern productions was so competitive that after the first term, half the speech majors (theater was part of speech) defected to other departments—and even more left after the first year. Those who stuck it out, along with Paul and me included Bill Daniels, his future wife Bonnie Bartlett, Cloris Leachman, and of course Patricia Neal.

I wanted to be a classical actress like the legendary Eleonora Duse whose subtle approach to expressing—rather than indicating—emotion revolutionized the craft of acting. I wanted to make a life doing Shakespeare and the rest of the classics.

Professor Walter Scott taught play analysis with American and continental dramas—everything from Ibsen to O'Neil to Chekhov as well as Sophocles and the other Greeks. He wanted us all to be well-rounded and cultured. He said the New Yorker magazine was, "the undergraduate's bible." We all loved Professor Scott and learned a lot about acting from studying all those great plays. Nevertheless, after my second year, I was so anxious to get to New York and try my luck at the big stage that I almost dropped out.

Cloris Leachman did leave after her sophomore year. She won the Miss Chicago beauty pageant, headed to New York, and never looked back. Patricia Neal also left after her sophomore year. I visited Pat in New York during the summer that year. She had an apartment in Washington Heights with actress and fellow Northwestern alumn, Jean Hagen. Jean was a little older than we were. She just finished grad school but she'd always been friendly toward us undergrads. Soon enough she went off to Hollywood and had a great film career. She was in *Adam's Rib* and *The Asphalt Jungle* and she played opposite Gene Kelly in *Singin' in the Rain*. But for now she was just Jean, Pat's roommate. They seemed to get on smashingly as New York roomies. There was a real camaraderie, I think. They would tip each other off to auditions and help each other however they could. Not that competitive back-stabbing nonsense some aspiring actors fall into.

My trip to New York that summer marked my first time in the Big Apple and I loved the excitement. We walked the busy streets and rode the hot, crowded subways. We went downtown to see Ethel Merman in *Annie Get Your Gun*. We sat way up in the balcony and marveled at how far up she projected every word (no mics in those days). We walked to Sardis afterward for drinks and a late snack and the place was alive with the energy of performers just off the various Broadway stages. Jean Hagen had a giant hickey on her neck and seemed completely unselfconscious about how it had gotten there.

I didn't want to leave New York and was tempted to follow the lead of my peers—and stay there. But I was afraid. I didn't know how I was going to make a living and didn't want to disappoint my parents who wanted to see their children get the educational opportunities they hadn't had. My great daddy had promised to support me for a year in New York if I finished college first—so I went back, though I did make more trips to New York. On one of those trips I saw Patricia and Jean in a production of *Another Part of the Forest*, Lilian Hellman's follow-up to *The Little Foxes*. I was so envious to see my friends on the New York stage!

I cannot tell you whether those last two years at Northwestern helped me as an actress—I mean, more than two years in New York would have—but I think finishing college helped me as a person. It made me a little more well-versed in things beyond the stage. Education is a gift, one I'm profoundly thankful to my parents for providing me with.

When I had a free moment or two I'd hop the el to one of the radio studios in Chicago and audition for a show. I got a small part on Pepper Young's Family for CBS radio. The producer, Burr Tilson saw my last name and told me I couldn't use it. Too ethnic. He asked if I had a stage name. I hadn't ever thought of it. It had never occurred to me that my heroes in the stage, screen, and radio might have changed their names. "Lubotsky is my name," I told him. He asked if I had a middle name. "Rae," I told him. "That's it," he said. "Charlotte Rae." And that was that.

When my father found out he was very hurt. "I don't understand," he said over the phone, after he heard my radio debut. "Who's Charlotte Rae?"

I explained the problem with Lubotsky. "Too many syllables. Too complicated."

"It's a good name," he said. "An honest name. A respected name—all over Milwaukee!" He was right, and I felt awful about it, but he never said another word to me about it.

A few years later, in New York, I was looking for material for my nightclub act and met with Shelley Berman to see about working together. He asked about my background and I ended up telling him about my father and how hurt he was that I had changed my name. Shelley never did write anything for my act but he used that story as part of his own act. He made it about his own father and did a beautiful job. It was very touching—but it was my father's story!

I got a few more small parts on radio programs out of Chicago, but my most important experiences during those years were on campus. That was where I met Sheldon Harnick (who wrote the lyrics and music to *Fiddler on the Roof*). He wrote for the Waa-Mu show and played the fiddle (what else?) in the orchestra. Waa-Mu—which stood for Women's Athletic Association/Men's Union—was a comic musical revue, a cross between vaudeville and Second City (before there was a Second City). I still had my sights set on being a serious actress and almost didn't audition for Waa-Mu. But I'm glad I got down off my high artistic horse long enough to do so—high drama is great, but in my book there is always room for comedy. I also learned a great lesson about comedy. I delivered every line of every sketch with great seriousness—never straining for the humor—and always got lots of appreciation from the writers and audiences.

Waa-Mu was a wonderful experience for me in so many ways and it turned out to be a family affair. Mimi, who also went to Northwestern, also joined the Waa-Mu. She played piano along with Brooks Morton—they had a two-piano orchestra—and the two of them became musical directors. By then I was already in New York but I was so delighted to know that Mimi was a part of the very talented Waa-Mu—and that Waa-Mu was benefiting from her talents.

I know that for me Waa-Mu was unforgettable. The writers were all wonderful, especially Sheldon Harnick. He was a music major and way ahead of his time. He played a mean fiddle and wrote brilliant music and lyrics. I remember in particular a tribute he composed to the women across America who had manned the factories in the recent war effort. I started the number with the curtain closed. I crawled under it and out onto the edge of the stage wearing overalls like a factory worker and sang Sheldon's original, "I've Got Those Gotta Go Home Alone Tonight Blues." We brought the house down with that number, but like I've always known, nothing trumps brilliant material. Nothing.

Paul Lynde wrote and performed in those hilarious sketches. My favorite was when we played a drunk George and Martha Washington trying to figure out why our son had cut down the cherry tree. In a really wild sketch, Paul played a Good Humor ice cream man who abused his wife. I kept telling him how good he was to me while he dragged me around the stage by my ankles. Then he put on his white Good Humor suit and went to work. Pretty tasteless by today's standards but somehow his cruel sense of humor and wicked sense of irony worked.

A lot of us drank too much. We'd stay up late and barely make it to our rooms, to collapse on our beds. We thought nothing of it. I remember lying in the dark spinning room tossing my clothes off and hearing them fall gently next to my bed, then waking up with a hangover and thinking nothing of it. No one else did either.

Drunk or sober, those were wonderful days. I still remember so many of my classmates, my comrades. Joe Bova who went on to become a really fantastic actor. He was on Broadway in *42nd Street* and gave wonderful performances in Joseph Papp's Shakespeare in the Park. Jerry Friedman who became a top-notch director and also worked with Joe Papp. In fact he directed me in *Henry IV parts i and ii*. And Jan McCrady, Peggy Loft and Helen Horton. I'll never forget her characterization of Viola in *Twelfth Night*.

Anxious as I was to get to New York, I look back on that time now with great fondness and tremendous affection and respect for all my classmates, those who went on to have big careers in the business and the many others who went on to do other great things in the world and who, I have to believe, brought that Northwestern spirit with them to everything they did. Our camaraderie went beyond the work, beyond the laughs. We were all there finding ourselves as artists, performers, and as people. Many of the friendships started there have lasted a lifetime.

# NEW YORK AT LAST!

Shortly before I left Northwestern for New York, I participated in a mock presidential election put on by some political science majors. After four years on the Northwestern stage, I was something of a campus celebrity and as such I campaigned for former Vice President Henry Wallace, the progressive candidate.

Wallace was a man way ahead of his time. He was skeptical of our country's obsession with the Cold War and anti-Communism. He realized we had more serious problems with justice and equality and human rights. In 1948, he campaigned on a platform to end segregation. He called for civil rights to be extended to everyone regardless of sexual orientation. Even political moderates regarded him as a radical Communist and when my endorsement helped him win our mock election—though in the real election later that year he got less than 3% of the popular vote and not a single electoral vote—I was afraid I might wind up on someone's black list before I'd even begun my career in the theater in New York. Boy, wasn't I self-important, thinking anyone was keeping track of my political affiliations or influences. But those were the times we were living in. Everyone lived in terror. Like actress Marge Redman and her husband, the actor Jack Weston. They told me they would cross the street to avoid talking to someone who was blacklisted. They wanted no association whatsoever with any of "those people." It's pretty shameful how actors turned away from their fellow actors who'd been blacklisted because they had the courage to stand up for what they believed in. In years to come I would be humbled to meet the brave few who never backed down from the anti-democratic criminal conspiracy of Joseph McCarthy—who I'm ashamed to say came from my home state—even when it meant not being able to work or going to prison.

I almost didn't make it to New York. By the time I'd graduated, my sister Beverly, after studying opera for a year in Cincinnati, then four years in New York, and opening with the Pittsburgh Opera to favorable reviews, had come home on a visit and fallen in love with Jules Levin, a neurosurgeon finishing his residency. Now they were engaged.

She was under contract with the Pittsburgh Opera and scheduled to perform in park band shells all over the country with Thomas

Hayworth—a Metropolitan Opera audition winner. My father had spent a small fortune to pay for her dream of being an opera singer—and he had to buy her out of the contract. For her part, Beverly didn't seem to agonize much about her decision—nor did she challenge her fiancé about giving up her singing career to be a housewife and socialite.

Beverly encouraged me to follow her lead. She urged me to get "secretly engaged" to my boyfriend, Jack Zuckert. We would live near each other with our husbands and raise our children together and live happily ever after in Milwaukee.

But I've always thought there was more to it. Beverly had the talent—more than enough of that and her opera coaches had assured her of that—but I think she didn't quite have the courage to face all the uncertainty of a career as an opera singer. Not that she didn't love Jules. I just think she was scared. Now she'd had her one big successful performance and good reviews to prove it. She'd never had to fail. She'd chosen security over the dream and I think she didn't want to be reminded of that by seeing me go to New York and chase my dream.

I guess I had my own doubts because Beverly's idea had some appeal to me. I asked my father what he thought I should do. He refused to say. He told me marriage was a decision only I could make for myself—not for him or my mother and not for Beverly. He was so wise. I wasn't in love with Jack. I was in love with the theater. "Don't make your decision on my account," he said. "It's your life, Charlotte. No one else lives it. Only you." When he put it that way, there was no more dilemma. What a relief! What a great father!

Once I made my decision I couldn't wait to get to New York. I sublet a basement apartment in the dead of summer on 81st Street, between Amsterdam and Columbus from a Northwestern alum who had enough sense to leave New York for the month of August. I arrived on a humid night, one of those noisy, hot, undershirt New York nights. People were sitting on the stoop above my basement sublet and I could hear someone playing jazz on a flute somewhere. My new home smelled of mildew. Roaches crawled up and down the walls and clung to the bathroom ceiling. I went to an all-night grocery and bought a can of Black Flag and sprayed until I could hardly breathe, then opened all the windows and let the hot stinking sidewalk fume down into the apartment. I got in bed with a single cotton sheet and pillow and opened *The Fountainhead*, the book I and everyone else was reading that summer.

That book might seem a funny choice for someone who had supported Henry Wallace, but I was young and naïve and didn't realize that Ayn Rand was a right wing fascist. I was a dreamer with big dreams and I found the book inspiring.

I recall hearing a noise that first night and looking up and saw a self-determined man leering in my window, peering down at me, his hand reaching in through the metal security bars, beckoning me to him with his finger.

I screamed and ran out the back door of the apartment into the basement hallway. I stood there screaming until neighbors came down from their first floor apartment, a man and his wife—Mack and Joan. Mack had a flute in his hand and all I could think of to say in my terror and embarrassment was to tell him I had enjoyed his rendition of *Cherokee*. Then I burst into tears and told them what had happened. They never asked me if I'd just gotten off the bus from the Midwest— I guess they didn't have to—or if I was ready to get on a bus straight back there (I pretty much was). They were very nice—not the stereotype of New Yorkers one hears about in Milwaukee. They assured me that I was safe and then took me around the interior of the building to show me how secure we were. "And at least the guy wasn't taking a leak," Mack added.

We became instant friends. Joan was a painter and a few weeks later I posed for her. Mack often had other musicians over, sometimes for jazz and other times for chamber music. The building and the neighboring buildings were full of artists and I loved the community and the fellowship—with all those sensitive creative people—and even with all those damn roaches all over the place. I felt like I had found a home.

Cloris Leachman managed to avoid the New York artist's poverty that summer by having a romance with financier Hy Sobiloff. She took pity on me and on Paul Lynde—who had also arrived in New York and jobless like me—and invited us on the yacht Hy was renting for the summer at $600 a day plus the cost of a full crew and a well-stocked bar and kitchen. I told Cloris thanks for the invite but I couldn't go because I had to get out and start meeting people as soon as possible so I could get a job in the theater. "It's the dead of August," she told me. "No one is in New York. You'll meet more interesting people on the yacht," she told me, and she was right.

We left early, from the 79th Street Boat Basin, with the sun still rising over the elegant apartment houses along Riverside Drive. For me it was thrilling—being on that luxurious boat and looking out over the shimmering surface of the Hudson River and the green Jersey cliffs. I felt like I was in an F. Scott Fitzgerald novel—in fact, the boat might have been named for F. Scott's wife: "The Zelda." We sailed beneath the George Washington Bridge, then around the Harlem River and over to the Long Island Sound. We anchored outside New London, Connecticut for a while, then sailed on to Montauk and out into the Atlantic.

The food was great and plentiful. Paul and I, hungry actors that we were, stuffed our faces with deviled eggs and caviar, marinated herring, cheese and crackers, beer and cashews and melon and grapes, then ribs and corn on the cob—and when the boat reached the Atlantic Ocean, our deep-sea fishing destination, we threw it all up. Then, a little while later, stuffed our faces again.

Hy was a charming man. Very nice. I could understand why Cloris liked him so much. In addition to being a millionaire he was a poet and we were obliged, as long as we were enjoying his hospitality, to listen to him read his verse on the high seas. We kept stuffing our faces while he recited his verse. It wasn't half bad—his poetry or his food. Hy had a poetry tutor named Milton. Milton brought his girlfriend. She sunbathed on the deck the whole time.

Also on the boat were the daughter of British actress Gertrude Lawrence, and her husband, a doctor. They took turns holding court. Pamela impersonated her famous mother and told us unflattering stories about Gertrude and her close friend Noel Coward. I wish I could remember those stories—they were quite naughty—but alas… Her husband told us about the latest developments in medicine—which I don't remember either—while we cast our fishing lines and waited for the fish to bite.

Paul turned out to be a pretty decent fisherman. He and Hy hit it off with the bait and tackle and the hooks and lines and all the fishing talk. I objected to the whole business. It just didn't seem fair. Lure the poor things with some little piece of a sardine then reel them in and beat them to death. The fresh sea bass was delicious though.

Hy and Cloris wanted to sleep outside on the deck, but Hy was afraid he'd get robbed by one of his crewmen so he gave me his wallet to keep for him. I was honored that he thought me that trustworthy. I shared a tiny cabin with Paul. That night, lying next to each other in our little cots, swaying with the sea, Paul came out to me—as if I didn't already know! Perhaps he felt self-conscious about sleeping so close together, or maybe he was just dying to tell someone. After knowing him four years, it was hardly a revelation. He told me about the boy he was in love with and I felt bad knowing that he couldn't have just brought his boyfriend along with him. He asked to see Hy's wallet. I refused. He pleaded. He said he just wanted to see how much was in it, but I wouldn't let him. I slept with the wallet under my pillow. It was a huge leather thing. I woke up with a stiff neck.

At the end of the summer, Cloris and I decided to find an apartment together. On our budget most of them were dark and drafty. There was one really nice place on east 68th Street, in the old Guggenheim mansion which had been parceled into apartments. The one we looked at—for $375 a month—had been the mansion's sitting room. It offered beautiful parquet floors, window seats beneath ceiling-high windows, a high dome ceiling, and a fireplace big enough to roast a pig—or even an ox (it was at least six feet high)! But there was no bedroom. No privacy! It was crazy. We asked Paul to come over and give us his opinion of the place. He took one look at the floors, the ceiling, the fireplace, and those wrap-around window seats and said, "Take it!"

So we did. Why we even asked him is beyond me. He wasn't going to have to live there!

Waking up the first cold morning in October—and with Cloris away at Hy's apartment—I smelled smoke through the walls. I remembered a story Father had told me about a business trip to Chicago and how he had smelled smoke while checking into the La Salle Hotel. The desk clerk and manager had told him everything was fine but my father walked out of the lobby with his luggage and found another hotel. An hour later the La Salle had a deadly fire. So I wasn't taking any chances. I went out in the hallway and the smoke was stronger. I followed it to a stairwell and down to an apartment half a flight below us. I pounded on the door and our neighbor opened up and apologized for the smoke. Her apartment had a beautiful fireplace and she'd put too much wood in it. Her name was Dr. Marie Nyswander and she invited me in for coffee. She had just moved to New York City from Lexington, Kentucky, where she'd just finished her residency as a psychoanalyst working with drug addicts. It all sounded terribly exotic to me. Marie was fascinated with the theater and actors and the craft of acting. She'd read about the Actor's Studio and was intrigued about the idea of emotional sense memory. We became good friends and she helped me get my first day job filing and answering telephones for Nejelski & Company business consultants in an office on East 38th Street.

A few weeks later, Cloris told me about a saloon that was looking for performers. I auditioned and got the gig. I was ecstatic! The Sawdust Trail was on 46th Street, between Broadway and 6th Avenue, across the street from the Actors Equity headquarters and next to the High School for the Performing Arts. I told Paul Lynde about it and he was insane with envy that I'd been hired as a singer. Eddie Bernard was the pianist and he was terrific. Theresa Brewer and I would do alternating sets to a crowd that mostly just wandered in off the street and sat at small round tables on a sawdust floor. At least we didn't have to mix with customers between sets; we just had to sing and then were free to go upstairs to our dressing rooms. The waiters were all ex-vaudevillians and would sing when we were taking our breaks. The owner paid me sixty dollars a week and I was thrilled. I was singing and they were paying me! I loved to get there early and walk around Broadway and look up at all the lights and think, *I'm part of this. I'm singing around the corner from Broadway shows and being paid for it!* Theresa arrived every night by taxi cab. She was only sixteen so her aunt accompanied her. They always left immediately after her last set. So did I—back to that crazy apartment I was sharing with Cloris.

It was a blast, though we probably got to know each other a little too well. One night, lying in our beds, I asked her what an orgasm felt like. Living with Cloris, I'd *heard* enough of them—though I was still a virgin. Cloris tried to explain the feeling but none of it quite made sense to me. I tried to fake it—fake understanding what she was saying, I mean, but Cloris saw right through me. She seemed exasperated by my inability to grasp it all at my age. Finally, I asked her if an orgasm was like those sparkling mirror balls in a ballroom. "Yes," she said. "That is exactly what it is like."

I wondered when I would find out if she was right. I had grown up believing in chastity. It was what nice Jewish girls were taught to believe in. I dated in college and kissed guys, but never wanted to go any further than that and they were all gentlemen about it. One guy stuck his tongue out when we kissed and I was so shocked that I called my mother the next day and asked her if that was all right. She rolled her eyes and said, "Your father tried that with me, but I told him never again." I asked my sister Beverly too, but she wouldn't discuss it. I assumed I would be a virgin when I married. I didn't judge young women who had sex before marriage. It just wasn't for me. But seeing how free and open Cloris was about sex started to make me wonder about what I was missing, and if I was being foolish and old fashioned. My new friend and neighbor, Marie also talked to me about it and answered a lot of my questions.

Meanwhile, I thought I would never get beyond being a saloon singer. I tried to develop a cabaret act to perform in night clubs—and get seen—and like pretty much everything I tried, that proved to be a long-range goal. First I had to find some original material. I knew someone who knew someone who knew Dick Miles, the song writer who had penned "There's an Awful Lot of Coffee in Brazil." He recommended a friend of his, Paul Secon, a talented young composer and music critic (and, a few years later, one of the founders of Pottery Barn). I called him and he invited me over to talk about maybe writing special material for me. He lived on 71st Street, between Columbus and Central Park West. I brought ice cream, which we shared, and I ended up in bed with him. I guess I was ready, and he was a really nice guy. I was too embarrassed to tell him it was my first time. I felt like such a square to be losing my virginity at age twenty-two. Cloris had told me I was really missing out on something—and she was right.

The next morning, when I got on the bus to go downtown, I looked around at all the other passengers and realized that some of these strangers had, like me, done it the night before. I almost wanted to congratulate them all.

Cloris and I were starting to outgrow our cozy little apartment. One day I opened the door and found her pressed against actor Martin Balsam. They jumped apart and said they'd been working on a scene from Streetcar. They were both students of Lee Strasberg at the Actors Studio and I was so naïve I actually believed they'd been rehearsing that scene. Cloris really did love Hy Sobiloff but she had a naughty streak. When Paul Secon came over to visit me, Cloris would walk around in a transparent negligee. She always had a great body (and probably still does) and was never shy about it. We'd had fun sharing that place and I think we managed to inspire each other with our big dreams, ambitions, and our lust for life. But it was time for each of us to move on.

I moved in with Paul on 71st Street near Central Park, but he didn't want anything serious and neither did I, so we decided one of us should move out. He was a real gentleman. He packed up and left me the apartment. I enjoyed the adventure of living on my own and it was around this time that I first somehow started to feel the possibilities of a career on the stage, though I felt I was off to a slow start.

One night, without warning, my Dad walked into the Sawdust Trail! He seemed horrified at the sight of all those men nursing drinks and looking at me. He watched me sing with tears in his eyes. The next morning, he came to my apartment. He sat on the bed and felt the firmness of the mattress and then pleaded with me to come back with him to Milwaukee. He said that New York was not a good place for a young, single woman. I tried to assure him that I would be all right. I told him how nice everyone had been to me and how, beneath the big city coldness, were some of the warmest, most neighborly people in the world. Just then came a knock on my door. It was the landlord. He saw my father inside the apartment and apologized for the intrusion, then said, "I saw the older gentleman paying you a visit and just wanted you to know that I would also, you know, that I would…" He winked frantically, and said, "You know!" I politely rushed him off my doorstep and I don't think my father heard enough of the exchange to know that my landlord had taken me for a hooker!

Still, Daddy kept trying to convince me to pack up and get on the train with him. He said he was concerned about me. He had heard that I'd made friends with a lesbian. It was crazy—that anyone thought they knew a thing like that about my friends and that it should matter. I knew it was Beverly. I'd told her and Mother about my new friend, Marie, and now Beverly was making things up about her and using it against me. Beverly had once had a singing teacher at a summer music camp during high school who she'd heard was a lesbian and so she understood the stigma and how my parents would react. Now she was trying to manipulate our father and trying to get me to come home. I couldn't understand why Beverly would do such a thing. She'd had her chance to follow her dream. Why would she begrudge me mine?

I gave my Dad a big hug and promised to be careful, and walked him outside and hailed him a taxi to Penn Station.

Over the next few years, I would face a steady diet of rejection—interrupted only briefly by the taste of a few minor successes—but I'd think about Beverly and how she'd tried to throw cold water on my dream and I'd resolve to stick it out and make it somehow.

In the meantime, I decided I would try to enjoy myself. I saved up to buy a record player and some LPs. I'd come home late and spin some

June Christy and Nat King Cole and Frank Sinatra. I kept the volume down but I think someone in the neighborhood was listening. Within a few months my apartment was robbed—the Victrola gone. The thief must have figured out my schedule—when I came home from my filing job and when I went back out for my singing gig.

It sure was a creepy feeling having someone invade my little sanctuary and take my jewelry and leave me in an eerie silence, unable to play my records. I guess I shouldn't have been surprised—and maybe I should have been glad they didn't steal more than they did, or come in while I was home and tie me up—but I was angry. I felt violated. Paul Lynde cheered me up. He invited me to a party at the Park Savoy on 58th Street between 7th and 6th where he was living. He said other people from Northwestern would be there. Paul was still looking for a job, but that didn't stop him from having fun, so why should I let a little robbery stand in my way? It was the perfect diversion for me—a big mob of actors and other creative types crowded into a few rooms, drinking and smoking and talking about ourselves and how great we were—or weren't *quite*—doing. Marlon Brando showed up. We could hear his motorcycle through the walls of the hotel revving and then yawning off. He'd come from the Saturday night performance of Streetcar still wearing his undershirt and khaki trousers. He was young and gorgeous and he was the toast of the town. People offered him their spots on sofas but he waved them off and sat on the hard floor. About a dozen women sat around him and he held court. He only stayed about an hour and I overheard the woman he left with asking the hostess if she could borrow her diaphragm.

After the break-in I didn't want to stay alone in that West 71st Street apartment anymore. I also wanted to economize—and buy more time in New York until I broke through—so I found an old college roommate to go in with. Barbara Shamansky and I found a cold-water flat across town on 72nd Street and 1st Avenue, in what was then still the Czech part of Yorkville. It cost $50 a month and had a bathtub in the kitchen, but at least the apartment had its own toilet in the bathroom! Barbara's parents came to inspect the place and immediately made her move to a hotel—and I was stuck with all the rent. I stayed anyway. I found a place on 2nd Avenue that made potato pancakes almost as mouth-watering as my mother's, and landed a part in a melodrama at the Old Nick Music Hall a few blocks away on 2nd Avenue. Paul Killum ran the place, and he knew people, and out of that connection I got my first agent, Leonard Jacobson. He got me a spot for the summer of 1949 in the performing ensemble at Maud's Summer-Ray, a left-wing resort in the Adirondacks.

I thought I knew a little something about politics, but I learned a lot that summer, on and off-stage. I heard about Emma Goldman and got a little education on the struggles of labor unions and equal rights. I also sang in a chorus of pop and folk songs, some English, some Yiddish, and performed in comedy sketches. I had to learn the Yiddish songs phonetically because I'd never learned Yiddish, I'm sorry to say.

Some nights we were sent to entertain at other resorts—at the fur workers union resort, we performed right before Pete Seeger. It was thrilling to stand backstage in the wings and watch him sing all the songs he'd written. He was a wonderful, courageous and resourceful man. He built his own house, helped clean up the Hudson River, and never backed down from those sinister un-American politicians who tried to label people as subversive because they challenged the status quo and stood up for people who were hungry and vulnerable all over the world. I was proud to cross paths with him. Many years later, I got in touch with Pete through my friend Harold Leventhal who was Pete's manager. Mrs. Pfeiffer, the miracle worker who did so much to help my son Andy, asked if I could find someone to come and sing for all the developmentally disabled children she worked with in Bellevue Hospital's day program. Pete agreed without hesitation and did a beautiful show for those children in the facility's tiny auditorium.

When the summer was over I returned to New York determined to make the next year a turning point, a breakthrough year. It turned out to be—though not quite in the way I'd planned.

Acting and singing jobs were still few and far between, and my cabaret act took much longer to develop than I'd hoped—the better part of the fall and winter—and then I had to find a way to get it in front of the right people. Fortunately, Paul Killium, the same man I'd worked for at the Old Nick Music Hall on Second Avenue, had a connection at the Blue Angel on 55th Street. It was a very posh little club, a little intimidating for me at first. I went on a Sunday night when acts came to audition for Max Gordon and Herb Jacoby.

I saw Marilyn Cantor, one of Eddie Cantor's daughters. She was good but I thought I was just as good, and that gave me the courage to return on another Sunday night and audition. They liked me and offered me a two-week engagement in the fall on one of their other stages, the Village Vanguard, which was still a popular cabaret club—years before Max Gordon turned it into a legendary jazz club.

I was thrilled—and anxious to get my material ready for this great opportunity. I went out to the Vanguard and other clubs to see what all the different acts were doing. I wanted to be original but I also wanted to see what worked. One of the most influential acts was Wally Cox who became a comic icon before his untimely death in 1973. He was on just about every television show, including his own *Mr. Peepers*. He was the voice of cartoon hero *Underdog*. I watched him at the Vanguard doing a series of character studies, all of them hilarious, and it got me thinking about what I could come up with, different characters that I could do.

Wally was so brilliant. And there were so many great acts. It made me think I needed to get some better material for my act.

I looked around for someone who could write some great stuff for me and it turned out to be harder than I thought. I just wasn't impressed with any of the writers I was meeting. Then I remembered my friend from college, Sheldon Harnick. He'd written for the Waa-Mu show at Northwestern and he was so talented. I wanted him to write for me. I thought the whole club scene could probably use more writer/composers like Sheldon.

So I called him. He'd just graduated and was living in Chicago. He said he was playing the fiddle and there was plenty of work for him. He was happy, didn't see any reason to come to New York.

I let it go, until I saw Yip Harburg's *Finian's Rainbow* on Broadway and it reminded me of Sheldon's work. I don't mean exactly but I could hear elements of Harburg's work that reminded me of Sheldon and it made me think Sheldon was artistically cut from the same cloth. I bought the *Finian's Rainbow* show album and sent it to Sheldon and told him this was the kind of show he could write.

Sheldon listened to that album and had the same reaction I had. He called to tell me how inspired he was. He said, "I want to write like that. That's what I want to do with my life." And he moved to New York and became one of the most important Broadway composers of his generation. He gave us *She Loves Me, Tenderloin*, and many many others, including, of course, *Fiddler on the Roof*. Sheldon always tries to give me credit for his career, for bringing him to New York. It's very sweet of him to say that but Sheldon brought himself to New York. I was just the messenger.

And what a spectacular reward I got for delivering that message. Sheldon—before he wrote any of those Broadway shows—gave me one of the most brilliant songs ever written, The Shape of Things to

Come, a hilarious take on geometry, infidelity, and murder. I still sing it sometimes when someone asks me to perform. Sheldon also gave me a beautiful little number called *Gus the Gopher* which he'd originally written for the Waa-Mu show at Northwestern.

The summer before I was to open my cabaret act, I worked at Crystal Lake Lodge in the Adirondacks. It was a beautiful resort with a great group of performers. They kept us busy with musical revues and full length theatrical classics like Chekhov's *The Boor*, but when I had the chance I'd work on the act I was going to perform at the Village Vanguard. One morning, some of us were rehearsing a new song in a recreation room near the theater. I don't know what got into me but when I walked in and saw our cute pianist at his bench playing "Blue Skies," I went over and sat on his lap and sang along from memory.

If he minded my weight on his legs or my arm around his shoulders, he didn't let it show. He politely softened his chords under my voice and seemed to enjoy hearing what verses I could remember, and what I made up when I couldn't. His name was John Strauss, and he wore round, black-framed glasses as was the style for artists and musicians back then. His hair was dark and curly, thick and short. His lap felt nice. Warm. It reminded me of my father's which I'd never gotten enough time on.

He took me for drinks that afternoon and we hit it off. He had a great sense of humor. Witty, and very dry. I think John appreciated my sense of humor and I think we both admired each other's talents. He was a classically trained pianist and composer. He was a music student at Yale on the GI Bill after serving overseas in the war, but he also loved musical theater, and when I told him about my act being booked into the Village Vanguard in the fall, he offered to help me. I was happy to have the help and thought it was so sweet of him to offer.

I worked on my opera singer imitations and John knew enough about opera to really appreciate what I was doing and to make suggestions. He also knew how to improvise on the piano and play just the right notes and phrases to help the satire along.

In addition to music and comedy John and I also shared an affinity for hard liquor and became drinking buddies while we were falling in love that summer. John was smart about money, and so after that first date we always bought it by the bottle and drank in either my room or his room. Romantic, huh? Anyway, it gave us more time alone together and also more time to work on my act. John had some great ideas and really helped put a musical shape to the program. We got to try out a lot of the new and newly revised material at the resort and it all went over very well. But best of all John was kind and he was gentle and he was all mine.

After the summer, I returned to New York and John went back for his final year at Yale. I used to ride the train from Grand Central Station to New Haven for the weekend. John had a tiny apartment near the school. Very cozy.

One Saturday night he brought me with him to the home of his professor and mentor, the renowned composer Paul Hindemith who'd invited us over along with some of his other Yale students. On the way there, John described Hindemith and his wife and everyone else who would be there. All their speech quirks and physical ticks. He described them so well that when I met everyone I couldn't keep myself from giggling. At one point I had to excuse myself to the powder room just to let out some laughter.

I sang for Hindemith and his wife and some friends of theirs and performed my opera impressions and they really seemed to appreciate it. They really got a kick out of it.

Other weekends, John would come down to see me in my one bedroom at 427 West 51st Street, between 9th and 10th, next to St. Claire's Hospital. If either of us had a little money we'd go see a show. Otherwise, we'd drink and make love and sometimes we'd rehearse my act together.

John was there at the Vanguard for my opening night and gave me great moral support. I was the opening act on a bill with English folk singer, Richard Dyer Bennet, and I got a good response. I sang some of my very favorite songs, including "When The Idle Poor Become The Idle Rich" (from *Finian's Rainbow*) and "The Shape of Things," the brilliant song Sheldon Harnick wrote for me, and also did my opera singer impressions, my garden club ladies, and the comedic sketch about dieting that was a satire of the TV cop show *Dragnet*, called Sagnet, which John had helped me put together over the summer. This was quite a few years before eating disorders were in the public consciousness, and the idea of treating a candy binge like a crime spree was quite daring and got a lot of laughs.

The house band was the Clarence Brown Trio and they were top-notch and after a while I developed a nice little repartee with Clarence. During one of the opera impressions I'd sing a shrill high note and he'd play it, I'd sing another and he'd play it, and we'd get faster and higher until it got ridiculous and we'd have a laugh. Then I'd lean over and give Clarence a little kiss. Everyone loved it—except for my sister, Beverly. She and her husband Dr. Jules Levin were visiting New York and came to see my show and afterwards, Beverly told me I shouldn't kiss the pianist because, as she said, "He's a Negro." She said it would hurt my career and that anyway I just shouldn't be seen kissing him. I was surprised. I really wasn't expecting anything like it. I was ashamed of my sister and, of course, ignored her advice.

Max Gordon seemed to like my act and so did audiences. My two week engagement turned into a regular gig. His headliners came and went. Anita Ellis, Maxine Sullivan, Irwin Corey. Professor Corey, as he was known, used to drive Max crazy because he would ignore the lighted signal to wrap up the show so the waiters could settle everyone's bill and clear the room for the second show. Max was a short guy with a big cigar. He knew talent and helped launch many careers. He also knew business. After a few months, seeing so many headliners come and go while I stayed on as the warm-up, I thought Max must really like me, maybe I was worth more than $150 a week so I asked him if it was possible that I could have a raise. I walked into his smoky closet of an office and said, "You know, it's been nearly three months and I was wondering if it's at all possible, if maybe I could get a few more dollars." Without missing a beat, he said, "You know, I think I should change the bill." Tough negotiator that I was, I immediately pleaded with him to keep me at the same pay.

Max sent me uptown to the Blue Angel—55th Street between Lexington and 3rd—where I'd originally auditioned and I opened for Eartha Kitt. Eartha had been a Katherine Dunham dancer and had become accustomed to changing in front of everyone else in a small space. She and I shared a tiny dressing room and on opening night when John came back to see me after the show, Eartha stripped naked to put on her gown as she was introducing herself to my boyfriend. She caught herself and apologized but John told her he didn't mind.

One night, after our shows, John and I had Eartha come to our apartment for drinks. On our way there, a policeman pulled John over. He didn't say why but he kept poking his flashlight around, shining it on Eartha and on John and me. He asked us where we were going and we told him we were entertainers going home after a show. He scrutinized us again and then let us go. John and I weren't sure what was going on. Eartha seemed unfazed.

Another night, a photographer came to our dressing room and asked Eartha if he could take a picture. When she said yes, I moved away from her, ducking out of the shot. Eartha scolded me. She told me never to do that. What a generous colleague. I've never forgotten that. I love Eartha.

The next time Max sent me to perform at the Blue Angel I was the opening act for Pearl Bailey. We shared the same closet they called a dressing room and on opening night Lena Horn came back after the show to congratulate Pearl. At one point, Pearl, who was dating the famous jazz drummer, Louie Bellson, asked Lena, "How is it being married to Lennie?" (Lennie Hayton, the American composer and jazz musician). And Lena replied, "Oh, they treat you like a queen." I was still so naïve I didn't realize what Lena meant.

Soon John graduated from Yale and moved in with me. He was teaching at the High School for the Performing Arts on 48th Street. There he met Bob Joffrey and Gerald Arpino. Joffrey was a teacher/choreographer and Gerald was his assistant. John wrote two ballets for the Joffrey Ballet. He loved working with them and seeing his work performed on the stage.

We had talked about marriage that first summer together at the resort and I guess we both felt it was inevitable. It just seemed the natural thing to do. We were compatible and we loved a lot of the same things and so it was easy to fall in love and imagine a life together.

We flew to Milwaukee together for my baby sister, Mimi's wedding. Mimi's new husband, Donald Guten, was such a nice guy. He was what we call *haimisha*, a real gentleman. I was so happy for Mimi. For both my sisters and me. We'd all found ourselves great guys.

During the party, John and I announced our engagement. John was Jewish, which did matter to me and mattered a lot to my family, though John's family was hardly religious. Like many German Jews, they had assimilated long ago. Neither John nor his brother had had a bar mitzvah—though John told me he'd once had a brief ceremony in what was called a "Mitzva Mobile," a sort of ceremonial ice cream truck of Judaism.

John's parents and I hit it off. They seemed to like me and they seemed very happy that John was getting married. I figured they'd worried about him because he was kind of shy.

They had come from the Midwest. His mother from St. Louis, his father from Minneapolis. But they were real New Yorkers now. Marie

Haberman had a dress shop and was very chic in her style and manner. John's father, Maury Strauss was in management for Bloomingdale's department store up in New Rochelle. He used to tell stories about catching shoplifters trying to waddle out with pieces of clothing between their thighs.

John had grown up in Washington Heights but now his parents lived on 57th, between 9th and 10th Avenues. They loved their penthouse apartment and hardly ever went anywhere. They loved their neighbors, especially the ones right next door whose morning glories crept in through their windows. Maury and Marie entertained on their terrace. They had a lot of parties. John and I even went to some of them. We met people in the arts and other interesting people and I thought his parents were pretty sophisticated, a lot more so than my parents. John had no problem telling them that he and I were shacked up. Whereas when my family came to New York for our wedding, John had to move out—for appearances—and stay with his parents until after the wedding.

I didn't want my father to go broke throwing us a big wedding. He'd already done that for Beverly and Mimi. So John and I were married in his parents' apartment on West 57th Street.

It was a beautiful, simple ceremony for our parents and a few other relatives on both sides. Mimi was there with her new husband, Don. He was working for Daddy in his tire business and Daddy thought maybe he would run it one day. This was a great relief to my father who had three daughters and no sons. Beverly couldn't make it. She was very pregnant. But my cousin Marcella was there with her husband Jack Gallub, a foreign correspondent for one of the newspapers. John's parents were there, of course, along with his favorite cousin, Julia and her husband, Dr. John Waller and John's favorite Aunt Hattie and her husband Percy. Their nicknames were Hat and Purse.

Everyone got along well. The reception was in a small room at the Waldorf Astoria Hotel. Friends of ours played a jazz trio and we all danced with each other.

Great things were ahead, we were certain.

# HIGHS AND LOWS

John and I lived on Madison Avenue between 97th and 98th Streets, just a block from Central Park. Those were busy days for us. We were anxious to get our careers going, but, weather-permitting, we always found time for walks, sometimes uptown toward the Harlem Meer or downtown to the reservoir. In the spring and summer we were surrounded by lush green and when the leaves started falling we could see the panorama of the New York skyline that surrounded the park, the power and promise of the city we were going to claim.

I loved New York and even began to forget that I'd ever had another home. I clung to my dreams and endured my disappointments. One of my lowest moments in those early years came at Café Society, the famous cabaret club at Sheridan Square in Greenwich Village. What a thrill to be performing in this legendary room where so many greats had shown their stuff, what an honor that owner, Barney Josephson, had booked me onto the stage where Zero Mostel and Hazel Scott had performed.

It was a late-arriving audience and it never got quiet. People kept talking through my act until it seemed that no one was listening. I couldn't believe it. The great Fletcher Henderson Jr. was my accompaniment and maybe we were a bad combination that night. My God, it would have been fabulous to be singing jazz standards with Fletch, but that wasn't my act. My act was special material and comedy and Fletcher struggled to get with it—and I felt stupid wasting his genius on my silly routines. The audience was talking during the show so no one could even hear the funny lyrics. They couldn't get the jokes even if they'd wanted to.

To make matters worse, my old boss from the Sawdust Trail showed up with some people. I saw him sitting there and I was absolutely mortified. I mean, there he was trying to show me off to his friends, and there I was, background music to people's conversations. I was so upset, so humiliated and frustrated, that as soon as I was finished I ran off the stage in tears.

When I got backstage I was even more embarrassed, realizing what a fool I'd made of myself for taking it so personally. I knew I had to develop a much thicker skin about audiences—about everything.

Later that year—1951—I had an even worse experience. My agent Jules Scharr booked me into the Mocombo Room on the Sunset Strip in Los Angeles. Charlie Morrison had called William Morris and asked for "the girl with the Zsa Zsa routine." I guess he didn't remember the name and, as it turned out, there were two of us making fun of the Gabors but I was the one Jules mentioned. Charlie flew John and me out to L.A. and put us up in a hotel. We arrived late on a Thursday night and slept in the next morning and did a little sight-seeing with our rented car on our way to the club. We walked in and I asked for Charlie Morrison. He came out of the back and looked me over. "You're not the one I booked," he said, shaking his head. "You're not the one I wanted."

I just stood there, dumbfounded.

He said, "I want the girl who did the Zsa Zsa Gabor..."

I told him that I had a routine about the Gabor sisters but he wasn't interested. He didn't even want to see my routine. "You're the wrong girl," he said. One of his partners asked what they were going to do and Charlie said, right in front of me, "We're stuck with her for tonight. Then we'll see." Then he turned back to me and said, "You'll go on tonight and then you can go back to New York."

You can imagine how excited I was to perform that night. It was pretty depressing.

So I went on. I really gave it my all, wanted to show Charlie what a fool he was. He never even spoke to me after the show but a couple of colleagues, Jack E. Leonard and Phil Foster were there and came back to tell me how much they enjoyed my act. They were old school borsht-belt comics and I'd seen them around New York. They did all the good clubs. They were pretty big, very successful. I told them what had happened—how I was being dismissed. Phil said, "Charlotte, just remember, this club is just a toilet." *Tur-let*, he pronounced it. It was probably the sweetest thing anyone could say to me at that moment.

The next morning John drove me to the William Morris building in Beverly Hills so I could pick up my check from George Dresher. He greeted me at his receptionist's desk and I broke into tears. "If this is show business I want out," I told him. "I don't want to get hardened like Sophie Tucker. I don't want to lose my life to this awful business."

He listened to me weep for a few minutes and told me he understood, then handed me the check. What else could he do? Nobody had put a gun to my head and insisted I be a performer. Thank God for friends like Jackie and Phil. "It's a tur-let." Those four words really cheered me up. Henny Youngman was another angel for me in those early years when my thin-skin and insecurities came up against the little cruelties of the business. Henny was a genius. He'd play the fiddle and crack a relentless string of one-liners. He was one of my biggest fans. He came to see my act whenever he could and always had nice things to say afterwards. He taught me how important it is for performers to support each other. Without the support and camaraderie show business can be overwhelmingly lonely.

It was a struggle, those early years. There was always just enough work to eke out a living and not have a day job—or a night job. I never waited on tables, and I'm not sure I could have even if I'd tried. The funny thing is that I always kind of wanted to. I've always admired my peers who took food orders and carried trays and cleared dishes. I couldn't fathom how I would manage with my short legs and short arms and small hands. Just the thought made me imagine the sound of crashing china and glass. I'm sure women shorter than me with smaller hands have done it brilliantly but I can't imagine doing it. Through the years I've fantasized waiting tables for one shift, just to know what it is like. Maybe in another lifetime. To this day I marvel at waiters and always try to strike up a conversation with them and tell them when they're really outstanding. Usually they're either actors or college students. I want them to know that either way I'm pulling for them—and I hope they remember I want water with no ice and dressing on the side.

I enjoy giving people the praise they deserve. So many people work so hard. I like to acknowledge them. Why not? We all need to hear it. Whether it's a waiter or a tailor or a make-up artist or another performer. I remember when I met Jackie Mason. It was after seeing his one-man show on Broadway in the late 1980s. I nearly peed in my pants he was so funny and went back stage to tell him. "Oh, Miss Charlotte Rae," he said, "you're big with the compliments." I knew it meant a lot to him to hear it from a colleague.

But getting back to 1951, my husband, John had his own battles for respect. He took a job teaching, first at the Dalcrose School of Music. He enjoyed it but discovered that working with a classroom full of small children was exhausting. He moved on to the High School of Performing Arts and found out that teenagers could be just as difficult to work with. He also picked up odd jobs arranging music and playing piano and sometimes, when he was available, still accompanied me when I sang. He was always my best accompanist.

I'm tempted to look back on those days fondly, as a time of young love and passion and possibility, but at the time it didn't feel much like that. Mostly, for me, it was a time of youthful angst and impatience. I just couldn't wait to "make it"—whatever that was going to mean. I did not stop to smell the flowers very much or appreciate all the wonderful people I was meeting and the richness of my experiences in the cultural and artistic renaissance of New York City in the 1950s— when the Broadway Theater was still going strong and the golden age of television was in full swing. For John and me it was a time of great uncertainty. We were newlyweds who spent our evenings drinking and trying to unwind in our tiny apartment. We never thought either of us might be problem drinkers or might ever become that. Buy a bottle and pour a few and then a few more—it was what people did after work. A cigarette and a whiskey or a scotch or a martini. It was a big part of what it felt like to be a grown up. No need to worry about driving anywhere. Not in New York. Hardly anyone we knew drove a car. A pack of cigarettes was a quarter and every restaurant in the city—or anywhere else—allowed smoking. You marked the end of a meal by lighting one up, flicking the ashes on your plate until the waiter cleared your dishes. It was a different time, a very different time.

Early in 1952, things started to pick up—a little. Jack Rollins, a talent manager who'd just gotten out of the army, saw my act at the Village Vanguard and offered to represent me. Jack eventually went on to produce all of Woody Allen's pictures and he and I were lifelong friends. His wife Jane too. I'm so glad we got to celebrate Jack's 100th birthday before he passed away.

The first thing he got me back then was a TV show called *Once Upon a Tune* with Reginald Beane, Gordon Dilworth, Phil Hanna, Sondra Lee and Holly Harris. Each week we'd do an original half-hour musical. Most of them were satirical send-ups on what was on Broadway. We had a ball—and it was cancelled after three months.

Jack also introduced me to Broadway producer, Leonard Sillman who went to see my act and liked what he saw. He was trying to raise money for a new musical revue called *New Faces of 1952* and he asked me to do all their backers auditions along with Leonard's sister June Carroll, pianist Arthur Siegel—who'd written some of the songs— and Ronnie Graham—who was also one of the writers and who years later went on to write for the comic genius Mel Brooks. Ronnie was a brilliant writer and performer.

Leonard guaranteed me a part as soon as he got all the financing together and we were all confident that he would. Then Abe Burrows, who had directed Guys and Dolls and Two on the Aisle and was very hot, came to one of the backers auditions and the next afternoon I got a call from my agent. He said Abe fell in love with me and wanted me in his new musical, *Three Wishes for Jamie* with John Raitt and Anne Jeffries.

I was thrilled—mostly to know that someone of Abe Burrows' stature appreciated my work. I asked when I could read the script but my agent said it wasn't ready yet. I'd have to decide sight unseen. How could I do that? What kind of part was it?

"It's a part in a Broadway Musical," my agent told me.

"I've already got a part in *New Faces!*"

"Which has no backing—and probably never will," he said. "A job in hand is worth ten in the bush."

What else could he tell me? But I was torn. Leonard was a friend. He'd given John and me a beautiful antique set of Minton crockery. New Faces was something I felt like I was a vital part of the show having been in it from the very beginning, unlike my agent, I believed in it. He kind of bullied me. I mean, he was right about a job in the hand, but also I just wasn't strong enough to have the courage of my conviction. "Do I have a song?" I asked, about the new offer.

"Yes," my agent told me. "You have a song. And it's an Abe Burrows show!"

I took it. The right decision for many reasons but I felt terrible. I knew Leonard would be upset and I was right. I mean, he understood but was very very disappointed and I felt terrible. I almost offered to give back the antique set of Minton crockery—it must have cost a small fortune—but didn't want to further insult Leonard so I kept it. The next time I had my new in-laws, John's parents and his brother and sister-in-law, over for dinner, I made beef stroganoff and served it in what I thought was a big bowl from the antique Minton but turned out to be the chamber pot. I had no idea. My in-laws did—and were sure to let me know to my complete mortification.

*Three Wishes for Jamie* was a beautiful story from the book, *Three Wishes for Jamie McRuin* by Charles O'Neal about an Irish tinker who gets three wishes from a fairy, but still struggles in America with a wife who cannot bear children. I played the daughter of another Irish tinker. My father was played by Bert Wheeler, a Vaudevillian with no formal acting training and not much experience. We were supposed to be the comic relief. One of my songs was about love having nothing to do with the way a person looks—one of the lines was, "When it's dark all cats are gray." My other song detailed qualifications for a wife. I wasn't crazy about the part—when I finally did get to look at it—jokey stuff.

But it was a Broadway musical! Proof that I belonged. So I was thrilled.

John Raitt and Ann Jeffreys were great, even if the comic relief material Bert and I had to work with was weak and kind of broad.

Opening night was pure excitement—and I was too busy to get nervous. The flowers, the telegrams, and then my brother-in-law, John's older brother, Bill, came back stage to have me intervene about his tickets, which the box office apparently couldn't find! Later, I was still trying to get all my flowers in water and arrange them in my tiny corner of the dressing room when I noticed, a few feet away, Grania O'Mally, an Irish actress from the Gate Theater in Dublin, quietly putting on her makeup. She was so calm, so quiet. Almost in a trance. Her performance that night was flawless. As for me with all my flowers and telegrams and headaches, I actually blanked out and had to ad-lib part of one of my songs.

I got better, but the show didn't last. Luke warm reviews and too many great shows just up the street. By the time it closed, though, it was too late for me to go back to *New Faces*. By then Leonard had cast Eartha Kitt, Robert Clary, Carol Lawrence, Paul Lynde, and, to replace me, Alice Ghostley. When I had given Leonard the bad news about my leaving, he'd asked if I knew of anyone who could do my songs. I told him Alice Ghostley, and she turned out to be great—and the show launched her career. Sheldon Harnick wrote her the song *Boston Beguine*. She deserved every bit of that success, and thinking back on it now I'm so glad that my mistake became her good fortune. At the time, of course, I resented her for it—and wondered what would become of me now that my first big show had unceremoniously closed.

Actually, I was offered the touring company of New Faces. Alice had moved on and Leonard, ever the gentleman, held nothing against me and called me first and even offered to give John a job in the orchestra. It was tempting but I wasn't sure I wanted to go on the road, especially with Paul Lynde in the cast. I loved Paul and we'd been through a lot together but he was drinking more and more and he could be so abusive when he was drunk. He scared me a little.

My next job was with Michael Howard and Tony Holland in a production of Eugene Ionesco's *Victims of Duty* and *The New Tenant* at the Fourth Street Theater with Michael Kahn directing Michael Howard, Tony Holland, Joe Chaikin and me. It was Michael Kahn's first time directing and we could see how nervous he was. Michael Howard had been his acting teacher and I think he was a little intimidated by that. Sometimes, if we—the actors—would be looking at each other while he was staging something, he would stop and ask, "What are you doing?" He'd say, "I see it. Don't think I don't see it." Like he thought we were judging him negatively though not one of us had that in mind. Michael Howard and Tony Holland and Joe Chaikin were the consummate professionals and we had fun working together. Over the years I'd see them occasionally and it was always hugs and kisses. I was heartbroken to learn what had happened to Tony, years later. He got AIDS and committed suicide because he couldn't bear to let his mother discover that he was gay.

On a positive note, the last time I worked in Washington D.C.—did a play at the Ford's Theater—I went to see a production of Othello at the DC's Shakespeare Theater. It was absolutely marvelous, and guess who the director was? Michael Kahn. He had completely mastered his craft. He's a superb director—and I've been meaning for years to write him a note about it.

But back to 1952—and after the Ionesco plays came *Three Penny Opera*.

*Three Penny* is a show with timeless themes that in the early 1950s were considered dangerous—and therefore very timely: the struggles of ordinary people against greed and inhumanity. There were two versions of Brecht's opera. I had done the original Eric Bentley version at Northwestern. Leonard Bernstein had put together a concert version in 1952 for the Brandeis University Creative Arts Festival of Marc Blitzstein's version of *Three Penny*. Brooks Atkinson, a New York Times theater critic, liked it so much, and believed it so important, that he told producer Stanley Chase and director/producer Carmen Cabalbo that if they mounted Three Penny Opera anywhere in New York he would guarantee them a good review. An unusual promise from a New York critic but these were strange political times and he really wanted for the work to be seen on this side of the Atlantic.

I found out about it from my dear friend Leon Lishner, a wonderful singer and actor who I'd met at Maud's Summer Ray a few summers before. We'd stayed in touch and John and I socialized with him and his girlfriend. I'd phoned him to say how wonderful he was as the Villain in Benjamin Britten's opera of *Billy Budd* on the NBC TV opera program, and he told me he'd been cast as Mr. Peachum in *Three Penny Opera*. He told me they hadn't yet cast Mrs. Peachum and suggested I call the producers. I loved *Three Penny*. I'd done it at Northwestern. The only problem was that I was already committed to George Abbott's new musical, *Pajama Game*. Leon told me to look into it anyway. Maybe they can work something out. Who knows? So I called my agent the next day and he called the producers and they offered me the part.

I told them I had to start Pajama Game two weeks after the opening of Three Penny Opera—and that I had a nightclub commitment that would last during most of the Three Penny rehearsals. Carmen said that was no problem. He'd love to have me longer but he'd take me for the opening and the reviews. He was very reassuring.

It was an exciting time for me—rehearsing *Three Penny* during the day and still performing my act in the evenings in Carnival Room uptown at the Sherry Netherlands, a fancy 5th Avenue Hotel. I was starting to believe that I wasn't just wasting my time in New York, that my dream of stardom might actually be possible. I was also exhausted.

I went to my doctor at the time, Dr. Gilbert. He examined me and said that I had an enlarged heart. He said it very matter-of-factly.

I asked him what that meant and he didn't really have much to say. He told me that usually an enlarged heart was found in men who did rugged heavy work. He never did say it had anything to do with why I was always so tired.

I finished my run at the Sherry Netherlands right before the opening of *Three Penny*. Rehearsals had been wonderful and hectic at the Theater de Lys. This tawdry little hole in the wall of a theater was the perfect setting for a play about the poor and working class struggling against oppression. Backstage was even more dilapidated and crowded than the theater. Everyone was crammed into a few small dressing rooms. I dressed alongside my pal Leon Lishner and Bea Arthur, John Astin (who most people know as Gomez on *The Addams Family* TV sit-com of the 1960s), Jo Sillivan (who was married to *Guys and Dolls* composer Frank Loesser and later appeared in *Most Happy Fella*) and the incomparable Lotte Lenya.

My big number was the *Ballad of Dependency*, also known as the Ballad of Sexual Slavery. It's a brilliant lyric, subtle in its double *entendres*, all of which had to be explained to naïve lil me by Mark Blitzstein.

> *Now there's a man, the living tool of Satan*
> *He charges forth while others are debating*
> *Conniving, cocky knave with all the trimmings*
> *I know one thing will trim him down: women.*

Tool. Cocky. It all went right over my head. But once I understood I wanted to make it play. I felt that I should convey Mrs. Peachum's own sexual frustration along with her contempt for Mr. Macheath and his wandering lust. I asked Carmen if I could have something to do during the song. He was open to any ideas I had. I asked for an iron, an ironing board, and a pair of men's trousers—and I pushed that iron across those trousers and jammed the point of that iron into that crotch.

Toward the end of the show, Macheath returns after being pardoned from his execution and though urgent matters await, he stops off to see Susie Tandem for a quick fuck. To that I sang a reprise of the *Ballad of Dependency*. Afterwards, as he lay there spent, I said, "What a man!"

But also what a play! And Leon Lischner was so wonderful as the captain of our proverbial ship. So full of ideas and support for all of us. What a great experience.

During previews, the famous director, George Abbott came to see *Three Penny Opera*. He met me at the backstage exit and said, "Charlotte Rae, you are the cutest!" Was he really saying that to me? Here I was playing Mrs. Peachum, this bitter, angry woman—and he thought I was cute?

Rehearsals for his new show, *Pajama Game*, were starting right around that time, and thus began the greatest challenge of my young career—rehearsing all day for *Pajama*, then rushing downtown to perform in *Three Penny*. It was wonderfully exhilarating. Rehearsing with George Abbott and theater stars John Raitt, Janis Paige, Carol Haney. A dream come true. And exhausting! I started getting cranky. I remember sitting in a taxi going down 9th Avenue worrying about both parts I was playing. Each wonderful in its own way. A classy off-Broadway show. Working with Marc Blitzstein and Lotte Lenya. And a Broadway show. I kept thinking I should be on top of the world. But I was so tired it felt like I was dying. I mean, if this was success, I wasn't so sure I wanted it. Thinking back now, I have to wonder if it was my heart. At the time, of course, I had no idea. I was just so tired.

Mr. Abbot let me out of *Pajama Game* rehearsal early on the opening night of *Three Penny Opera*, early enough for the dress rehearsal of Three Penny. Afterwards, I thought I might find a quiet corner and catch some shut-eye, but I was too wound up. I remembered my opening night in *Three Wishes for Jamie*, how I gave in to the excitement and let it distract me from the work. I was determined not to let that happen this time.

So I got out of the dressing room and went outside and walked. No particular destination. Just walking the narrow streets of the Village, walking out the nerves and thinking about my character, Mrs. Peachum. Muttering in my head and occasionally uttering aloud my contempt for Macheath and my bitterness about life, thinking about all the disappointments and frustrations that were piled up inside Mrs. Peachum. Crossing Hudson Street I passed Lotte Lenya. She was in a similar state, muttering her rage as Pirate Jenny no doubt. We silently acknowledged each other and went on our own private paths, concentrating on our characters.

Opening night was electric. Inspiring—to be performing this subversive opera at the height of red-baiting and black-listing, to proudly sing out a big to hell with you in the direction of that very un-American senator, the disgrace of my beloved Wisconsin. The reviews were great. I was so proud to be involved, but sad that I would soon be leaving.

And I had never been so exhausted in my life. I was rehearsing *Pajama Game* all day and performing *Three Penny* at night and I often found myself lying down on the nearest couch whenever I could and I have to admit that my attitude was not great. The work became a burden and I felt overwhelmed by it, and I'm embarrassed—even now—to say that I found myself at the run-thru for *Pajama Game* still holding my script! I could hear my sister Beverly's voice in my head reminding me how stupid and useless I was. Everyone else in the cast, of course, had their parts down. Carol Haney and John Raitt and everyone else was nearly flawless. And there I was with the damn script in my hand. It is something I've tried to forget and God knows I never thought I'd be admitting it to the world. But there it is. I was TIRED!

Harold Prince approached me the next day after the run-thru. He said, matter-of-factly, that they had decided to combine my part with

Carole Haney's (Gladys). I was more than welcome to stay on as one of the factory girls—a much smaller part. I probably deserved it—for coming to the run-thru unprepared—but I was in no frame of mind to accept the truth. I was deeply hurt. And furious. I was an up-and-coming star. I deserved better. Dick Adler, one of the lyricists, overheard Hal and me and came over, afterwards, to sympathize with me, but I was inconsolable and humiliated. The part they were offering me had no song, nothing interesting. I decided to leave.

*You'll be sorry*, I thought, foolishly, defensively. *Pajama Game* went on to become one of the most successful musicals on Broadway. Carole Haney did a great job with her newly enlarged part and got great reviews. Her understudy was an unknown actress in the chorus named Shirley MacLaine, who got a chance to go on for a while when Carole broke her ankle. Three months after that, Carole got injured again and Shirley took over for her again. Hal B. Wallis, the legendary movie producer just happened to be in the audience. He brought her to Hollywood and the rest, as they say, is history.

Many years later, I apologized to Harold for my lack of preparation on *Pajama Game* and for my bad attitude about it. He accepted my apology and didn't disagree with anything I said about myself, so I guess he thought I was pretty out-of-line. And he was right. I should have understood my limitations. Performers often spend so much time waiting for an opportunity that when two or three come along at the same time—and they often do—it is hard to be realistic.

So I went from being in two shows at once to being unemployed. I think I learned my lesson from that experience and while I've tried to never back down from a creative challenge and pursue formidable acting roles, I've also been careful not to over-extend myself physically. It isn't fair to all the other people involved in a production—and it isn't fair to myself.

Things were quiet for a while. I got some club dates and got my act back on stage. I got a nice long run at the Bon Soir downtown. It was a great way to make a buck and get showcased. So many extremely talented people were working the club circuit along with me. Jerry Stiller and Annie Meara, Alice Ghostly, G. Wood, James Kirkwood, who became a novelist and who wrote the book to *A Chorus Line*. A mainstay at the Bonsoir was the incomparable Mae Barnes, a short, chubby African American personality and singer. She was simply terrific. Funny in a sophisticated way. John and I became great friends with her and husband Dave and used to visit them at their home in St. Albans quite often on Sundays.

Meanwhile, John was still teaching. Somehow we managed to get the rent paid. I got a few calls for small parts on television shows—*The U.S. Steel Hour* (with a very nervous young Jack Klugman), The *Armstrong Circle Theater* (with Fred Allen, we played opposite each other—he kept laughing at me when I'd sneer at him, found it very funny), and *Philco Playhouse*. Live television was strange and exciting. I had to keep reminding myself that thousands of people were on the other side of that camera. I doubt too many noticed me as the party snob in Fred Allen's sketchbook. It's a little sad that so many of those early TV shows are now gone, evaporated before anyone could make recordings of them. But there is something kind of pure and wonderful about that. It belongs only to us and always will—the writers, producers, directors, and actors who created it all.

I'd almost forgotten about the *Three Penny Opera* cast album when I got a call from Leon Lishner. He told me that the producers had offered him only a small recording fee, almost a token amount, and no royalties. He said he had refused to do it and hoped I'd do the same. I was a little heartbroken. I'd been looking forward to getting back together with the cast and making that record. But when Carmen called me, he gave me the same lousy offer he'd given Leon, and just as Leon had hoped, I told him no thank you. I was negotiating. I figured they would come around and make all of us a reasonable offer. I was proud to stand in solidarity with Leon.

Then Marc Blitzstein came to see me at the Bonsoir and back stage, between sets, he pleaded with me to reconsider. I told him I would happily reconsider if I was made a reasonable offer. He shook his head and said they weren't going to offer any more. They were nervous the album might not sell many copies and they couldn't risk a lot of up-front money. Fine, I told him. Cut us in on a share of the royalties if the album does sell. Marc shook his head again. He broke down, weeping. He said, "I've lost Leon and if I lose you I'll lose the deal! No album. No recording of all the great work we did."

Incredible. I almost asked him if he appreciated the irony—here was the man who had written "Joe Worker," a song about the exploitation of the working man and he was asking us to allow ourselves to be exploited. Maybe he just didn't see it. Maybe because we weren't on the floor of a factory or in a field of cotton or lettuce. Or maybe it was just too personal for him and he was blinded by his own artistic ambitions.

I can hardly fault him because, despite my convictions about it, I'm ashamed to say I allowed his tears and pleas to convince me.

To this day it remains one of my greatest regrets, though the regrets are mixed with pride that I helped bring those important songs to a larger audience. *Three Penny Opera* is a great album—and in a way that almost makes up for the unfortunate circumstances around it. But it is hard for me still to listen to it without thinking that I had sold out.

In the spring of 1954 I was offered the role of Mrs. Juniper in The Golden Apple, a delightful musical—based on the epic Greek poems, *Illiad and Odyssey*—by John La Touche (book and lyrics) and Jerome Moross (music), directed by the brilliant actor and director Lloyd Richards. The show had started off-Broadway at the Phoenix Theater with G. W. Hambleton and his partner, a theater professor, author and scholar Norris Houghton. It was the same theater where *The Littlest Revue* had started out.

I was actually brought in as a replacement for someone they weren't happy with. I played two characters. In the first act, I played Mrs. Juniper, the mayor's wife. In act two I was Madam Calypso. It was a great cast—Portia Nelson, Bibi Osterwald, Priscilla Gilette, Jerry Stiller and Kaye Ballard. We had so much fun working together. All those fun, warm-hearted, talented people.

Hanya Holmes was a wonderful choreographer, though we had our differences. She wanted me to play my part the same way as the actress I'd replaced. I wanted to find my own truth in the movements of my characters. I was a little intimidated. Hanya had an impressive list of Broadway credits—including Kiss Me, Kate and Out of This World, but Mary Tarcai, my wonderful acting teacher, worked with me on it and I found that truth and Mary helped me have the confidence to stand my ground. In the end, Hanya respected the work I'd done and we came to an understanding.

We had a great time together. I mean the whole cast. So many great people. My husband, John and I got to be very good friends with John La Touche who wrote the book and lyrics. We had him over to our apartment a few times. We'd sit on the floor around our cocktail table and drink and John would tell stories about all the weird people in his family and growing up in the south.

What a genius he was. He wrote that great standard, "Taking a Chance on Love" and he wrote the "Ballad of Americans" that Paul Robeson sang. The two Johns—my husband and La Touche—were going to collaborate on an opera for me after The Golden Apple. It never quite came to fruition but they did collaborate on a piece of comic special material for me about a patron of the opera, a woman who knows everyone and thinks the opera isn't the opera without her. It was called "A Nail in the Horseshoe" and it became a regular part of my routine, one of the songs we chose for my album a few years later.

The Golden Apple played the Alvin Theater on Broadway, then toured at the Carter Baron Theater in D.C. We all got great reviews. But the show closed less than six months in and after just 125 performances.

I was turning 28 that spring and had lots to be proud of and much to look forward to—but I was disappointed. I had always imagined becoming a big star by now, then perhaps taking a break to start a family with John. Beverly had a son and a daughter. Her husband was a prominent neurosurgeon and they were part of the Jewish social life of Milwaukee with a beautiful house near the lake. That wasn't the life I'd ever wanted but I felt like I didn't have much of any life.

Mimi and her husband, Don, were trying to start a family too. All I had were a lot of small successes that didn't feel like they added up to anything. John and I were as financially unstable as could be. We were still trying to build up our professional reputations. John was still teaching, picking up odd jobs arranging music and playing piano when he could. Our two bedroom was inexpensive and we still did most of our drinking at home out of the bottle—avoiding those expensive bar tabs. We knew that children could be expensive, but it didn't seem like waiting was getting us anywhere. Thinking back, of course, 28 seems so young to me now. But at the time it felt so old.

I got pregnant in the early spring of 1955 and realized it by the early spring. It was an exciting time. More exciting than I'd thought it would be. A validation of myself as a woman. And John seemed more excited about it than I might have thought he would be. All of our concerns about not being ready suddenly gave way to a new closeness between us and a wonderful sense of anticipation.

John became much more domestic. He went out to the hardware store and bought baby safety window bars. He scrubbed the floors and walls of every room in the apartment and painted the bedroom that would be the nursery.

At the same time, John landed a job as music supervisor and composer on the new Phil Silvers show. Nat Hiken gave him the opportunity. I'd met Nat a few years before when he'd come to see me perform at the Bon Soir. He'd introduced himself after the show, said he really enjoyed my act. He also said that we were related, distant cousins by marriage. I think that really meant something to him, that we were family. We became friends.

Nat was so loyal to friends and family—and he considered us both. He knew all about John's background with classical music, his studies with Paul Hindemith. But Nat also knew that John had written ballet music and that John loved Broadway. Nat just basically gave John carte blanche. Let him learn music cues and how to operate a Moviola and lay in the music tracks. It was pretty remarkable. That Nat had such faith in John figuring it all out and that John actually did figure it all out—on the job! There were no film schools in those days. Just ingenuity and hard work. There was some anxiety about it but it became his career and he became one of the best at it.

And it was steady income—though for how long we did not know. We still lived on Madison Avenue between 96th and 97th Streets. It was above an A&P supermarket and that upset my father. When I called to give my parents the news, he pleaded with me to move to a better place. I told him this one was fine and that it was what we could afford, for now, but that didn't satisfy him. He said it reminded him of when our family lived atop his tire store in downtown Milwaukee. He said, "I worked and worked so my wife and daughters would never have to live on top of a store again. And now..." It was sweet—my Daddy worrying about me like that. I looked forward to visiting him and Mother with our new baby.

Meanwhile, I was busy. Still doing my act at the Bonsoir and the phone was ringing from my agent with TV jobs, including a program called *Appointment with Adventure*. The director of my episode turned out to be Paul Lammers, a guy I knew from Northwestern.

He was hard-working and made the cast likewise, rehearsing us over and over. I could hardly blame him. This was live television. No one wanted to embarrass themselves. But I was already in the second trimester of my pregnancy and the seemingly endless rehearsals really wore me down and when we were filming, I forgot about my last scene. I finished the scene I thought was my last, said goodbye to everyone and everyone said goodbye to me, and lumbered outside to get a cab home. I saw one and flagged it down and reached for the door—and heard someone screaming my name. It was Joseph Papp, the assistant director (who would go on to found The Public Theater and become one of the most successful theater producers of our time).

I opened the taxi door and waved goodbye.

"Charlotte, wait!" he yelled. "You have one more scene!"

And it hit me—yes, my last scene with Sheila Bond. I slammed the taxi door and waved off the driver and ran like hell. Joe ran even faster and got to the stage door and held it open for me. Poor Sheila was on the set, alone, waiting, improvising, pretending to look for me in closets and under furniture, in drawers! Wardrobe had to throw a nightgown over my clothes while I ran to the stage. Somehow—me out of breath, Sheila surely out of patience!—we pulled it off.

I wasn't sure I'd ever work again after that, but Nat Hiken, who was now John's boss on the Phil Silvers Show, wanted me to do a guest shot as the wife of an Army General visiting the base where Sergeant Bilko (Phil Silvers) and his cohorts carried out their mischief. For those of you unfamiliar with that show, it was about a bunch of misfit soldiers who preferred to spend their time drinking and gambling. Sergeant Bilko ran interference for them with the officers. He was smooth with his superiors but underneath it he was as bad as the rest of the enlisted men.

Nat once explained to me that Phil Silvers was not a very warm personality for a series so he'd done whatever he could to make the character of Sergeant Bilko very likeable. Made him a lowly sergeant, wheeling and dealing and conniving and always losing out in the end. I think it was one of the funniest shows ever. On one episode, Bilko and his men had a monkey inducted into the army. Hilarious.

My character, in addition to being wife of a general, was a dilattante of high culture. Visiting a base with my husband enabled me to secure a captive audience for my lectures on Shakespeare. As you can imagine, that was not the way Sergeant Bilko and his men wanted to spend a Friday night, but they found a way to make the most of it. I had a habit of tugging on my girdle as I spoke. In fact, my lectures and the girdle-tugging had become legendary on bases throughout North America and the free world. Odds were made and bets taken on how many times I would tug at that girdle during my lecture. The episode—and my character—had the same name: THE TWITCH.

People to this day remember that episode. They come up to me on the street or in a restaurant and they say, "I remember the Twitch."

It was a joy working with Nat Hiken and Phil Silvers. They were comic geniuses. Nat had written for *The Grouch Club, The Fred Allen Show, the Martha Raye Show,* and of course he went on to write and produce *Car 54 Where Are You?* His suggestions were often brilliant. Sometimes he would come out of the booth and direct an entire scene. His timing was amazing. Being around him somehow made you funnier. I don't know why he's not in the Television Hall of Fame along with all the other giants like Norman Lear and Carl Reiner.

I loved being at the television studio where John worked every week. We got to eat lunch together a few times. He had to finish my sandwich—instead of me finishing his—because I was watching my weight. I'd stopped smoking and drinking for the baby. Alcohol and cigarettes were repulsive to me.

My body wouldn't let me do anything that would harm my baby. I was eating and drinking and breathing for two and it was a wonderful feeling. I still wasn't quite showing but soon I would be.

Mostly John and I talked about the album Vanguard Records wanted us to record. Nat Shapiro had been assigned to be our producer. He managed Michel Legrand, the French composer who worked with the Bergman's, and he knew his stuff. He helped us select the material and gave John great feedback on his arrangements. John assembled a nice little ensemble of musicians for the date—including a clarinet and flute—and Michel came up with the idea to call them "John Strauss and his Baroque Bearcats." We laid down the tracks at a church in Brooklyn. It was a magical day for me. Performing my material for posterity. My wonderful husband's stunning arrangements. His exquisite accompaniments. Felt like we were doing something really special and I knew that in a little while would come something even more special, the birth of our child.

# MY MOST IMPORTANT ROLE— NO REHEARSAL

John and I lived around the corner from Mount Sinai Hospital, so when my water broke, we just threw a few things in a suitcase and a few minutes later I was in the maternity ward.

I wish the ease of those first moments was a sign of things to come.

We were optimistic. Our Lamaze teachers had given us gold stars. We'd taken two birthing and parenting classes. Paul Newman and Joanne Woodward were in one of them along with some of our other friends. It was nice to share the experience with people we knew but mostly we all concentrated on childbirth. We were there to have healthy babies.

The teacher was a little old woman named Elsa. She told all the women to do our kegel exercises. "Contract and release your vaginal muscles," she said. "It's good for the childbirth. Good for the bladder health. And good for the husband. When he's in you just squeeze. It's a nice thing to do—like giving him a hug.

She'd made it all sound so easy, so… natural. And for the first few hours, it seemed it might be. I had all my notes, the outlines Elsa had dictated to all of us. I had everything all planned out. I was Marie Antoinette with the court around while she's giving birth… I even brought along a deck of playing cards. Why not? I figured John and I might play a few hands of gin rummy.

Meanwhile, I breathed deeply and held tight to my outlines and looked at them to see what to do next.

The contractions were painful but nothing I couldn't handle. After those first few hours, though, it started getting scary, really terrifying. I kept pushing but nothing was happening. It felt like my baby was too big to come out. I kept asking the nurses if they could do anything, but they all just smiled and offered to knock me out. I told them no. I was vehement. I wanted it natural. I tried to hang. Three hours, four hours, five, six. I didn't think it would ever be over. It was pretty agonizing. I was drenched in sweat. John was white as a ghost from sitting there, his eyes sagging, and somehow seeing his exhaustion got to me. It made me think this would never be over.

By the seventh hour, the pain of natural childbirth felt unnatural. It was too much. I gave in. I surrendered. "Knock me out," I screamed.

My doctor, Dr. Norman Pleshette, asked: "Are you sure?"

I'll never forget the look on his face. It was a tired look—him and his nurse both—waiting for me to answer. I answered.

"Knock me out!!!!"

I remember those moments so vividly because I've thought about them so many times over the years. Each second came to be fraught with meaning. What could I have done differently? What could anyone have done differently? Would any of it have mattered? No one ever wants to think there could be anything wrong with their child. And yet it happens. It happens to people every day. It happened to me.

I came to and was so relieved to have my son, Andrew Brian Strauss. He was very big. Twenty-three inches long. Nine pounds, ten ounces. And he was very beautiful. Holding him, I knew that everything was all right. The struggle and the pain and uncertainty, it was all worth it.

I was a little terrified by the responsibility of motherhood but somehow I felt ready. Who in the world is ever completely ready? I knew that I loved my son. It was a profound and beautiful experience to lock eyes with his little soul and smell the sweet scent coming off the top of his head and feel his weight outside my body. Beverly had always told me I was no good at anything—anything important at least. Holding my baby now I felt so strongly—more strongly than ever before—that she was wrong. I'd done something right. Something—the most important thing I could ever do. John and I had made a life and I'd brought him into this world. I was so proud. He had all his fingers, all his toes.

I couldn't get over the miracle of it all. And somewhere along the way I got to thinking about my own mother and what it was like for her. First Beverly, then me, then Mimi. Suddenly I understood, holding Andy, for the first time, how Mother and Father could have so totally surrendered themselves to their first born. Knowing how destructive that surrender had been for my family growing up I promised myself that I would never repeat that mistake. Little did I know how impossible keeping that promise would be.

John and I were both very excited. John was in such wonderment at being a father that he went home the first night, while Andy and I were still in the hospital, and scrubbed the walls of the apartment.

Again. He wanted everything germ free and I think he may actually have succeeded.

We hired someone to help us through the first few days at home with our new baby. Looking back I'd have to say she wasn't the best person for us. I would have preferred someone who taught us things and encouraged us. This middle-aged woman insisted on doing it all herself. Her only concern seemed to be that everything was absolute precision while she was on duty. She didn't see her role as helping us through the early challenges of parenthood and helping us to become capable caretakers of an infant. We only kept her a week. What was the point? We had to figure it out for ourselves, and of course, like all parents, we did.

So there we were up all night with the crying and the feeding. And then, when we could steal a few hours of sleep during the day people kept calling to congratulate us. Of course, the call that meant the most to me, the one I'll never forget, was from my father and mother. They were so delighted. Daddy could hear Andy crying in the background while he talked to me. He said, "You've got a beautiful baby." He just loved hearing his grandson and promised to visit as soon as he could. Daddy had just gotten over a bout of pneumonia. He and Mother were going to take a trip to a ranch in Arizona to relax. Then, maybe, when he was fully recuperated, they would venture east to see Andy.

He survived the pneumonia and before they left Milwaukee for Arizona my father's doctor gave him an EKG. Daddy had been having some mild chest pain and shortness of breath but the doctor assured him that he could travel. I know they were both really looking forward to their vacation. I'd always thought my Daddy looked like Gary Cooper (though I might have been the only person who really thought that) and he looked especially so (to me, at least) sitting astride a horse. Mother stood next to him looking more relaxed than I'd ever seen her. I still have the photos, though it has always been a little hard to look at them because of what happened just a few hours after they were taken.

They both ate a big barbecue dinner at the ranch and Daddy felt what he thought was indigestion. Tightness in his chest. He went to his room to lie down. One of the other guests at the ranch was a doctor. He came to check on Daddy. He had someone call an ambulance and said to my father—my mother told this word for word: "Mr. Lubotsky, you're having a heart attack. I'm not well myself. I can only tell you that the ambulance is clean. I want you to stay in bed. If you need go to the bathroom, just do it right there in the bed. Whatever you do don't stand up. Just wait for the ambulance." But Daddy didn't obey. He got up and he went to the bathroom. It took a while and the chest pain got a little worse but he was still alert and optimistic, my Daddy, and when the ambulance arrived, there wasn't much they could do for him except keep him still and take him to the hospital and put him in a bed and keep monitoring him. He chatted with the nurses and thanked the nurses for being so helpful and so nice to him and they all joked about ruining his vacation. They kept him comfortable and everyone seemed to like him. People always loved my father. He was just a really decent man. Hard-working, considerate, and always upbeat. He went to sleep that night and never woke up. He seemed to die peacefully. He was only fifty-eight. And to this day, whenever I hear the wail of an ambulance, I think of my Daddy.

I was holding Andy when I got the call and I felt so bad that Daddy would never get to meet my sweet son and that Andy would never get to meet his grandfather. What a terrible terrible shame. You really don't get to write your own script in this life, do you?

I flew alone to Milwaukee for the funeral. Andy was too young to travel so I had to leave him with John and a nurse we hired to help while I was gone. It's all a bit of a blur to me now. I was glad they had those little liquor bottles for sale on the airplane.

I loved my Daddy and admired him so much. He was such a kind and generous man. Not just to my sisters and me but to everyone. He was admired and loved throughout the Milwaukee community. His funeral was well attended. A huge crowd turned out and not just Jewish people, not by a long-shot. Probably more than one-hundred novenas were made in his name by local Catholics. Anyone who ever did business with my Daddy knew they had lost a great guy. Anyone who had ever known him.

One thing I know he was so very proud of was what he'd done to help Israel. Everyone was buying Israel bonds but he was more ambitious about what he thought he could do. He told us he woke up in the middle of the night one night with an inspiration. He went to a Jewish friend in Dayton, Ohio who had a tire factory and together they donated tire molds and other needed materials for Israel's first tire factory, Alliance Tire and Rubber. To this day, Alliance is still in business in the city of Hadera. There's an honorary tire with Father's and Mother's names on it. Israel was always very important to him, to both my parents. I don't know how he would feel about Israel today if he were still alive. I think the situation would have deeply concerned him. I think Daddy would have wanted—as I now want—to see everyone, Arab or Jew, able to live in dignity and peace. That was the father I knew. He didn't have an enemy in the world.

The world lost someone special when he died but for me there was a much more personal and devastating feeling. I never quite got the closeness I'd wanted or hoped for from him. I understand now that for me maybe it was more of a feeling than a fact. I mean that my disappointment might have been an emotional condition I fell into. It happens. Being a middle sister with a domineering older sister and really cute younger one. And it is so hard for parents to make all their children feel equally loved. My father always used to say, "I love you all the same," which was a nice sentiment, but not very personal, though I'm sure he meant it to be.

I found myself, in the days after his death and after the burial thinking back, remembering good times, happy times, but also very sad times. I couldn't help it. I remembered an afternoon when I was about eleven or twelve years old. We were living in Shorewood and it was just him and me in the backyard. Just sitting there. I was telling him something or other. I don't remember what. What I remember was the warmth of being there with just him and me and a moment later the deep chill when he said, "Charlotte, I hope you don't mind, but I'd like to be alone."

I understand that need now—especially as a parent—but at the time I felt so rejected. I just wanted something else, something more.

Maybe it's just a part of the human condition to want more.

I felt such emptiness on that flight back to New York, but then I returned home to my husband and my son and felt my love for them and the fullness of their love. What more could a woman ask for? A happy marriage, full of joy and laughs to a man I loved and admired and a perfect-looking, big beautiful hungry baby.

Andy was such a big and beautiful baby. I have so many pictures of him from his first months. John and I snapped a bunch and then Nat Hiken's wife, Amber, who was a photographer, asked permission to photograph Andy because he was so beautiful. And he really was. People on the street and in the park would marvel at him as I pushed him in his stroller every day. I used to sing to him while we strolled and he always smiled when I did—children's songs at first, and then the songs for Lil Abner which I was in rehearsals for in early 1956. He also sometimes seemed enchanted hearing John's classical records on the Victrola. He especially loved Stravinsky's Punchinella. The trombone part always made him laugh.

He seemed from a very early age to have a strong affinity for music and for light. He'd gaze up at a bulb on the ceiling or at reflecting sun coming in a window or he'd smile at the glow of a flash bulb from a camera. Related to music and light. At times it seemed perfectly natural but after a while I became concerned. Sometimes he just didn't respond to me or to John the way other babies appeared to respond to their parents. He always ate well. Took the bottle hungrily and drank it down. But there was often a vacant look in his eyes and a distance to his smile—and I could see it all the time when I held him. He didn't walk for a long time, till well past his first birthday. Sometimes, when he was in his bouncy seat, he would break out in little red dots. They'd cover his face and his back would arch up like a cat.

I took him to my pediatrician, Dr. Berenberg, who said it was nothing. It was the first of a number of such doctor visits when I was told my son was fine, that I was needlessly worrying. Doctors barely knew what autism was. And I believed them each time they told me not to worry.

Aside from my concerns I really enjoyed being a mother in those early weeks and months and was in no hurry to go back to work. So when I was offered Lil Abner I didn't think much of it. The last thing I wanted to do was leave my baby and my husband to tour the east coast playing a comic strip character. I wanted to do Shakespeare, Shaw, Ionesco. And what I really wanted to do right then was spend my time with Andy and John.

But John thought it was a mistake to turn down something headed for Broadway. He had a point, but I was still very torn about it. I didn't want to turn down a job like that so I told my lawyer, who was negotiating for me, to ask for $750 a week, an awful lot of money at that time and way more than I had any business asking for at that point in my career. He didn't think he heard right and when I repeated it he said I was crazy, but I insisted. What a relief to know they'd turn me down so I wouldn't have to turn them down. Only they didn't. They agreed to the $750 and I was stuck.

At least that's how I felt at the time but now I'm kind of glad I ended up doing the show. I got to work with a lot of terrific people and had some really good times. Lil Abner went into rehearsals in the summer of 1956. John and I hired a nanny to help with Andy. Mrs.

Holznagel, a middle-aged German woman was great with Andy and easy to work with, very flexible about everything.

We rented a house near the beach on Long Island and she agreed to go with us. I rode the Long Island Railroad into the city every morning and came back amid the crush in the evening. It was great to know that my baby could be out of the city in the hot and humid summer with John—and it was nice for me too, even if only for a few hours at a time to know our baby could enjoy the cool ocean breeze.

Rehearsals can be a little tense in the beginning. No one ever knows for sure if a show is going to be good until it gets on its feet. But it's so much more pleasant with nice people, like Edie Adams (who was in a bunch of movies, including Oscar-winning *The Apartment*). She was the consummate professional, always, and a real pal. One day at lunch I was fretting about what to wear to a TV audition I had the next morning. She took me to a wholesale house nearby and helped me find something to wear to the audition.

My other pal was Tina Louise (who most people know as Ginger from Gilligan's Island, though she had an impressive stage career also). After we opened the show, Tina told me to drink a large bottle of cold water instead of eating before bed. She was so helpful and so adorable too. One night when we were onstage, the audience was laughing somewhere they hadn't ever laughed before and when Tina and I were in the wings after the scene, she asked me if her boobs had fallen out. Yes, we had wardrobe malfunctions even back then. They were propped up so far she had trouble sometimes knowing what the audience was seeing. I assured her that nothing had escaped and that it was her comic abilities, not her breasts, that had the audience laughing.

Tina and Edie both were so tall. Well, not really, but I'll never forget sitting next to Edie one night at Sardis. In our seats, I was taller, then when we stood up she towered over me with my short legs. Sometimes I wonder how I ever made it in the theater with my stumpy little legs. I used to wonder how far I could have gone if I'd had beautiful long legs and was taller but now I've learned to appreciate my little legs. They're like little sausages. I've had so many wonderful and rich experiences and worked with so many brilliantly talented people.

Anyway, I just loved working with Edie. She was so talented and such a lovely woman. She and her husband, Ernie Kovaks, were madly in love. On her birthday he had three Mexican crooners come to her dressing room and sing love songs to her and give her champagne. He bought her a chinchilla coat that went to the floor. Sadly, he died in a terrible car accident not too long after. He was really an innovator in television. A real original on *The Ernie Kovacs Show*.

Joe E. Marks, who played opposite me as Pappy Yokum, was adorable and great to work with. He was an old vaudeville actor and almost seventy at the time and a consummate professional.

Stubby Kaye played Marryin' Sam and what a great comic actor he was. He'd played Nicely Nicely Johnson in the original *Guys and Dolls* and brought the house down with his now famous number, "Sit Down, You're Rockin' the Boat." While we were on the road with the show in Boston at the Bradford Hotel, he put his arm around me in the hotel lobby and tried to convince me to go to bed with him. He was kind of cute but I wasn't interested. I was happily married and had a little baby and a husband I couldn't wait to get home to.

I could go on and on about everyone in the cast of that show, how great they all were. Peter Palmer, our male lead, from my hometown, Milwaukee. He was discovered by the producers when he sang on *The Ed Sullivan Show* and did a great job. Julie Newmar, who was also an absolute pleasure to work with, used to joke with everyone that she was the highest paid actor in the show. She was only onstage 34 minutes so she figured she had to be making the most per minute of any of us. And everyone else, pretty much—sorry, everyone I left out—except for Bern Hoffman.

What a jerk, God bless him, and I have to admit that after almost sixty years I still remember how mean he was to me. I guess I was pretty sensitive but he really picked on me. He was kind of a bully. During rehearsals he would imitate my performance and mock the way I was developing my character. I guess he thought my movements were mechanical but I knew what I was doing. I'd figured it out with my acting teacher, the great Mary Tarcai, who also taught Ralph Waite of *The Waltons* fame and so much more, and Valerie Harper from *The Mary Tyler Moore* show—and so much more—and Florence Henderson (*Brady Bunch* and more).

Mary Tarcai knew that any show choreographed by Michael Kidd would have a lot of movement on-stage. It is what he was known for. He'd done *Finian's Rainbow* and a lot of other great things and he was truly a joy to work with.

Anyway, as Mammy Yokum I was supposed to be the leader of this fictional town. I was also the shortest person on stage. Mary suggested showing my power through minimal movement. To contrast the movement all around me by standing still and moving only slightly, only what was absolutely necessary. So I had this image. I thought of myself as the prow of a ship and every time I moved it was meaningful. Which meant that I was, admittedly, a little stylized. But, really, so was the whole show.

Bern, who coincidentally played Earthquake McGoon, arch enemy of my character, would parody my little movements, exaggerating them until he'd get a reaction from someone—usually me. At first I thought he was just being cute, a little friendly teasing, but he wouldn't stop and seemed to really want to ridicule me. I don't know why he picked on me. Maybe he was nasty to everyone. It made an otherwise great experience a lot less enjoyable. Don't get me wrong. He was a good actor and had a great sense of comic timing. Played on Broadway in *No Time for Sergeants, The Merry Widow, Catherine Was Great,* and *Guys and Dolls.*

When I ultimately left the show, after just a year, Bern came up to me and said, "Well, I guess because of our characters, I guess we didn't get along." I had to tell him that I didn't think it had anything to do with the script. I really wished him well and told him I hoped I never had to work with him again. Thankfully, I never did.

Lil Abner played in Boston, then Philadelphia and then down to Washington D.C. Adlai Stevenson, who was campaigning for president at the time, came to see the show one night and came back stage. He paid me a nice compliment and I threw my arms around him and someone with one of the papers snapped our picture. We were quite a pair—me with all my Mammy Yokum makeup still on and the buttoned-up presidential candidate. That shot ended up in the D.C. papers and elsewhere, including the New York Daily News.

Around the time the show opened on Broadway, John and I got the itch to move. We liked our little neighborhood on the upper east side. We were close to the park and though technically we lived on the Spanish Harlem side of 96th Street—Madison Avenue between 96th and 97th—that wasn't such a big deal in 1956. I used to run into David Suskind sometimes at the supermarket or just out walking. He and his wife lived in one of the fancy buildings on 96th  Street between Madison and Park Avenue.

This was before his iconic TV show when he was known as a big television producer and a pretty great one at that. Sholem Aleichem, which I'd been in, was among his many credits. He was very ambitious, I mean artistically ambitious, and full of energy and always with his thinking cap on about something or other. He once phoned me on a

Sunday afternoon because he'd thought up a sit-com idea—a bunch
of girls sharing an apartment—and had to tell me about it right away
because he thought I should be in it.

Another time I bumped into him and his wife at Sardis. I remember
it well because they both tried to have a different conversation with me
at the same time. It was exhausting. I was cross-eyed trying to focus on
both of them at once. But it was also hilarious watching the husband
and wife competing for my attention.

Anyway, so we were perfectly content to stay living where we were,
but it was kind of small—it was cozy but cozy gets old with a child.
And anyway my father, before he died, had made me promise him that
we would move just as soon as we could afford to. Our apartment was
on the second floor above the A&P grocery store and he didn't approve
of that. He said he'd worked and saved so that his family didn't have to
live above a store. John and I needed more room anyway and we liked
the west side so we looked around for a more spacious apartment. I
was busy with rehearsals and previews so John did most of the looking.
He carried around the newspaper photo of me with Adlai Stevenson
thinking that might make an impression on the building managers.
A few of them seemed impressed. One looked at me in my rugged
Mammy Yokum make-up and asked John if I was "colored."

We ended up at 27 West 96th Street, half a block from Central Park,
on the 15th floor. The building had a doorman and a canopy and a lot
of wonderful neighbors. We immediately hit it off with a couple a few
floors below—Natalie Priest, a very talented theater and television actress and her husband, a public relations executive, Dolph Silverstein.
Natalie was so warm, such a good person. She was a terrific actress
and I admired her for her commitment and activism in Actors Equity
and AFTRA, working for a better deal for all stage and screen actors.
She was a real trailblazer as far as I was concerned. Very community-
minded. She bought groceries through a food co-op and celebrated
diversity all those years ago. Her New Years Day open house always
had an international theme, foods from all over the U.S. and the world.
And she became a terrific friend to me and, later, when I needed it, a
terrific support.

Another wonderful new neighbor was Liz Levin and her husband,
George. They were so welcoming and through them I got to know
Liz's mother who had been a labor organizer many years before and
she told me about the dark side of New York, things I'd never known

and hardly imagined—sweatshops exploiting women and children and bosses who terrorized them for wanting decent wages and working conditions and who had strikers beaten, jailed, and even killed to preserve their profits.

My own father was a business man but he'd always been so decent to his workers—paid them a living wage and even loaned or given them money when misfortune struck them. He gave them bonuses and threw them a big party at Christmas. He gave them ham and roast beef sandwiches while they worked and gave away hams and turkeys, potato salad and kegs of beer for the holidays.

Liz's mother—who had eventually become a special seamstress for the famous designer, Mainbocher—had known Emma Goldman who was not only a labor rights and civil rights activist but one of the most outspoken feminists and humanists of the early Twentieth Century. It was so humbling to learn these things while I fretted over my small successes, petty disappointments, and grand ambitions as an actress and singer. How could I take myself so seriously now knowing there were so many more serious dramas playing out in the world? Easy—I decided I would one day do a one-woman show about the struggle for women's rights and worker's rights..

A few years later I found myself at the New York University Labor Library researching the struggle of seamstresses and other garment workers. I found out about the ILGWU housing where some of the survivors of that period still lived. I met an old woman who told me first-hand about getting cracked in the head by a police Billy club because she'd held a picket sign asking for fair wages.

Lil Abner opened on Broadway in November of 1956 to rave reviews. I was thrilled but even more thrilled to be back in New York with my big growing boy and my wonderful husband. Having a show on Broadway made it easy to get to know many of our new neighbors. People recognized me in the lobby and the elevator and soon John and I were right at home in the building. I was even able to get my first cousin Marcella and her husband a third floor apartment. They raised their daughter in that apartment and stayed there until Marcella died in the 1990s.

Lil Abner was a big hit, and I could have stayed on and made a lot of money but I wanted to spend more time with John and Andy who I was starting to worry about more and more. My lawyer tried to convince me to stay for at least another six months. He said he had a great investment opportunity that could set me and John up for a long time. Stay with Lil Abner for six months or another year and buy Venezuelan bonds with the money. They were paying 20%! But I thought it was unconscionable to gouge a developing country like that. Maybe I was naïve. Maybe that's just the way business is done in this world and I was just foolish to squander this chance to get mine. But I'm still glad I didn't do it.

I didn't care about money. I was concerned about my son. Andy didn't seem right. He cried but never seemed to be trying to make the sounds that would become speech. Sometimes he would seem to look right through me, almost like I wasn't there and then I'd see him smile up at a glowing light bulb or the light reflecting off a wall clock. He loved the sharp flash of a camera flash bulb and would always smile beautifully when we snapped a picture of him—and so, in almost all of his early pictures, he looked perfectly normal. He seemed to love the classical music John played on the phonograph all the time but as he got older I noticed that his greater fascination seemed to be watching the record spinning around on the turntable before I even put the stylus down on the groove. One night Andy became so agitated when we tried to turn the record player off that we ended up having to let him sleep with the record. When Andy finally fell asleep John and I just stared at him. It was so crazy, our son sleeping peacefully next to a phonograph record instead of a teddy bear. We didn't know whether to laugh or cry. John took a photograph of it.

Our pediatrician, Dr. Berenberg, never seemed too concerned about any of this. I don't think he knew much about developmental disabilities. He suggested I put Andy in a pre-school. He said that maybe being around other children would bring him out of his shell. Andy was around other children at the park and that had only seemed to drive him further into himself but I thought maybe if he was in a more controlled environment it could help. Perhaps the park was too chaotic. I was willing to try anything. I found a pre-school at a synagogue near our house and they invited me to bring Andy in to try it out. We got there in the morning, just after all the other children had arrived. Someone was hanging their little winter coats on hooks in a corner and I thought it was so lovely. I hoped to God that Andy would fit in and that one day soon he'd be hanging his winter coat on one of those hooks. The teacher had all the kids walking around in a circle and told Andy to join them. He smiled and tilted his head and then he went around in the other direction, dodging all the other kids. I thought it was adorable and laughed and cried with joy. I thought he was going to make it, he was just a big, funny, creative kid who everyone would love and laugh along with. But afterwards the director of the school came beside me and said she didn't think Andy was ready yet. Maybe it wasn't just that he walked against the tide. Perhaps she saw something in him. Or noticed that he didn't really speak. But she didn't share any of her thoughts or any of the reasons for her reservations.

Suddenly I felt terrified that there was something really wrong with my son. I took him back to Dr. Berenberg but the doctor just seemed annoyed with me. He said I worried too much. He said that a lot of parents did. He was always very rough with Andy—and probably all his other patients. He'd grab kids and throw them on the scale to weigh them. It was fine for most of the kids but I think it shook Andy up. "Your son is fine," he told me now. "He'll probably be another Einstein. He'll talk in full sentences!" He added, "I didn't really say much till I was older and I'm a doctor now." I started crying, partly from the relief of what he was saying, partly from embarrassment that I was being so nervous about it, and partly from the frustration and dread of it all.

I didn't do much professionally at that time but I did manage a few roles on soap operas. On *From These Roots*, I played a social worker therapist. One of my patients was played by Richard Thomas who was a boy at the time, long before he was John Boy on *The Waltons*. It was the perfect job for me at the time. I only had to be there a few days a week and not too many lines. I didn't have to be on the road or even get home late for dinner. I turned down a lot of work around that time, Broadway shows, off-Broadway and television work with long hours. Another soap opera, *Brighter Day*.

I got to know the star of the show, Nancy Malone. She came over for dinner. She was very interested in Andy. Didn't know anything about developmental disabilities, had never been exposed to a child like that. Autism was still a big mystery to everyone, including people who were supposed to be experts. And anyway Andy never really quite fit any autism diagnoses available at the time. He showed signs of autism—and he was clearly cognitively impaired as well as epileptic and schizophrenic. His condition was fascinating. I mean once you got past the obvious sadness of his limitations. And he was adorable. Of course I would say that. I'm his mother. But a lot of people told me so.

After my guest appearance on Brighter Day, star Nancy Malone wanted me to be a regular on the show. I was flattered and I would have been tempted but the show was moving to L.A. and I didn't want to uproot our family. John was still working for Nat Hiken on *The Phil Silvers Show* and anyway Andy was always very sensitive to change.

Andy needed a lot of love and attention and I wanted to do everything I could to make him happy and whole. That was the most important thing in my life.

So there we were, John and me, with our beautiful son and his strange behavior, his slow development and all our fears but also our desperate hopes, faith in what we were being told. He'd grow out of it. He would be okay. But every trip to the park with Andy or anywhere there were other children hammered me with doubts. Just seeing how those other children were next to Andy, their curiosity, their grasp of language, the way they interacted with each other and the way they reacted to Andy, sometimes with mockery, sometimes with curiosity. He was afraid of garbage trucks and dogs and pigeons and on the street or in the park he might suddenly get all jittery and try to run away crying. One afternoon we were at the park and I ran into Abe Feder, the great lighting designer from *Lil Abner* and he and I started to chat until pigeons swooped down around a woman with a bag of bread crumbs. I didn't even get a chance to say goodbye or excuse me—I was off with Andy helping him get away.

John's Aunt Julia and her husband were on the board of a place called the Child Development Center and when we saw them for dinner one night I think that they could sense our concern about Andy and they could probably see that something was wrong with him. They made some calls and got us in to see Dr. Alpert who was the director.

The Child Development Center was in a small building on the east side, near the 59th Street Bridge. Dr. Alpert assigned one of her assistants to work with Andy for an hour every day. Her name was Mrs. Friedman and Andy seemed to like her. Mostly she just seemed to be interacting with him, trying to pull him out of himself. After a year of that, she said, "Well, we've had him for a year and I haven't observed any change in his condition. We can't really do much else for him."

She recommended a doctor who diagnosed childhood cognitive disabilities. Dr. Ackerman worked for Jewish family services. I made an appointment. By then I was pregnant with our second son, Larry.

When I phoned Dr. Ackerman for the results of his evaluation, he told me to come see him after I delivered. At the time I thought he just didn't have much to tell me, just like the pediatrician. But of course it was something else. He didn't want to alarm me, wanted me to go have my baby with a clear mind and not the dread that I was going to feel when he told me about my older son.

The day I finally met with him, I'll never forget. It was a beautiful spring day. Late May. The car windshields along 57th Street shimmered in the blinding sun. I walked into the narrow building and waited for the elevator and I tried to keep a positive attitude about what he was going to tell me—though Andy hadn't shown a lot of improvement in the months since I'd spoken to Dr. Ackerman. He sat me across from him in his office and told me his diagnosis with great seriousness but also great warmth. He said, "Your son is autistic."

I'd never heard that word before. Few people had. The word had only existed for a decade-and-a-half and was only really known to people in the psychiatric field and those families unfortunate enough to have to hear it and use it to describe someone they loved. So I was overjoyed when he said the word because I didn't hear it. What I heard was this: "Your son is artistic."

I heaved a sigh of relief and almost got down on my knees. "Yes, that makes sense," I said. "His father and I, you know, we're both artists."

"No," Dr. Ackerman said. "I said autistic. Your son has autism." He wrote the word on a piece of paper and said it again. Then he got very detached. He probably had to deliver this kind of news all the time and couldn't get too sentimental about it. He seemed matter of fact. He said, "See if he improves in the next few years. If he doesn't get any better by the time he's six then institutionalize him."

I brought Andy back to Dr. Berenberg to tell him what he should probably have figured out a year before and to see if there was anything that he or anyone else could do for my son. I don't know what I expected him to say or do. Apologize? Tell me I wasn't such a crazy person for having thought there was something wrong with my son? Give me some encouragement or comfort?

Maybe that's what he thought he was doing. I don't know. He told me he had just told one of his oldest patients that she had cancer and that she would probably die within a few months. I understood the subtext. A lot of people have misfortune—and a lot of it is worse than mine. I guess that was supposed to cheer me up.

# THE KINDNESS OF STRANGERS

When I first saw *A Streetcar Named Desire*, on the stage of the Ethel Barrymore Theater in 1948, I never imagined I would one day paraphrase Blanche DuBois's famous line as a way to understand my life as a mother, but having a developmentally disabled son made it a reality. I have often relied on the kindness of strangers. And I'm glad that so many strangers have been so kind. More about that later.

Life with Andy was no picnic though there were still quiet times. He was a beautiful child and sometimes had a twinkle in his eye and he always had love in his head.

Now we had the added blessing of our baby boy Larry. He was so adorable. Such a beautiful baby. It was a shock now to have two but also Larry was so different from his brother. He seemed to notice everything and respond to everything. It made us realize how closed off Andy had been so much of the time.

We tried not to dwell on the sadness of Andy's condition. What else can you do? You try not to think too much about what your child might not be able to do in his life. Just accept what is and work with it. But sometimes the weight of the sadness was overwhelming. And on top of that there was all the crazy wondering, the sinking feeling, haunting voices inside asking what might have been if only I'd done something differently.

John felt the same way. Or maybe worse. He blamed his genes—he had relatives on both sides of his family who'd had nervous breakdowns. A cousin of his had a developmentally disabled daughter.

I tried to reassure him. I had a cousin who'd suffered a mental breakdown after coming back from combat in World War II. He'd been a tail gunner and had basically lived in terror for his entire deployment. But who knows why anyone loses touch with reality? It certainly wasn't doing John or me any good to second guess ourselves.

What mattered, anyway, was what we were going to do for our challenged son.

I never forgot what the doctor told me, his suggestion to have my son locked in an institution, to throw him away like garbage. I never forgot that and I was determined never—never!—to follow that advice. John felt the same way. Determined to help Andy improve as much as he could and to give Andy the best life possible.

But it wasn't just our doctors telling us to institutionalize our son. My sister Beverly's husband, Dr. Jules Levin, was a prominent neurosurgeon in Milwaukee and he warned us that a child like Andy could be a devastating burden on our family. I loved Jules and I knew that he was a good man—a very very decent human being—and that he loved me and would never have said that if he didn't believe it was the best advice for us. But I just couldn't reconcile what he and our doctors were saying about my little boy with the cute little boy I loved with all my heart. Sometimes thinking about it all was just too depressing and alcohol was my drug of choice; and when the boys were gone or sleeping in their beds, I just drank and drank to get through it. I can still vividly remember a cold night in the kitchen with the window open and the chill pouring in while I drank vodka and ranted, "My boy! My cute little boy! My son is insane!"

John and I really didn't know what to do with Andy so we went back to Dr. Alpert and the Child Developmental Center and I wept in her office and pleaded with her to do something for my son.

She said, "We aren't equipped for children like your son." That was that. I wept again. I asked her what I was supposed to do. I wept and wept.

I wasn't going to leave her office until she gave me something, some direction, something. I don't know what right I had to do that but I was desperate. I didn't know what else to do.

Finally she said, "There is a woman…" I still remember those exact words. There is a woman. I remember those words because as she was saying them I was thinking that if there was a woman who could help then why did I have to practically coerce it out of her? I think I know the answer to that question now. People don't like to be wrong and they don't like to admit they don't have the answers. That is especially true for people with titles like Dr. in front of their name. Autism is a humbling illness for all of us. It's easier to chase people out of your office than to risk failing again and again to find a solution.

"There is a woman," Dr. Alpert said. "Elsbeth Pfeiffer. She is a psychiatric social worker specializing in working with deviant children. She worked with Anna Freud. And now she works here once a month and she seemed to really like your son. She seemed to like Andy. I think you should call her."

Deviant children? I almost told her no—what a terrible thing to call someone's child, a child who's never done anything bad and didn't ask for his disability! I went home and drank. I'd been drinking for a long time. In the family basement, in college, drinking alone and with friends and my drinking buddy and husband and now that my son was in trouble, I mean real trouble, I mean madness, I only knew one place to turn for comfort. Whiskey or vodka and the occasional Milltown.

But drunk or sober I was willing to try anything or anyone to get help for my son. I called Mrs. Pfeiffer that afternoon. I reached her at Bellevue Hospital where she worked when she wasn't at the Child Development Center or training therapists at the Bank Street School and her voice—with that soft Viennese accent of hers—was just about the sweetest I'd ever heard. She remembered Andy from the time she'd spent with him at the Child Development Center and said, "Andy, oh, yes, Andy. He is a delightful child. I am so happy to see Andy. Bring him. Bring him tomorrow." It was so wonderful to hear. I wept with joy! And not only did she see him the next day but every weekday after that for a long time.

Entering Bellevue Hospital the first time and for a while after that was a shock. The old building looked like a Dickensian orphanage from outside. It was a dreary old place, and sometimes I had to cover Andy's eyes so he didn't see the drunks or the psychos that were all over the place. No, it wasn't exactly the Waldorf Astoria lobby, but it was worth it. Mrs. Pfeiffer was on the fifth floor in the Bellevue Hospital nursery and always very welcoming to Andy and me. She put all the autistic children in a small area. She told me, "Yeah, I put them all in a small place so they cannot avoid each other. They just have to smash into each other and experience the human contact." Elsbeth was cheerful and loving but forceful. She seemed to understand Andy and the other challenged children and knew just how much to push them and just how to push them and challenge them in a loving way.

She loved Andy. She loved all the children she worked with. And she was so kind and warm and generous toward me and John and all the parents of the children she tried to help. She was truly a God-send. She never judged me or John. She was smart enough and she'd worked with enough challenged children to know that their challenges were not the result of bad parenting.

I needed to hear that over and over because kept wondering if I'd somehow been the cause of Andy's problems. Elsbeth reassured me that we had done nothing wrong and that I was a good mother and that my instincts about how to relate to Andy were the right ones. She told me that she could see how to be with Andy from watching me. Patience and love and good humor, which was how she was with Andy. She was a miracle worker. She understood Andy's challenges but she managed to always push him to relate to her and to me and to the rest of the world. Andy loved her. And so did I.

She taught me so many things about how to parent a child like Andy. And about love and acceptance and patience and understanding. She told me, "Big, broad, animation! Make him pay attention to you. When you speak to him, use a cheerful voice, loud, big smiles, make the world a happy place for him to be in." And it worked. Everything good that ever happened to Andy—and there were many good things throughout his life—we owe to Mrs. Elsbeth Pfeiffer.

She was also a hell of a diagnostician. Better than any doctor we ever took Andy to. She was the professional who figured out that he was having auditory hallucinations, that he was developmentally disabled and schizophrenic. It wasn't easy to hear about his dual diagnosis but it was information essential to understanding Andy and providing him with what could do the most to help him improve. I cannot imagine what we would have done without her. I have never forgotten what she did for us.

Every morning I would deliver Andy to Elsbeth and wait while Mrs. Pfeiffer worked with him for a few hours. Sometimes I'd walk around the block once or twice but often I'd find myself at the payphone in the lobby, amidst the drunks and psychos, and I'd be talking to my neighbor and friend, Natalie Priest. We'd talk about acting and give each other advice on scene work or auditions, though at the time I wasn't doing much professionally. It was a strange place I was in. I'd been so driven by my desire to be a star and now I didn't want to sing or act or anything. I felt like I couldn't do any of that until Andy was better, until we could get him on the right life path.

Sometimes I felt so angry. Sad and angry. Sad for Andy. Angry at God. Why did God pick on me and my son? I drank a lot in the evenings but every morning I was just as sad and angry. Andy was six years old and still not potty trained. Everything was an ordeal. He ate like a maniac and got so fat it was hard to find clothes that fit him. He had tantrums and frightened Larry. Somehow John and I coped with the day-to-day struggle of it but what was much harder was thinking about his future. I worried so much about what would become of my son.

Natalie helped me so much. Mostly she just listened and commiser-
ated while the drunks lurched around the lobby and the crazy voices of
lost souls bounced off the walls of the stairwell behind me. On many
mornings Natalie saved me from despair. For one thing, she was much
freer than I was about her career. She loved the theater and she loved
to act but somehow she never seemed to tie her self-worth to what
roles she got or what others thought of her work. She worked at her
craft and pursued her passion.

But more important was her absolute love and acceptance of Andy.
Of both our sons, but particularly Andy who was so difficult for so
many other people. Natalie was just a genuinely good person who
knew that the greatest gift she could give me was to treat Andy like
he was part of her family. Her husband and her children did likewise.
Her son Jaimie and daughter Esther were so patient and kind to Andy
from a very early age. Good people. Just really beautiful people. They
really enriched our lives. And Jaimie was like a big brother to Larry
who really needed that since Andy just wasn't up to the task. I'm sad
to say that we lost Natalie and Dolph years ago but I know that their
son Jaimie is a successful DP (director of photography) on a lot of
New York based movies and television shows and that their daughter
Esther is a terrific jazz pianist (she goes by Esther Blue).

Elsbeth Pfeiffer truly was a miracle worker but she was much in
demand and only worked with Andy and the others a few hours
each day and it wasn't enough. He needed stimulation. He needed
to be with other children. This was the early 1960s and the public
school system had nothing for children like Andy and parents like
us. Nothing. My son, Larry, who is a public school teacher now, tells
me that there are special needs schools and special needs classrooms
within regular schools and that there is a federal law that requires full
inclusion for all our children. Still hard for me to believe it—and I'm
delighted to hear. But fifty-some years ago there was almost nothing
for autistic children and their parents. Mrs. Pfeiffer saved us.

So did a local minister who started an informal special school for
his developmentally disabled son and a few other children including
Andy. I cannot remember the minister's first name but his last name
was Melon. His son's name was Peter. Reverend Melon's church and
his house were on Lexington Avenue downtown and in one of the
church buildings he set up a classroom for the three autistic children.
He found teachers and figured out how to hire them and how much

to pay them. I still remember all the children. Along with Andy and Peter Melon were Dossy (I don't remember her last name but I do remember that her parents were orthodox Jews) and Stevie Selsnick from Staten Island. He was asphaisic. Couldn't talk.

They were all such nice people. After school one day Peter's mother, Barbara invited me and Andy up to their house after school for a snack. I was so thrilled that Andy had a playdate. I stopped on the way and picked up a Neapolitan brick of Sealtest ice cream. I'll never forget how short I felt amidst their family. They were all so tall and thin. And when Barbara served the ice cream everyone got a thin sliver—about what I might eat standing up before I served everyone. I thought to myself, no wonder they're so tall and thin! But they were such warm and wonderful people. We were so blessed to have met them.

Eventually the school grew and we moved from the Lexington Avenue church to another church property on 12th Street and 5th Avenue. We called it the 12th Street School or Jerry's School because Jerry was the name of the man Minister Melon hired to run the school. We all paid $2000 a year to cover the operating expenses and that was no small sum in those days. John and I were happy to pay it but getting Andy downtown every day was sometimes an ordeal. The subway noise often agitated him as did the loud street noise coming out of the tunnel downtown. Taxis were expensive and where we lived they were often hard to find. In a snowstorm it was almost impossible to get Andy to school. It was on one such morning, almost a foot of snow and bitter cold, that a kind angel came to our rescue.

I was tugging Andy along. Desperate for a cab, hoping otherwise I'd somehow get him to the subway station before we froze to death. I saw a taxi heading toward us. The TAXI light was off which meant the driver had a fare—or didn't want one—but I guess I still waved at him and maybe he saw the desperation in my eyes or the trouble engulfing my son. Whatever it was he pulled over. "You need a lift?" he asked.

"I sure do," I said, and he told me to get in.

There was a woman sitting next to him. She turned around and introduced herself. She said, "I'm Clare and this is George. He drops me to work in the mornings. We usually don't pick up but you looked so cold out there with your son." She had a high-pitched voice and a Bronx or Queens accent. George sounded more Brooklyn. He asked where I was headed and when I told him he nodded, said, "That's right on my way."

Clare gave him a playful shove and said, "No, it's not," then turned and winked at me. "But it's no trouble, ma'am. Be our guest. You got a nice-looking kid."

I couldn't believe it. New York cab drivers were never known for their generosity or hospitality, but perhaps that's unfair. I broke down and cried with joy and gratitude and when they dropped us off I had to drop the money on the front seat to get George to take it. Angels in my life.

By the next morning, the snow had stopped, it was still bitter cold when Andy and I walked out our building. I was already dreading the ordeal of standing in the cold, trying to hold onto Andy and hail a cab. But one was already there, at the corner, waiting for us. A cloud of exhaust billowed up out of its tailpipe. George and Clare were inside. George tooted at me to be sure I saw them. I got in and they told me they'd be there every morning. Rain or shine. The kindness of strangers.

For months, they gave us a lift downtown and we became great friends. George sat on a special cushion Clare had made for him. "Hemorrhoids," she'd whisper. "It's from sitting too much." George always had an extra donut for Andy. Chocolate glazed, Andy's favorite. George and Clare didn't have any children of their own. Clare said she couldn't have children. George said, "But we got Andy in the back seat." He turned around and said, "Hey, you!" And Andy laughed his head off.

We got a little spoiled, Andy and me, with our private taxi service in the mornings and when George needed to have surgery on his hemor-rhoids, it was especially tough getting Andy downtown every morn-ing. We missed the ease and convenience but I think we both missed George and Clare most of all. My angels.

We weren't the only family that had a hard time getting to school each morning. I think it was a big challenge for pretty much all of us and we decided as a group to ask the City of New York for help. The public school system at the time had nothing for our children. Nothing. Zilch. Nada. Just a sad smile and an apology. Sorry, your child doesn't belong, isn't ready. And we all understood. We blamed our children and ourselves, not an indifferent public school system. We willingly paid two-grand a year to operate our own school for our children. But we thought the least the city could do for us was give us a bus. Just give us what every other school child in the city got. So we went to City Hall. Rita Rabinowitz, whose son's name was Robby, was outspoken and de-termined. So was I. Other parents came to support us.

Back then Mayor Wagner used to have town hall meetings that were televised on Public Television. The other parents and I held signs and walked outside City Hall for an hour or so, then attended the televised meeting and made our demands. Because of my background in the theater and because I'd been on television before, I was elected to speak for everyone. I didn't know if I was really up to it. I mean making this kind of political performance, but it was easy because I believed in our cause and because I was speaking for all the mothers and fathers like me who just needed a little help. I thought Rita could speak as meaningfully as I could so we went up together and stood up to the microphone and looked Mayor Wagner in the eye and told him how it was. We told him, "Our children matter too, Mr. Mayor." We told him that our children hardly had anywhere to go, that if not for a few remarkable people in our city that our children would be completely left out in the cold and us all with them. I tried to let him know what it was like for us. To have children who couldn't just go to school and dream about being a fireman or a policeman or an astronaut or maybe even the mayor or the president one day. We really laid it on thick. And then said that all we were asking for was a bus. Of all the things we needed all we asked of our city was one little bus to get them to and from school.

I was really proud of Rita and everything she and I said. It had come from the heart and I thought it was damn good and I was right—my acting teacher, Mary Tarcai happened to be watching on television and later she told me how moved she'd been. But back to the moment, I stood there waiting for Mayor Wagner to say something about what I'd said. And wouldn't you know, the first thing out of his mouth was:

"Excuse me, but are you Charlotte Rae?"

"Yes," I said.

"I've seen you on television," he said. "We'll see what we can do for your children."

It was a strange thing. I was glad that he wanted to help—that anyone wanted to help! But I wondered, almost immediately, so what if I hadn't been an actress, what if I hadn't appeared on *Ed Sullivan* and *The Phil Silvers Show* or wherever the hell it was that Mayor Wagner had seen me? What if I'd been a housewife or a secretary or whatever? Why should that matter? Don't get me wrong I was glad it helped but it felt strange. Here I'd been so ambivalent about working. A part of me always felt like I couldn't go back to work in earnest until we figured out what to do with Andy, until he got better, and here I was being told that because of my work the mayor of New York actually gave a damn and was willing to help.

# LIFE GOES ON

Andy never really did get better. Not in the way we'd hoped and dreamed. That was a fantasy. It's easy to believe in the miracle and we prayed and prayed for it. Maybe it's what kept us going. There were very tough moments for John and for me. I remember one night when Andy was little. John and I were drinking and sitting around. I don't know what we were doing. Reading the trades, paying bills. John had something on the phonograph, something depressing to go with our mood. Anyway, we lost track of Andy and somehow he got out on the window ledge. I don't remember which of us saw him there first or if we saw him at the same time but I swear there was a moment— maybe just a split-second—when we looked at each other and seemed to both be wondering if we all wouldn't be better off if… I can't even say it but you know what I'm talking about.

Of course we grabbed Andy off the ledge and continued for the rest of his life to protect and care for our son. During those early struggles with Andy, I turned down a lot of work. I don't regret it. I don't regret any of the other times in my life when I've said no to an acting or singing job. I'd always been so driven, it was good for me to slow down anyway and make my family the priority. Life should always take priority—life and the people we love.

*Songs I Taught My Mother* sold enough copies that Vanguard Records wanted me to go back in the studio and record another album, but I said no. My focus was on my family and I didn't think I was ready to sing again. I wouldn't audition for anything on Broadway—too much of a time commitment, too much of an emotional commitment. I just didn't have it in me. I did agree to play sister to Sid Caesar's German professor on his new show. The producers liked the way we worked together and wanted me to be a regular after that but I turned that down. I wasn't ready to commit to working every day every week. I didn't feel much like doing anything. Not for a while. It was Elsbeth Pfeiffer who finally convinced me to go back to work on a more consistent basis. She didn't want me to give up my life, not if there was any way I could avoid that. I think she could sense the despair I so often felt and believed that getting back to work would be good for my spirit and that if my spirits were lifted it would be better for Andy.

So in 1962, when I was offered *The Beauty Part*, I said yes. John was very supportive of my return to the stage and that made it much easier. We hired a college student to help take care of Andy and John fixed his schedule so that he could help out more, especially getting Andy to school each morning and after a while Andy felt so comfortable with George and Claire that he didn't need us to ride along anymore. They would pick him up in their cab and then take him into his school like he was their own son.

*The Beauty Part* was written by the great S.J. Perelman, humorist for The New Yorker and author of the Marx Brothers' *Monkey Business* and *Horse Feathers*. I played four different roles in the show—as did others in the cast—which was a great challenge for me made not so difficult by a really wonderful director, Noel Willman, who'd just won a Tony Award for *A Man for All Seasons*. "Remember," he told me on one of the first days of rehearsal, "the audience is intelligent. Don't hit them with a trowel." I have always remembered that advice and always tried to respect my audience in that way.

Bert Lahr had the lead and had many roles of his own—a different one in each sketch. What an instrument he had! Most people know Bert as the cowardly lion in *The Wizard of Oz* movie but he had an extensive career on Broadway before, during, and after that and before that he'd done burlesque. He was great but not the easiest actor to work with. "Are you gonna do that?" he'd ask if you did anything at all while he was delivering a line.

Everyone was afraid to move while they were on stage with him. Alice Ghostly. Larry Hagman. David Doyle. Arnold Soboloff. And me. All terrified to breathe if Bert had a line.

Noel, the director took me out to lunch one day during rehearsal. I can't remember the place. We were in Philadelphia at the time. Noel said, "Bert is an old old man. You only really have one scene with him. Give it to him. Give him the scene." I took his advice and played the scene with my back to the audience. Bert never seemed the least bit concerned. Never suggested I turn slightly sideways so the audience might see a little of my face. Years later, my dear friend, Eddie Lawrence worked with Bert Lahr on the film *The Night they Raided Minsky's*, and as they were chatting between takes, Eddie asked Bert how he had liked working with me. "Charlotte Rae," Bert said, smiling, "oh, she's a brilliant actress." That really taught me something. It had been so easy to defer to Bert on that stage years before. I hadn't really given up anything and it had felt good at the time to be generous, to show that kind of respect. And then to see how much he'd appreciated it.

Being on the road with a show can be lonely but not this show, not with Larry Hagman and his wife, Maj around. It was Larry's first big show, his big break long before *I Dream of Jeannie* was even a dream and longer still before he created the most despised character on network television—J.R. Ewing. He was still very much an up-and-comer, a complete unknown at that time. After the show sometimes, Larry and I would drink vodka while we were taking off our stage makeup. Usually Maj was back there and would join us. She had an electric frying pan in the dressing room. She'd plug it in and make us the most wonderful quiche.

When the show got to New York, Larry and I became roommates. I was supposed to share the second-star dressing room with fellow co-star Alice Ghostly. It was a big dressing room on stage level but Alice needed her own space, room to focus on the work. She was the consummate actress and I had great admiration for her. I offered her the star dressing room all to herself but she wouldn't have it. Instead, she moved upstairs and left me the big dressing room downstairs.

Well, I wasn't alone in there for long. Larry came in the first week and asked if we could share. He had a lot of fast costume changes and the dressing room they'd assigned him was upstairs. He promised to stay out of my way if I just gave him a corner of the dressing room. I was happy to give him half of it; he was such a nice guy.

First thing he did was bring in a big electric coffee-maker which, in 1962, was still a bit of a novelty, and a blue can of Chock Full of Nuts coffee. Every evening before curtain he brewed a big pot of coffee for the two of us. Burt Lahr must have gotten wind—or smelled the aroma— because an hour or so before each night's performance Lahr's dresser, Earl, would walk in with an empty mug and, without a word, fill it. Larry and I thought that was the funniest thing. We had lots of laughs. Noel, the director, thought it was strange that Larry and I shared a dressing room. He said, "Even Lunt and Fontanne had separate dressing rooms!" But it worked out great and we became great friends.

When I was out in L.A. with a show a few years later, Maj and Larry came over for dinner and we ate and drank and laughed all night. Years later when I moved to L.A., Maj and Larry had John and me over at their beautiful home on the beach in Malibu Colony.

I wish I'd seen more of them. But that's life. Suddenly you turn around and it's twenty years later. In 1995 I read in the paper that he'd gotten very sick and had to receive a liver transplant and I wrote him a note letting him know how much I missed him and how glad I was that he was still with it. He wrote back such a lovely note to me. Very warm and wonderful.

Larry was such a good actor. Not just the TV work. In the film, *Harry and Tonto* he played Art Carney's son, a guy who'd never really amounted to much. Very sad, moving, particularly the scene in which he reveals that he's broke. Larry and Art did it with such plain, simple honesty. I'll never forget it. Larry did so much great work—on stage, in film, and on TV; I followed his career the whole way—but that one really stands out for me.

So sad to have lost track of each other or just lost track of time. You know, you always think you'll finally get back together with someone sometime but that sometime never happens. When I went to his memorial, I found out he and Maj had moved from Malibu to Ojai and had a beautiful place there. I spoke to some of his neighbors at the memorial and they all couldn't stop going on about how generous Larry and Maj were. For example, they would invite teachers up to their place for a nice weekend, a get-a-way and cook for them and serve them. No star-sized egos for them. They understood who the real stars are in this world.

The last few years, Maj had gotten Alzeimers and it was very very tough for Larry. He loved her so much. He used to say, "You know, she's my mummy," because she was four years older but they just loved each other like crazy.

Getting back to the old days, *The Beauty Part*, somehow, during rehearsals and previews I managed to do some episodes of *Car 54 Where Are You?* Nat was just getting that show off the ground. He hired John again to write the now well-known theme song. "There's a hold-up in the Bronx," etc. He'd already cast Al Lewis as Leo Shnauser and thought Leo should have a wife. Nat wanted me to create the character. He said, "You know, she's from The Bronx. They've been married awhile." I asked Al if we could get together and do some improvising. He said sure so I asked Mary Tarcai if I could rent her studio for a couple hours. I'll never forget, the two of us pacing back and forth by the window, like a husband and wife in mid-argument. Then he started calling me names. He called me stupid. Said, "What the hell is wrong with you?" Very convincing, very specific. I kept pacing, taking it, not going to let it bother me, not going to stoop to his level, then he said, "What are you, retarded?" And that set me off—maybe because of Andy, maybe because Beverly had called me stupid my whole childhood—and I let loose on him, crying and yelling and calling him names. By the time we saw Nat, it was like Al and I had been married for years. We were ready to start filming.

I loved working with Al and I especially loved working with Nat Hiken. Who wouldn't want to work with a comic genius? But it was hard work—shooting a TV episode in the day and then performing in a Broadway show at night. A lot of actors do it, I know, but I don't know how they do it. For me, it was so exhausting. I was relieved when it was over and all I had to worry about were the nine performances a week in *The Beauty Part*—and then I didn't even have to worry about it for long.

What a terrific show it was and we got great reviews. I mean really great. The staff at the Music Box Theater congratulated us and said our reviews were even better than the reviews for William Inge's *Picnic*, which had been a huge hit. We were all so relieved, certain that we would have a long run on Broadway. We were scheduled to move in a few weeks—the Music Box had already booked another show in March (*Dear Me, the Sky is Falling*, it was called) but nothing to worry about; the producers would put blurbs of our golden reviews in the theater ads of the New York Times and the Daily News and we would fill the Plymouth Theater, a few blocks away.

But then the newspapers went on strike and the producer couldn't afford radio or television advertising so he had a giant hit that was one of the best kept secrets on Broadway. At one point he asked the cast and crew to take a pay cut and every one of us agreed to it. Then he still closed the show.

What a disappointment for all of us. Alice Ghostley, Patricia Englund, and of course Bert Lahr. And too bad more people didn't get to see us. It was a hell of a show and just like that, poof—gone forever. But I was still a semi-regular on *Car 54 Where Are You?* and more than that I was happy to have a little time with John and the boys.

We got some good news about Larry, our younger boy. We'd applied for him to go to the Ethical Culture School, one of the most prestigious and progressive schools in the city—and he got in! Not only did he get in but the school gave us a partial scholarship. It was such a joy for us to know that Larry was all right. Andy was doing better though I often worried about what would happen to him as he got older. He was making progress but it was so slow and in the meantime there were always new challenges. He became terrified of dogs and pigeons—in New York City! He would obsess over things. He'd lay out toy railroad tracks on the floor of his room and if anything got moved or upset he'd have a fit. Sometimes it seemed that almost anything could shake him up.

We'd been warned that a child like Andy could affect his siblings. The two boys seemed to get along. Larry was patient with his brother and they often played together and had lots of laughs, but it was still a relief to know that our younger son was all right and that he had such a great opportunity.

Life goes on. It's not always the life you imagined it would be. Maybe it's never that for anyone. Mine was certainly an adventure. The career I'd spent my youth obsessing about was happening, sort of. I'd just been in a terrific Broadway show—that closed after a short run. I would soon be in another—that would also close way too soon.

But I was blessed. I had my two terrific boys and a wonderful husband. John was busy working as a sound and music editor and writing music for Nat Hiken—who I'd introduced him to—and learning on the job. We were supportive of each other and shared the parenting duties and John never looked at another woman—little did I know why.

# LOOK UP AND LIVE

The fall of 1963 was a time of great joy and uncertainty for us. Andy was doing well at school. He was talking more, doing more for himself. He seemed slightly more engaged with us and with the rest of the world around him but his future was still so uncertain. Larry was attending one of the best schools in the city but John and I sometimes felt out-of-place amid all the fancy east side and Central Park West parents. We hoped Larry would fit in.

I guested on the Sunday morning religious inspirational program, *Look Up and Live*, and on the Dupont Show of the Week. Dupont put on an original show each week. The one I appeared on involved an amusement park heist in which a real robbery is to be concealed by a robbery staged by the amusement park.

Then came the call from my agent. Ray Stark and Garson Kanin wanted me for the role of Fanny Brice's mother in *Funny Girl*. It was between me and Kay Medford, a wonderful actress who went on to create the role of Mama in *Bye Bye Birdie*. But my agent said they really wanted me, I was their number one choice. I was excited. Barbra Streisand was a spectacular talent and surely this would be a hit show. Sure enough they offered me the role but my agent said he could get more money and urged me to hold out. I trusted him and maybe he was right—but we never got to find out.

A few days later I was on my way home from exercise class. I'd called my answering service from a payphone to see if my agent had settled with *Funny Girl*. No message. I was tired and caught a cab uptown and when I got out Joe the doorman looked pale. He hardly made a move to open the door for me, just stared ahead as I approached. "Hi, Joe," I said, and he said back: "The president's been shot."

John already had the TV on upstairs. Walter Cronkite. I think it was his voice and the CBS News logo. It took a while before he announced that the president was dead. It was devastating for me and John and everyone we knew. JFK gave us all such hope for the future and he was just a young man with such small children. Heartbreaking. I didn't even think about *Funny Girl* for a week and when I called my agent to see what had happened he said the producers had closed the negotiations because of the presidential assassination; they'd already made a deal with Kay Medford.

Naturally I was disappointed, but also relieved. More family time. Less stress. A little less stress anyway. Andy, bless his heart, always gave us a challenge, even on his good days. He was so fragile and so easily agitated. Sometimes he seemed oblivious to everything and everyone. Then a moment later the most arbitrary thing would set him off, a spot on his shoe or a shadow on a clock. He was terrified of garbage trucks which made walking the sidewalks of Manhattan an adventure. We worried about him with Larry. Most of the time Andy was gentle and cooperative with his brother. They always found things to laugh about. But if something went wrong—and we weren't always sure why they did with Andy—then he could be a danger to his brother. So we thought Larry should have his own room. We hated leaving 27 West 96th Street, my best friend Natalie and her family, my cousin Marcella and her family, and quite a few other friends. But we knew we had to do it. Three bedroom apartments weren't cheap. I mean, by today's standards they were, but for us back then, without steady income, the extra bedroom meant moving ten blocks uptown and to a building without doormen. Not that we had to have a doorman but in those days 106th Street could get a little scary. We could tell by the lack of warmth and friendliness of our neighbors. Everyone walked our street with their heads down. Everyone hurried into and out of the security door and double and triple-locked their apartment doors; and no one talked to anyone in the lobby or the elevator. Muggings were common. John got mugged right on our street. Larry was nearly abducted by a strange man just a few feet away from me on the sidewalk. I screamed so loud I think you could have heard across the river in New Jersey— and I managed to scare the guy off.

No way to live, I tell you. Certainly not the way I wanted to live. So I started a block association. I started with our building. I went around ringing doorbells and getting people to sign up. Not everyone would answer the door and not everyone who opened would sign up but there were enough people. I asked someone in charge of the Buddhist temple around the corner where Larry took jujitsu classes if they had space for us to hold a meeting. They said sure. I found a teacher in the building who had access to a ditto machine and she agreed to copy a flyer to pass out to everyone on the block. I called the police and asked if they would come talk to everyone about safety. I set up our big coffee pot in the temple social hall and we had our meeting. More than one hundred showed up. We planned a block party and got a permit to close off the street. We had food and music and games for kids and best of all we got to know our neighbors. A few weeks later, John got hold of a 16 millimeter projector and speakers and prints of *The Red Balloon* and *Casablanca*. He set it up in the window of an 8th floor neighbor and people across the street hung sheets out of their windows to form a movie screen and everyone—from our block and elsewhere in our neighborhood—sat on folding chairs or stood on the sidewalk and ate popcorn and drank soda and beer and watched the film.

Neighbors in our building signed up volunteers to man the lobby and make it safe for those of us coming home at night. We took up a collection and got a table and a chair for the volunteers to sit on while they guarded the entrance. One night, when no one was there, someone broke in and stole the table and the chair. We took up another collection and got another table and chair and chained it to the wall. A month later, late one night, someone stole the table and the chair—and the chain—and left a big hole in the wall. The building superintendent told us that the landlord said we couldn't tie anything to his wall. So we got a folding chair and a folding card table and we stayed in that lobby and no one was mugged—at least not coming into the building or going upstairs. Old people watched the street from their windows, making sure no cars got stolen and they checked the hallways on their floors for burglars.

It was the best of what New Yorkers are—courageous, resilient, together helping each other. By the time we left the city ten years later we knew people up and down the street and had a real sense of community and shared experience. Even years later I'd go back and visit someone on the old block and it seemed we still knew everyone.

Over the next few years I got on some interesting TV dramas. It was the 1960s but still, to me, the golden age when programming was driven by quality as much as ratings. I did an episode of *The Defenders*, a court-room drama ahead of its time tackling social issues of the time. I also did *Journey of the Fifth Horse*, Ronald Ribman's play based on a Turgenev story, with a young Dustin Hoffman who played an obsessive man. Years later he told me that part had influenced the way his character in *Papillon*, one of the most magnificent performances I've ever seen. I kind of enjoyed the TV work. It was quick and interesting and sometimes I was home in time for dinner—and it was all local.

Then I was offered *Half a Sixpence* with British star, Tommy Steele and Carrie Nye (Dick Cavett's wife). It was lots of fun and Carrie and I became great friends but then my agent called with an offer of a much bigger part in *Pickwick*, an original musical based on Charles Dickens' *The Pickwick Papers* and produced by David Merrick. I didn't want to do it. I mean, it was a great part, *a lead*, and I knew I could do a good job with it, but I wanted to stay close to home. I did not want to leave my boys—and taking this show meant being on the road for six months!

John urged me to do it—with *Oliver* setting records on Broadway this had 'big hit' written all over it and God knows we could have used some steady income and my career could certainly have used a shot in the arm. He was right—it was important for my career to take it—but still I wished I hadn't listened.

The first six weeks were in San Francisco and I drank like crazy from loneliness in the evenings. I wasn't the only one. All the British actors were drinking like mad, partying on boats in the bay. Maybe I should have joined them but I was too down in the dumps. When my mother flew out to visit I got her a separate room so she wouldn't see what a mess I was. One night I took Mother out to see the show at the famous Finocchio's night club in North Beach. She was mesmerized by the performers, their voices and make-up and glamour, and at the end of the show, when these female impersonators lifted their tops and showed their masculine chests, she nearly passed out. She never got over it.

Everyone in the cast of *Pickwick* was really nice so I still managed to make friends. With Anton Rodgers and his wife, Morna. What a wonderful actor and person and what a sweet couple they were. And Oscar Quitak and his wife. A few years later when I was in London I stayed in their flat. I mean they insisted—they were in Surrey for the summer and their place was right in the heart of the theater district. I watched the first lunar landing on their telly and felt like a real Londoner, walking to all their neighborhood shops for everything.

Soon *Pickwick* moved from San Fran to L.A. and by then I knew I couldn't do it—couldn't be away from John and the boys that long so I used my per diem money and little extra to rent a house in Encino so when summer came John and Andy and Larry could join me. Did I leave out the cats? We had two cats, Max and Frisky, and they came too. John was quite a sight getting off the airplane after a six hour flight with Andy and Larry. The cats were traumatized for a few days. After that everyone had a great time in the sun. The house had a pool, which meant keeping an eye on both boys but they loved being in the water and John and I didn't mind staying in there with them. The cats loved their new freedom and took full advantage running all over the neighborhood but always coming back in time for dinner. It was a wonderful few weeks having my husband and Andy and Larry around. After the boys were asleep, John and I would get drunk together. John's father visited for a while and he'd get drunk with us late at night.

As for the show, it was a great experience. For one thing, all the writers and the director, Peter Coe, Cyril Ornadel who wrote the music and Leslie Bricusse who wrote the lyrics and Wolf Mankowitz who wrote the book were all Brits. So was director Peter Coe and pretty much everyone else except the renowned producer David Merrick who, like me, was a yank. Anyway, the Brits all seemed to think I was a big star in the U.S. and treated me like I was one. They really listened to what I had to say and let me have real input and when it became clear that my character needed one more song and I suggested John for the job, they listened. We worked on it together and they paid John $18,000 for it. He used the money to buy me my first mink coat. We played to full houses and they were huge. In L.A., we were in the Dorothy Chandler Pavillion at the newly built music center, a massive place that's now home of the L.A. Opera. Too big for a play of any kind if you ask me. I can still remember what it was like, looking up toward the balconies from the stage. The people were so far away. Their heads looked like dozens of eggs in their cartons. But the audience—near to us and far away—seemed very much to love the show. We were sure we had a hit on our hands.

Sir Harry Secombe was a joy to work with. Actually he hadn't been knighted yet but that's what I'll call him. He was famous in the UK and for good reason. So brilliant. So funny. Such timing. And he had a gorgeous voice. He was part of The Goons along with Peter Sellers and Spike Milligan. Funny and crazy. Look them up on YouTube and laugh your head off. Some of the times in L.A. I'd go into Harry's dressing room so I could listen to him and his pals—like Davey Jones and Roy Castle. They would talk so fast in their British accents that I couldn't keep up with them. Still, somehow, they were hilarious. I couldn't stop laughing.

But Harry was more than a great actor and a comic master. He was a great human being. So warm-hearted. He could have given lessons in napping. He could doze off for a few seconds or a few minutes, then jump up and be ready for anything. And he taught me something more important. He once told me something his father told him and it really stuck. He said his father told him never to forget who he was and where he came from. "We're just plain folk from Wales," his father told him. "You're popular now. Big stuff and everyone's kissing your arse but that's not who you are. Watch out who your friends really are. Watch how your new chums handle the waiter, the bus boy, the boot black. See how they treat those people and you'll know how these people really are."

I've never forgotten that. Or anything about Harry. Such a warm-hearted man. And his wife, Irma was a sweetheart. They had two adorable little kids. Pickwick was a large company made up of some of the nicest people I'd ever worked with, except for Peter Bull. I never felt any warmth from him. He was a very talented actor and looked like his last name and with a personality to match. He was in *The African Queen, Doctor Doolittle*, and *Tom Jones*. He played the Russian ambassador in *Dr. Strangelove*. During our *Pickwick* run, I didn't think he liked me. I was right. Years later, he wrote a memoir and summed me up as "Jewish" and "terrible." Well, now it's my turn. He was a good actor but I don't think he was a very nice person.

After our very successful run in L.A., *Pickwick* moved on to Cleveland, then Detroit and Washington D.C. and in each city we played to packed houses in huge theaters. And what a crazy family odyssey it was for us—our two sons and two cats, Frisky and Max, in three cities. Then the summer ended and John and the boys and the cats went back to New York. I only had a month or so on the road without them but it was really hard. Many nights, I'd go home to my hotel room and drink and eat while the others were out partying. I'd get drunk and wish I hadn't taken the show.

Still, I looked forward to a long run on Broadway in a show that had 'hit' written all over it. It's what I'd always dreamed of and it meant time at home and a little financial security.

But it never happened. We opened in New York and the reviews were good but not great and David and the other producers decided to close rather than risk losing anything on a Broadway run. Just like that. Here were all us actors touring the country working our asses off to get the show ready for Broadway and little did we know that the producers had other ideas—and their bottom line was all that really mattered to them. They had already made a lot of money touring the show in all those enormous theaters, enough to satisfy the writers and their investors. I guess that's why they call it show *business*.

I got a Tony nomination for best featured actress, which I guess is a decent consolation—but lost out to Bea Arthur in *Mame*. So there I was, from a hit show to the unemployment line. Fortunately for me, there was television. Series and commercials. I shot a funny commercial promoting oil heat where I'm taking a shower and being interviewed about how much money I'm saving using oil instead of gas or electric. I wore a strapless swim suit so it looks like I'm not wearing anything. It was a long commercial with a lot to say but we nailed it in one take and the crew applauded me. You can see it on YouTube—the commercial, I mean, not the applause.

Commercials were fun and they helped pay the rent and probably helped keep me sane until my next big chance on the stage. It turned out to be Shakespeare—Shakespeare in the Park to be precise. It was the second season at the Delacorte Theater in Central Park and it was very exciting—though I'm not sure any of us imagined Shakespeare in the Park would still be going there at the Delacorte almost five decades later. Joseph Papp hired me for the whole summer—*Henry IV Parts I and II* and then *Romeo and Juliet*. I was absolutely thrilled to be able to do both productions.

In *Henry IV I* was Mistress Quikly. Stacy Keach was Fallstaff. He was so young then, just out of Yale. A slight man but a profound actor. He had a hare lip and he was wonderful at playing character roles. His Fallstaff was the best I've ever seen—and I've seen dozens. He was so young—twenty-two years old, had just graduated from the Yale School of Drama—and so good, completely believable. He understood what it meant to get inside the character and be that character.

I never worked with a better actor. And so generous to those he shared a scene with. He let us all find our way, never concerned about being upstaged or distracted. Lots of actors feel threatened, territorial. Or they put up barriers. Don't want you to touch them, for example. Stacey never worried about any of that. He understood that we had to all trust each other and let our characters live within us, whatever that meant, wherever it took us. Young Sam Waterston was Prince Hal. He was great too, but I had a crush on Stacy. There was something special about him.

We all had a wonderful time, all of us in the cast. Hard work but wonderful. Barry Primus played Pistol and he was marvelous. Rae Allen was terrific as Doll Tearsheet. I could go on. And our director, Jerry Friedman really knew how to work with actors and how to guide a great cast. He appreciated that I'd done my homework, reading the play and finding all the little motivations and thinking about the character. He said he was proud of my hard work. I'll never forget that. Such a kind thing to tell an actor. What better way to inspire someone to work extra hard. He had a great career in the theater and then headed up the theater department at the University of North Carolina.

One night we were scheduled to do *Henry IV parts I and II* with an intermission between them—starting at 6:00 p.m. and ending around 2:00 a.m. We were already rehearsing for our second play of the summer, *Romeo and Juliet*. Every day in the morning and afternoon before performing *Henry IV* at night. It was tiring but we could survive doing part I or part II. Rehearsing all day and then doing both parts was daunting. Everyone in the cast was dreading it. We were exhausted just thinking about it.

So little old me, I decide to be spokesperson for the cast. I went to Joe and told him it was too much, really too much, too many hours not enough rest. If we were going to do back-to-back shows from six till two in the morning he ought to at least let those of us who were in both shows take the afternoon off. Everyone else—who wasn't in both parts of *Henry IV* could rehearse. So what did Joe do? He sent everyone who was in both shows home—except me. He told me to stay. He said he wanted to work on my scenes in *Romeo and Juliet*. I couldn't understand. Did he really have to work with me that day? Was it worth my health and sanity? I asked him, "Why are you doing this to me?" His answer:

"Well, after you've experienced this you'll know you can survive anything." He was doing me a favor, right? But I got the message. Don't tell Joseph Papp how to run his operation.

Somehow, I survived that day. We all did. We were exhausted but I don't think the audience noticed. I doubt they would have known if we'd gone off-script and improvised the entire last act. They had managed their own collective intoxication. By the time we got to that last act, we were performing Shakespeare in a cloud of marijuana smoke.

After the show we were so elated—relieved to have survived the endless ordeal of an eight hour rehearsal followed by two three-hour tragedies. Then, to burst our elation, came a real tragedy. We heard the news from L.A.—Bobby Kennedy had been shot and killed.

*Romeo and Juliet* opened in the middle of the summer and got a great reception. I played the nurse, one of my favorite parts. Shakespeare always knew just where to put the comic relief. The nurse provides that but she also delivers the tragedy when she believes she's discovered Juliet dead. I tried to do justice to his words. Young Martin Sheen played Romeo. He was a darling. So easy to work with and such a strong performance. He used to bring his cute little sons Charlie and Emilio with him to rehearsals.

Joseph Papp made it all happen. He was a superstar among theater producers and his contributions are staggering but no one is perfect and Joe's big weakness was firing his director and taking over the show. He did that with *Romeo and Juliet*. I can't even remember who he hired but whoever it was he fired him and took over. Joe wasn't a bad director but he wasn't great either and he was often not as good as the people he replaced—though he was immune from getting bad reviews because he was usually a last-minute replacement for whoever he'd fired. Still, despite that, he was an amazing man and we all owe him a great debt.

Central Park's Delacorte is a wonderful theater. It seats about 2000 but is still very intimate and audiences got all the subtleties. We performed in almost any weather. Blinding sun or rain—unless the rain got really bad, which it never quite did. On one wet night I skidded down the raked stage, skidded toward a table and delivered my line as if nothing had happened. The audience applauded.

That was such a wonderful summer for me. Every day I would take a bath and go over my lines and Shakespeare's words and my character's thoughts. The words and ideas sparkled always like diamonds and I felt so alive working with them. We were always discovering new facets of the play and our characters and scenes. What a joy performing Shakespeare with so many wonderful people, and then there were all the joys of our family, the small joys of family life. Being together at the end of the day. Sharing the triumphs and frustrations along with a home cooked dinner, watching the boys grow up. It was a happy time for all of us.

Andy was doing really well. I didn't know it at the time. I mean, in a way I knew because I could remember how hopeless everything had once seemed. He talked a little to us now. He was calm most of the time. And he had joy, real joy. He loved to listen to John's classical records, especially Mozart and Hayden. He did it a little obsessively.

Sometimes he'd move the phonograph arm a few centimeters back over and over and it drove us all a little crazy, but it was still beautiful music and it was beautiful to see how it moved him. John took him to the New York Philharmonic and Andy behaved. He loved it. John said Andy smiled through the whole thing.

It was around that time that Elsbeth Pfeiffer called me one afternoon to say that Andy was ready to move on from Jerry's school. Move on? I couldn't imagine what she had in mind. Honestly, I was a little frightened. I was so grateful, so happy for that little school we called Jerry's School and those wonderful people who worked so hard with Andy and the other special children. I was so fond of all those children and their families that we'd gotten to know. Andy had friends. He went to birthday parties and his friends came to his birthday parties. I still have photographs of him blowing out the candles on his cake. We were like a big family in a wonderful community.

"He's ready for Camphill now," she told me, and she sent me a brochure.

It was a beautiful sprawling place in Pennsylvania Dutch country. Elsbeth recommended Andy to them and that was enough for them to invite us down. It was about a two-hour drive from New York. Mostly just dull thruways and turnpikes but then, off the concrete highways it was like another world. Fresh green and kind of never-never-land. The Camphill school was very big. The houses on it were simple and beautiful. The people were German and Swiss and their little houses seemed to have been designed by someone from that part of the world. Families lived in those houses—husbands and wives and their biological children and then developmentally disabled people like Andy lived with them, were a part of the family.

When we parked and got out of our car, Mr. Peizner, who ran the school, called out to us. He stood at the bottom of a hill looking up at us and as Andy stepped away from the car, he opened his arms and said, "*Velcome*, Andy!" And Andy ran down that hill smiling. Into his arms. It was amazing. It was a miracle. Like Andy knew this man. Like he belonged to this place. He ran down that hill and into Mr. Peizner's arms and John and I knew we were doing the right thing bringing him there. Our son had a home in the world. People who cared about him and would care for him. For the first time I could imagine his future in a way that didn't make me weep. That day, even though he was only about twelve I could see the path of his life. He would live there and work and be a part of a family and a wonderful community.

I remember the drive back to New York. The profound relief that Andy had a place in the world. I was happy for Andy and for Larry and John and me. What a relief. Thank you, God.

# ON THE CUTTING EDGE

In many ways, those next few years were some of the best of my career. Not exactly what I had dreamed of but definitely some great roles and some of my best work.

I did a PBS television drama called *Apple Pie* by playwright Terrence McNally. I played a woman on the verge of a nervous breakdown because her son was MIA in Vietnam. Her husband takes her to Italy to get her mind off her torment but all she can think about is her son and all the terrible things that might be happening to him. It wasn't hard for me to imagine her mental state. In my own way, I'd been there. In a way Andy had been mentally and emotionally MIA. I wanted to represent all the mothers of all the young men in Vietnam fighting in that terrible war and I wanted everyone else to understand, to empathize, to realize that—like Arthur Miller so eloquently showed us—they were all our sons.

I also, finally, got to play the part of Rose in *Funny Girl*. It wasn't Broadway. It was summer stock. It was Barbara but not Streisand. Fanny was played by a dear and very talented—if a lot less famous—Barbara Minkus. You might recognize her from *Love American Style*—she was a regular for six seasons. We spent a summer in New England performing in tent theaters. John got hired to play piano in the pit. All our entrances were down the aisles. One night a mouse made an entrance. It ran up on stage and Barbara fainted. The other actors improvised until she regained consciousness. Then the poor little mouse jumped into the pit and the drummer ended its career in show business with his bass drum pedal.

Larry came along with us on tour that summer and got to experience some nature, New England style, and have a summer on the sand and in the water and even got to go out in a boat with a real lobster man checking his traps. Andy didn't come with us but spent the summer at a nearby camp for special children so we could see him every few weeks. Sandpiper Camp is where he developed his love of seafood, especially lobster. After that summer, whenever we took Andy to a restaurant, he'd always ask for lobster. We could be at the Carnegie Deli and he would ask for lobster—though he was always happy to settle for a corned beef sandwich piled high.

John's father, Maury, joined us for a few weeks also so Larry got to spend some time with his grandpa. It was an exciting and wonderful summer for our family. It ended with our car, an old green Rambler, dying on a bridge in the middle of Connecticut. We just left it there on the shoulder of the highway and somehow got to the nearest New Haven Railroad station and got back to New York.

That fall I was offered a role in another terrific show. *Morning, Noon, and Night* was three one-act plays—by three different authors—and it only ran for a few months but it was still thrilling to be a part of it. These plays were probably ahead of their time. Maybe way ahead of their time. Yes, *Hair* was still on Broadway and *Oh! Calcutta!* But so was *Hello, Dolly* and other traditional shows.

In *Morning*, by Israel Horowitz, we played an African American family that takes a pill and turns white. I played the mother, a cleaning woman, who—upon turning white—sings to her employer, "Fuck off Mrs. Robinson. I ain't gonna scrub your floors no more." I tried to sing it like Mahalia Jackson.

In *Noon*, by Terrance McNally, we played a bunch of sexual deviant practical jokers. And in *Night*, written by Leonard Melfi, four people pay respects to a friend at a cemetery while someone else buries a dog. Robert Klein was one of our co-stars. He was still starting out but I think he impressed all of us, as an actor and a person. After we opened he used to tease me because I got singled out in a positive way in the New York Times review. He'd say, "How did you get such good reviews?" As if I had bribed or coerced a New York Times theater critic. He was teasing of course, and I agreed with his sentiment. Everyone was great. I don't know why I got singled out but years later I saw Woody Allen at a screening and he said, "I know you. You're the one who gets good Broadway reviews."

One of the highlights of that show for me was a dinner party John and I held for the three playwrights and some of their colleagues, including my dear friend, Oliver Haily. It was so wonderful having those brilliant writers all at one table.

The lowest point during any show would be when I got bronchitis. It was winter and a cold winter at that and someone kept one of the upstage doors open—probably because the backstage area was a little musty—and a really ferocious draft blew in on us during a performance. There we were sweating on stage under the hot lights while the wind was chilling us from behind. I developed a sore throat and pretty soon after that it got so bad I could hardly speak. I didn't know what

I was going to do. I drank tea and lemon and hot water and breathed steam and nothing seemed to be working. At the time I was working with my sister, Beverly's voice teacher, Professor Korst. He was a wonderful man and a great teacher and he sent me to a friend of his who was a doctor and could see me right away. I had a fever and felt so weak I had to lie down in the waiting room. The doctor examined me and said, in his German accent, "You must stay out of the show. You have bronchitis. It could become pneumonia."

Well, I had a thing or two to explain to him! This was the theater and I was a professional. The show must go on! "You don't understand," I told him. "I never ever miss a performance."

He said, "Miss Rae, you vill miss the show until you are better or you will be dead!"

"Dead? I'll be dead if I *don't* perform. But there's no understudy!"

But he scared the shit out of me—and I really felt like I was going to die—so I did the unthinkable. I couldn't talk anyway. Ted Mann, our director, got his wife, Patricia Brooks, to fill in for me. Of course she didn't have time to memorize the part so, for two days, she had to do my part holding the script. Patricia Brooks was a famous opera singer with City Center Opera, too famous to be anyone's understudy so she went incognito under a different name—Amy Kleinsinger, I think it was. As soon as my voice came back I was back. I still wasn't 100%--or even 50%--but the show must go on.

Actually, the show only lasted a few months—like I said, ahead of its time—but it was worth every performance. And *surprise surprise* I got another Tony nomination!!! This time I was up against Estelle Parsons, Brenda Vaccaro, and Julie Harris. John and Larry put on tuxes and came with me. I was so naïve, I had no idea you were supposed to hire a limo to get dropped off at the big event. So we rolled up in an old Morris Minor (which was our new car). John had the VIP parking tag displayed but the cops still wouldn't let us on the street. They kept screaming at John to turn around. Finally I leaned out of the window and screamed back at the cops, "I'm Charlotte Rae! I'm up for best actress! Please *please* let us in." Fans saw me and screamed with laughter at our teeny Morris Minor. It was quite a spectacle. Finally, the cops let us in.

It was a wonderful night. John and Larry looked so handsome in their rented tuxedoes. It was such an honor to be on the same list with Estelle, Brenda and Julie. All my friends and fellow actors had told me I was a shoe-in. They'd said no one could have outdone my

*My mother's family right after they emigrated to America; Mother is the baby on my grandmother's lap.*

*My father in World War I—he'd only recently come to America and was sent back to Europe to fight for his new country*

*Mother around the time she met Father*

*Father around the time he met mother; doesn't he resemble Gary Cooper?*

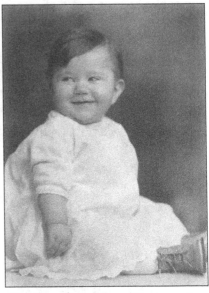

*That's me a few days old, propped up for my first close up*

*My parents' extended families on Hanukah 1930—I'm in the second row fifth from the right; Mother's mother Bubbe Ottenstein is in the middle with the shawl around her head and to her left is father's mother Bubbe Lubotsky; to her right is my big sister Beverly; little Mimi is in Daddy's arms at the left end of the long table*

*Daddy in front of his tire and appliance store .*

*Daddy was a proud American and a proud member of the American Legion*

*The three sisters*

*With Mother and Mimi*

*With Mother and Father at summer camp*

*The girls in my freshman dorm; I'm in the second row, second from the left; front row middle was my roommate Dorothy Davison*

*My high school portrait (don't ask me which year)*

*On stage, Northwestern U, playing President Truman's daughter in a spoof of the First Family*

*With Paul Lynde; they called us Lubotsky & Lynde*

*George (Paul) and Martha (me) Washington*

*Freshman year with Paul on the quad*

*John and me our first year together*

*Recording the album of* Threepenny Opera: *Paul Dooley second row,*
*second from right, Bea Arthur just left of me and left of her is John Astin;*
*Scott Merrill on my other side; Lotty Lenya first row all the way right*
*(CREDIT: Jerry Saltsberg)*

*Singing one of my opera impressions with John accompanying me on the Ed Sullivan Show*

*Live TV:* The Gary Moore Show

*A proud mother
with her mother
and beautiful
new son, Andy*

*Mom and dad
at a ranch in
Arizona just a
few hours before
daddy's heart
attack*

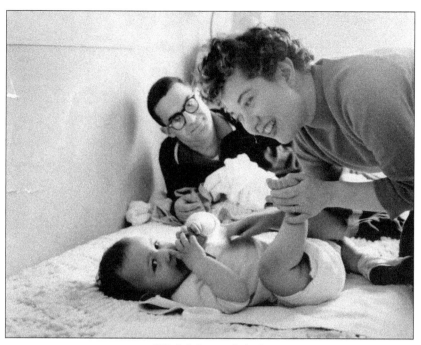

*With John and Andy*

*On stage as Mammy Yokum in* Lil Abner

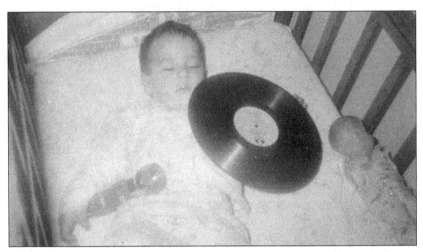

*Andy was a beautiful child but something was wrong; he'd watch that record spin around and around for hours, then wanted to fall asleep with it*

*Christmas card 1961*

*With Al Lewis as Silver Schnauser on* Car 54 Where Are You?

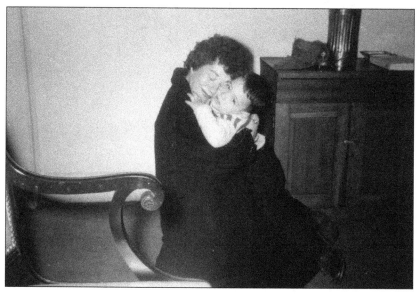

*Around the time it began to sink in that something was really wrong with Andy*

*My brilliant acting teacher,*
*Mary Tarcai*

*Even during the worst times there*
*were beautiful moments; together with*
*my two boys in Central Park*

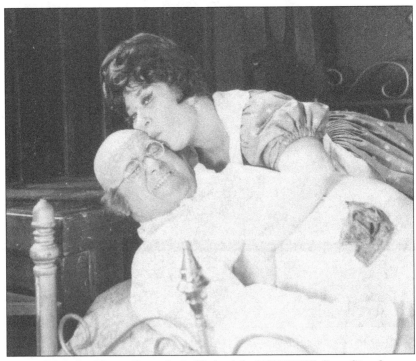

*With Sir Harry Secombe in* Pickwick *(CREDIT: Sam Siegel*

Henry IV Parts I and II *at the Delecorte Theater in Central Park,*
*1968, as Mistress Quickly on the lap of Fallstaff played by Stacy Keach*
*(CREDIT: Friedman–Abeles)*

*On Broadway in Israel Horovitz's* Morning *from* Morning, Noon, and
Night *(CREDIT: Friedman–Abeles)*

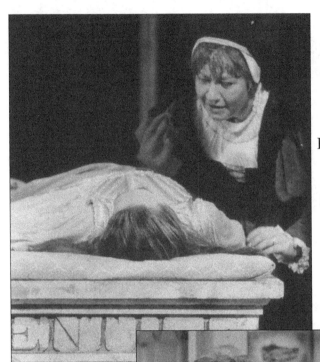

Romeo & Juliet,
*Shakespeare in
the Park 1968
(CREDIT: Sam
Siegel)*

*With Vincent
Gardenia in* Dr.
Fish *(CREDIT:
Carl Samrock)*

*As Lola in*
Comeback Little
Sheeba

*Lola's low point—*
*rejected by her*
*parents—but she's a*
*survivor*

*As Molly the Mail Carrier on* Sesame Street

*As Minnie Marx—mother of the Marx Brothers—in* Minnie's Boys
*with George Connolly as Harpo.*

*On stage at the Ahmanson in L.A. in* Time of the Cuckoo *with Jean Stapleton*

*With the one and only Rich Little on his variety show*

*A funny moment with Larry somewhere outside L.A.*

*With John on the set of* Hair

*With director, Milos Foreman on the set of* Hair

*With Gary and Todd on* Diff'rent Strokes

Facts of Life *first season*

*In Milwaukee as the Grand Marshall of their summer fest parade with my sister Beverly and her husband Jules*

*With Larry in Rome*

*With my sisters at our favorite
place: the piano*

*With my pal and colleague
Geri Jewel*

*Northwestern alumns assembled for a televised musical variety show
with Jerry Friedman, Bob Wright, Patricia Neal, Martha Hyer, Nancy
Dussault, McClain Stevens, Claude Akin, Peter Strauss, Sheldon
Harnick, Larry Grossman, Bob Banner (who produced the evening),
Carol Lawrence, Cloris Leachman, and others*

*With my dear friend, director John Bowab*

*With my old pal, Sheldon Harnick (CREDIT: Nathan Sternfeld)*

Facts of Life *all grown up*

*With Sister Joanna on the grounds of the Mary and Joseph Retreat Center*

*With little Carly in a parade at Disneyland*

*With little Carly; looks like it might be Easter Sunday*

*With my old pal, Sandy Ruben*

*Hanging out with geniuses during rehearsals for* Into the Woods—
*Stephen Sondheim and Cleo Lane*

*As Daisy Werthen in*
Driving Miss Daisy
*(CREDIT: Lisa
Howe-Ebright)*

*With my old pal,
Larry Hagman*

*At book signing for Larry's first novel with Carly and my dear dear friends, Judith Jordan and Gennaro Montanino*

*With Andy, looking at the elephants at the San Diego Zoo*

*As Winnie in Beckett's* Happy Days *(in a mound up to her waist, Act I)*

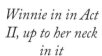

*Winnie in in Act II, up to her neck in it*

*With Andy and Larry On our old stoop on 96th Street in New York City*

*With Andy and Mrs. Pfeiffer standing in front of the old Bellevue Hospital after all those years*

*My two sons with their shades on waiting for our plane at JFK*

Pippin,
*summer of*
*2000*

*Backstage with Mimi, Larry, Eleanor, Nora, and baby Sean*

*At the piano with toddler Sean*

*With my dear friend and fellow survivor, Jackie*

*On vacation with Sean and Eleanor*

*With grown-up Carly*

*With my dear pal Betty*

*On the set of Ricki and the Flash with Meryl, Kevin, and Jonathan (CREDIT: Bob Vergara)*

*Filming my scene with the two generous stars (CREDIT: Bob Vergara)*

performance in those three one-act plays. Then came the big moment. And the winner is…

Oh, my God. I was going to have to get up there and give a speech. I wasn't even sure exactly what I was going to say. Just thank everyone. Don't forget anyone. I took the gum out of my mouth and tried to figure out what to do with it. I didn't want to stick it to the back of the seat or anything rude but I didn't think I should have a wad of chewing gum in my hand while I was accepting a Tony Award.

*Julie Harris, Forty Carats!*

And the music swelled and Julie made her way to the stage and I stuck the gum under my seat. I didn't feel like holding it anymore and I didn't feel like chewing it anymore.

Later, as we were all filing out of the theater, I looked across the aisle and there was Eileen Heckart, who I'd first met when I was in high school interning with the Port Players in Shorewood Wisconsin. Eileen looked at me—and I guess she could see my disappointment, and God knows she'd had her share of Tony disappointments. She held up nine fingers. Didn't say anything or try to say anything. Didn't have to. She'd been nominated nine times and hadn't had her name follow those words—the winner is—until the tenth.

Never hurts to have a little perspective.

My next stage opportunity was Murray Shisgal's *The Chinese and Dr. Fish*. Well, not quite. They were two one-act plays. My agent got me an audition for the part of Mrs. Lee in *The Chinese*. For the three days leading up to the audition I ate at Chinese restuarants once or twice each day and studied the women who worked there—their speech, their mannerisms, especially those who seemed to be in charge. I wanted to deliver a performance that was authentic, not just an imitation. They offered me the part on the spot. I was delighted but not exactly thrilled. I kept thinking that this was a dead-end part for me. It would show range but it wasn't as if I was going to have a future playing Chinese women.

So I asked the casting directors about the other play. They showed me the sides and I asked if I could audition for the part of Charlotte Mendelsohn in *Dr. Fish*, which was about a sex therapist. They agreed and then after I read, they offered me the part. I was so excited. What a terrific challenge to play such different roles in two one act plays. Mrs. Lee, the Chinese lady, and Charlotte Mendelsohn seeking sex therapy with her husband from *Dr. Fish*. But, no, my agent told me. That wasn't the offer. Murray insisted on separate casts! Why, I don't know. I mean, isn't it more fun for an audience to see the same actors in each of the plays, see the versatility and the relationship between the characters in each play? Since they were together on the same bill… But, no, Murray Shisgal didn't want that. So I chose to play Charlotte Mendlesohn in *Dr. Fish* and they hired Alice Drummond, a very wonderful actress, to play Mrs. Lee in *The Chinese* and that was that.

I think I made the right choice for me. I absolutely loved working with Vinnie Gardenia who played my husband, Marty. You know Vincent Gardenia—he played Cosmo Castarini in Moonstruck. What a wonderful actor and a wonderful person. The cast was full of terrific actors in both shows. Louise Lasser, Joe Bova, William Devane, Martin Lichterman, and Alice Drummond. We all really enjoyed working together and being together and Arthur Storch was a good director and a joy to work with. The only down side was Murray Shisgal. If a line he thought was funny didn't get a laugh he'd get all bent out of shape at us. He couldn't believe that any of the lines he'd written might not be that funny or that some audiences just didn't get it. It was all our fault. We weren't delivering the line right. We were all walking a tightrope with his ego which made an otherwise happy experience just a little annoying. The reviews were fair, not great, and the show didn't last very long.

That summer I got to play the part of Lola in William Inge's *Come Back, Little Sheba* in Cincinnati. It's a wonderful play. Very sad and beautifully written. Lola is so lonely, so desperate for affection and company. Doc isn't a bad guy. Just miserable in his own way. Lots of profoundly understated moments, lots of subtext and quiet desperation. Like when Lola finds the whiskey bottle in the waste basket in the kitchen and knows Doc started drinking again. Every night when I found that bottle I thought about Andy. Things had fallen apart for him at summer camp. He'd had a blow up and hurt himself and been sent home. John was taking care of him. And when I knelt down and saw the whiskey bottle in the waste basket I thought of Andy. I felt so desperate but I didn't get hysterical. I had a choice. I held it inside. It was a way to take back some measure of control in my life. Me and Lola. We couldn't change what had happened or the pain we were feeling. I kept it all inside as I knelt down and looked at that whiskey bottle but the audience knew what I was feeling. I could hear it in their silence.

I accomplished a few other things off-stage that summer—two things that should never go together.

I learned how to drive and let me tell you that was a big deal for me. I'd always been intimidated about getting behind the wheel. I think Beverly put that in my head that if I ever tried to drive I would crack up the car or something. But I was determined that summer to overcome my fear. I found a driving school and I learned on the streets of Cincinnati. I passed the written test and the road test on my first try!

I also tried smoking pot for the first time—though not, as I said, anytime close to when I was driving. It was 1970 and it seemed like everyone was at least trying it. Most of the stage crew seemed to be sneaking off to smoke between shows. I was still so naïve the assistant stage manager, Darryl, had to explain to me what the smell was.

I'd never smoked it, though I'd come close to ingesting it years before at a party of theater people. It was after seeing Brecht's *Mother Courage on Broadway* with Ann Bancroft. Her understudy, actress Tresa Hughes, was the hostess and she served drinks and chips and brownies and didn't bother telling people there was marijuana in the brownies! Thank God I was on a diet and didn't eat one. John didn't either. People got really freaked out. Some people had driven there from outside the city and had to figure out how to get home. But now, a few years later, I thought it was about time I tried this stuff and saw what all the fuss was about.

One afternoon, before the curtain, I approached the stage manager, Darryl, and offered to buy the weed if he would include me. He was delighted to oblige. I gave him extra money to buy "munchies." I'd heard that was part of the experience. So after the show that night, I joined him and a group of cast and crew for a get-together at my digs.

I think I was the only person over forty. A few of the cast members—who will remain nameless—got a real kick out of having me there while they were rolling joints and lighting them up. We were sitting around the living room on a long sofa and some big chairs. Someone lit a joint and passed it around. Darryl told me it was really good stuff. I wish I could remember the name he used. "Banana" something or other. Next thing I knew Darryl had the joint in his hand. People around us were leaning back in their seats. I was sitting on the edge of mine. Some people pinched the joint between their fingers and pushed it between their lips. Darryl put the joint between his fingers like a cigarette and slid it between his lips. He took a drag and I watched him hold in the smoke. He spoke from the back of his throat, his breath held in, and said, "Hold it in as long as you can, Ms. Rae."

I took the joint from him and tried it. Of course, I coughed up the first puff. Then I got used to it and did all right. I felt the buzz right away. I kind of liked it at first. I was floating and the colors in the room all got brighter. I got the munchies and scarfed down some M&Ms and some pizza someone put out and a banana.

Later, after everyone left, I could hardly stand up. I wanted to wash the smell off my hands and almost fell over doing it. Then I collapsed into my bed. I slept a long time but not a restful sleep. My dreams were all in technicolor. Kaleidoscopic shapes and stars. Orange, purple, red, blue, black, yellow. Even the words people spoke in my dreams were in bright rainbows. Nothing like this had ever happened to me before.

I woke up nervous. I still felt high. I drank coffee and took a cold shower but as my call for the matinee closed in I still didn't feel like myself. I got to the theater and told Darryl and the rest of my marijuana "connections" about my Technicolor dreams and how anxious I was about the upcoming performance. They tried to assure me that I was fine and that what I'd smoked the night before wouldn't affect my performance at all. But I didn't believe them. I was terrified!!! I'd never felt like this before in my life. I kept seeing those Technicolor dreams and when I got on stage I felt as if I was racing through my lines. The play seemed to go by in about twenty minutes.

After the last curtain call, Darryl met me in the wings to tell me I'd done great. But I'd felt so funny. I asked, him, "Wasn't I too fast? Wasn't I racing through it?"

"No," he replied, and he showed me a clock and assured me that the show had run the usual time.

It was a relief but it was a real lesson for me. No more pot for me.

A little later in the summer my mother visited. I picked her up at the airport and she was thrilled to see me behind the wheel. She couldn't get over seeing me drive for the first time.

She told me to be sure to get her a seat on the right side because she had a crick in her neck. Of course I wanted to do my best for Mother and it was never hard for me to get inspiration about the role of Lola. Anyone who ever saw Shirley Booth in the original knows what a powerful character Lola is and I had a particular affinity for her. I identified. There's one scene in which Lola's husband Doc comes home drunk and almost kills her with a knife. Two men from AA come and take Doc away and then Lola gets on the phone and calls her mom and dad and asks them if she can please come home for just a little while. They say no. What a horrible rejection. Devastating. Watching it you feel little hope for poor Lola. To be attacked and then to be turned away by her own parents. Yet somehow, in the last act, she pulls herself together and screws up the courage to face life anyway.

The critics had really appreciated my work and so, it turns out, did my mother though she never quite told me. After the show she came backstage and told me I was fine and then raved about all the other actors. Then she complained about her seat. How it was on the wrong side and made the crick in her neck hurt her. And that was that. Until many years later, long after Mother had passed, when Beverly let the truth slip out. She did it in the most off-handed way. Like it was nothing. I guess I mentioned *Come Back, Little Sheba*, and Beverly said, "Oh, that was a great show. Mother told me all about it. She said that by the end of the first act she forgot it was you, Char. She just felt so sorry for Lola, the character you were playing."

My God, how hard it must have been for my mother to keep silent, suppress all her feelings in order to protect me from the "evil eye," the *kenahora*, which she feared would zap me.

I got to see Mother again later that year when I did a movie called *Hello Down There*. It starred Janet Leigh and Tony Randall. He played a scientist who tries to save his underwater living experiment by volunteering to live in the deep sea compound with his family and some friends of his teenaged children who they are in a band with. Richard Dreyfuss played the band's lead singer. I played the family maid who helps deliver messages to and from the family via a bunch of very articulate dolphins. What a hoot.

I enjoyed working with everyone, especially Janet Leigh. She proved to be a particularly generous actress. I didn't have much movie experience and during one of our scenes she told me, "I'm in your key light." I didn't even know what she was talking about but she explained and pointed to the light that was shining brightest on my face. The way the director had blocked us put her in front of it. But not to worry, she said, and managed to twist her body so that she was no longer in the path of my key light while I was saying my line.

I was very touched to have another actress, one I hardly knew, make such a gesture. Years later we were both guesting on an episode of Angela Lansbury's *Murder, She Wrote* and I got a chance to thank her, again, for her generosity. I think she appreciated that I remembered. And why not? It's so important to acknowledge things like that.

Tony Randall was also great to work with and fun to be with. He was quite a raconteur. He'd hold court sometimes between takes and tell stories about the London theater and opera. He was a madman about opera. Loved it. We all enjoyed his stories.

We shot *Hello Down There* in Miami where Mother liked to spend some of her winters in those days so I had her fly down, rented a place for her where her friends were, and we got a chance to spend some quality time. I was really glad I did because it was the last chance to do that before she got sick.

We got to hang out in the evenings and talk about things and I got to let her know that Andy was doing really great. Life at the Camphill school was the best thing that could have happened for him. He was happy. He lost weight and seemed so much more relaxed. I don't think Andy was ever really suited for the city with its garbage trucks and other loud noises and crowds of people. Mother was so happy to hear that he was making progress and enjoying himself. And happy to hear me tell her all about Larry. He was a star athlete in his 6th grade class and musical too. Larry played the trombone and had formed a musical ensemble with some other boys, including Andrew Litton who is now a world famous pianist and conductor.

Mom and I had a great time in Miami. We ate at Wolfies a lot and Mom would always open her purse after we'd finished and put all the remaining rolls in there. I was so shocked and embarrassed but she explained that everyone did it—or at least a lot of people did. She explained how the restaurant cannot serve them again so they would just go to waste. I guess she was right. She was always quiet about it. My mother was never pushy. She was a really nice woman.

Talking to her—in a restaurant or in that room in Miami—I could tell, finally, that my mother was proud of me. She never exactly said it—she never could, of course, lest the evil eye get me. Whenever she had come to see a show I was in, she'd always tell me something about her seat or about someone else in the show. Could never admit I had done anything good—kenahora, evil eye. But at that moment, together in my hotel room in Miami, I knew. I could see it in her eyes. I felt her pride, her love. The comfort she took in my success and in the stability of my family.

I thought she'd live to see my sons grow up and perhaps to see me on stage at least a few more times. But pancreatic cancer doesn't often give a person much time. It absolutely didn't then, in 1970. There were no MRIs, no ultrasound. They could only diagnose by opening her up. By the time I got to Milwaukee she was about to go under the knife.

I got to her room. I rubbed her feet and hands with lotion and just tried to do anything I could to make her comfortable. She said, "Charlotte, maybe they can take it out and I can live."

And I told her, "I hope so, my darling mother. I hope and pray."

A few minutes later she was being wheeled off into surgery and not long after that the doctors told my sisters and me what they saw when they opened her up: tumors all over her pancreas. The final stages. Hopeless. The end.

It's unforgettable. The finality of it. A death sentence pronounced by a doctor in the waiting area of a hospital.

The next day, when Mother had regained consciousness, we were in her room trying to be lighthearted for her and having a tough time of it when she seemed to go cold, numb. Mimi first noticed it and Beverly yelled for the nurse. Mother had had a stroke.

At that point I didn't know whether to stay or go back to New York. No one had much hope that she'd ever come to—and, as it turned out, she didn't. She died on Mother's Day, 1971.

I took Larry out of school for a few days and brought him with John and me to Milwaukee for her funeral. I thought that was important. Larry hadn't known his grandmother very well—we'd visited Milwaukee a few times and she had visited us a time or two. But I think they were very fond of each other. It was a bittersweet time we had now back in Milwaukee. Sad to say goodbye to my mother but nice to be together with my sisters and their families. Everyone got along very well and when it came time to go through Mother's things we all did it with such grace and generosity.

We loved everything about her. Even down to the smallest things and couldn't bring ourselves to throw anything away. Her Q-tips and cotton balls and recipe cards and lists she'd written on white pads of paper. We divided it all up to remember her by.

Neither John nor I were working at the moment so we stayed the whole week and that was a blessing. Just to spend time in her lovely, spotless apartment and remember my lovely, beautiful mother.

Soon John and I were working again. John was hired as sound and music editor on Woody Allen's *Bananas* and I ended up in the same movie, playing Woody Allen's mother. Actually, I was Fielding Melish's mother. It wasn't in the script. Woody just got this idea while they were shooting. He wanted a farewell scene before his character flies down to the make-believe nation of San Marcos to join the revolution. He hired me as Mrs. Melish and Hy Ackerman to play Dr. Melish, the father. Woody's idea was that the doctor and his wife were in scrubs and surgical masks doing surgery when Fielding comes to say goodbye. I was my husband's nurse, I guess. We improvised the whole ridiculous scene. Woody kept getting ideas and we'd just go with it. I've never had so much fun.

Almost as much fun as improvising commercials for Victor's cough drops. I played a woman trying them for the first time. "Ooooh," I said, inhaling with my nose and widening my eyes with surprise and delight. "I can feel it. It's working!" The commercials were a big hit and people would recognize me on the street and mimic my reaction to the mentholated cough drops. But I think the company eventually pulled the spots because it seemed a little too suggestive of cocaine or something.

I also did those silly Charmin commercials where I'm supposed to check up on the workers in the toilet paper factory to make sure they're not squeezing the Charmin. Of course, I can't help squeezing it either—and neither can my boss. It was very sexual, everyone groping these packages of toilet paper. Watch it on YouTube. It's very weird but it was a lot of fun to be a part of it in those whacky days of the early 1970s. Teenage girls in our neighborhood would recognize me on the street and yell, "Don't squeeze the Charmin!" and laugh their heads off.

Sometimes people would recognize me in a store or on the street or on the bus but couldn't figure out where it was. Like that scene in Annie Hall where these two guys with thick New York accents recognize Woody Allen and won't let him get past them until they figure out where they've seen him. The worst time for me was at the Bronx Zoo. I was there with the two boys and things were already stressful. Andy loved the monkeys and the elephants but sometimes pigeons put him on edge and the zoo always had a lot of them. In the midst of that a woman accosted me. "Are you famous?" she asked. "You're famous, aren't you?" She wouldn't leave me alone.

Some people didn't even know they'd seen me on television. They'd ask if I had been their kid's kindergarten teacher or if I wrapped meat at Bohack.

That summer I toured with *Norman, is that You?* a play about a man from the Midwest whose wife dumps him for his brother. He comes to New York to visit and commiserate with his adult son only to discover that Norman is gay and living with another man.

Hans Conreid was our lead and he was such a good actor and a marvelous marvelous man. Totally devoted to his wife and five kids— you could tell when they came around—and somehow he was always touring with one show or another. On Broadway he did *Can-Can, Tall Story,* and *70, Girl, 70.* He'd also done a million things on television. Very versatile and always found the right details to bring his characters to life. What an honor to work with him.

The play itself was a little ahead of its time. It had flopped on Broadway but actually had been very well received in France and now we were getting good audiences in New England.

The best thing about that show was that I found a life-long friend in the cast. Judith Jordan, a very talented, beautiful—inside and out— and unsung New York actress who later moved to L.A. with her long-time boyfriend, talented director Gennaro Montanino. She did a lot of wonderful things, beautiful work.

I was still on the road with *Norman, is that You?* when I got the call from John that the Camphill School wanted Andy to leave. They'd told John that Andy was too old and too big, which seemed odd because this had always seemed like a good place for him as he grew up. But when John pressed them about it they admitted their real reason. They were afraid of him, afraid he would harm their young children. He'd grown violent and unpredictable. They had tried to work with him to get his behavior under control but he had thrown a chair and screamed and frightened all the children.

It was puberty. The physical changes and sexual urges that drive most of us a little crazy had taken control of our son. He didn't know how to control himself. He didn't belong there anymore. Just like that. I couldn't blame the people at Camphill. They really loved Andy and I know they were disappointed that they couldn't keep him there. I understood. John and I both understood. What I couldn't fathom was what we were going to do for our son? Where was he going to go now that he was a danger to himself and others?

And I was trapped in Westport Connecticut with eight performances a week!

John assured me that he could handle things with Andy while I fulfilled my obligation to the show but for me it was torture being stuck there, unable to be with Andy when he needed me. It was just a few more weeks but it felt like it would be forever. I felt so helpless. I was staying in a hotel but when I picked up John's message it was after a show and I was at the home of a friend I'd made, a woman who had contributed a lot of money to the Westport Country Playhouse. Helen often invited me over for a bite to eat after a performance. It felt awkward playing out my personal crisis on her telephone in her kitchen, but her heart went out to me about Andy.

John couldn't stay on the phone long. He had to drive to Camphill late at night and bring Andy back home. So I wished him luck and apologized for not being there. Helen asked me what was going on and I told her and she was quick to offer a solution. She said that the state hospitals were very good in the state of Connecticut. She offered to let us use her address so that we could get Andy in. Another angel in my life.

It was a beautiful gesture from someone I hardly knew. Bittersweet. Nice to know people cared and that there were hopefully options. But the word hospital broke my heart. I just wasn't ready to face the bleak reality of my son's situation. I wanted to go to him. I wanted to be there along with John. I wanted to put my arms around my son and comfort him and calm him down. I was in total despair and total anxiety about Andy and what to do and I couldn't just sit around this woman's comfortable house and talk about it. I felt a desperate compulsion to do something. I didn't know what. But I was going to go out of my mind if I didn't do *something*.

I asked her for a bucket. I asked her for a scrubbing brush and some soap. It was probably the strangest thing anyone had ever asked her but somehow she seemed to understand. She got me everything I asked for and showed me where to fill the bucket with hot water. I filled it and got down on my knees and I scrubbed and I scrubbed and I scrubbed that floor and my tears went into the wet floor and I just kept scrubbing.

It must have been a bizarre sight—her new actress friend scrubbing her floors and sobbing—but she gave me the space I needed to do it. God bless her.

# BOTTOM

The truth was John didn't know what to do with Andy. He was big now. Nearly six feet tall and very unpredictable and all that sexual energy. He'd get a hard-on and not know what to do with it. I've learned that this is a common problem for the developmentally disabled going through puberty. He would get agitated suddenly and he was difficult to control.

The morning after John brought Andy back home, he and I talked over the phone and decided he should take him to the psychiatric ward at Mt. Sinai Hospital. It was where Andy was born and I think I felt somehow more hopeful because it was a Jewish hospital. Silly of me but I was looking for hope anywhere I could get it.

John called me later and said they had admitted Andy for observation. Later that day when John went back to visit Andy, he was on some kind of tranquilizer. It was a shock to our system that our teenage son was being medicated but it was something we would sadly get used to. I remember thinking that we had failed. John and me and everyone who had tried to help us. We'd all failed.

For the moment, we wanted him off those drugs and out of that place.

I made some calls. There was a guy—I cannot remember his name now, all these years later—but I remember his voice. Soft and sincere, a Brooklyn accent. He ran a camp with his wife for the developmentally disabled in Upstate New York and Andy had spent a few weeks with them the previous summer. This summer was almost over now but the guy offered to take Andy. It wasn't a solution by any stretch but it gave us time to work on something else.

A few days later, on my day off from the show, John and I drove Andy up to the camp. I think the couple who ran it could see how stressed John and I were after just a few days of trying to find a place for our son. They told us to relax. "Take a trip or something," the wife said. "Go to Europe. Enjoy yourselves. You're good parents. You've taken good care of your son. You've got to live too."

It was a nice thing to say but we weren't going anywhere until we figured out Andy's future and helped him make the transition. But we were grateful to this couple and their camp for giving us a little time and for showing us kindness. God's angels.

We caught our breath. We kept calling people and asking for advice. There was no internet. No computers. The telephone and a yellow legal pad of paper and a pencil. I wasn't even thinking about my next job and neither was John but I was relieved when the Children's Television Workshop called to offer me a season on *Sesame Street*. It meant I'd be working in New York. I didn't want to go on the road. Not now. Not as long as there was any uncertainty about Andy.

It was a good thing John and I didn't go to Europe or anywhere else. A few days after the camp took Andy in, the camp director brought him back home. The guy was apologetic but he was firm. Andy was too agitated, too dangerous. I think that was when it really hit me how alone we were with our son. Thank God for our friends. Not only did we need a lot of consoling at the end of each miserable day, but the people we knew were our only hope of finding a good place for our son.

Somehow we resigned ourselves that Andy would have to be institutionalized. For us, it was a devastating defeat. We'd been told to put him away when he was little and we'd done everything we could not to and what had it all come to? All we could do now, it seemed, was find the best one. Not some awful dungeon.

By then Larry was home from summer camp. He was about to start the 7th grade at Fieldston, the Junior High School of the Ethical Culture Schools. It might have been a joyous time for our family but it wasn't that at all. Andy was out of control. We didn't know what he might do. He dislodged a bathroom sink from the wall. He threw a heavy glass ash tray out of the front window and almost hit Louie, one of the maintenance workers, with it. He could have killed someone. We didn't know what he could do. We had to call a neighbor to help us restrain him.

Bellevue was the only place that would take him. We got him downtown in a taxi, perspiring and holding our breath and clutching onto him, hoping we didn't pass a garbage truck or that a siren didn't come too close and upset Andy during the ride. The driver seemed to sense our urgency. He was brilliant, cut through midtown in five minutes and got us there in less than twenty.

I don't think there has been a more depressing sight in my life than that ancient Dickensian building, the old Bellevue Hospital. I remembered when Andy was little and I would bring him there to work with wonderful Elsbeth Pfeiffer. I would try to ignore those awful human sounds from the psych ward and hope that Andy didn't notice them or think about them and that neither of us would ever see anyone who'd wandered out somehow. And here we were—and I was afraid Andy was going to be one of them.

We had to sign a form requesting to have him committed. Neither John nor I read that whole form and if we had I doubt we would have understood it anyway. It seemed like just a heartbreaking formality to get Andy temporarily into a place that could handle him if he became dangerous to himself or anyone else. I remember that phrase on that paper: "Danger to himself and others." I cried seeing it and signing my name to it and for years after I cried inside every time I heard or thought about that phrase.

John and I were standing at an old varnished counter when we signed that paper. Behind us, slouched over on a vinyl sofa, a disheveled young woman in sunglasses seemed to be signing the same paper, seemed to be signing herself into Bellevue. I tried to respect her privacy and not look at her but I kept seeing her out of the corner of my eye. She seemed at the end of her rope and I kept thinking—and almost wanted to say to her—I'm right there with you, sister. I mean I was about ready to sign myself in too.

Had to sign him in.

I don't know how we got out of there, John and me. I don't know how we made it back to the apartment. I couldn't stop crying for Andy but we had another son and we had to be strong for him.

It broke our hearts to leave Andy there and we were desperate to get him out. I cried every night and I don't know how I pulled myself together every morning. We looked at Manhattan State Hospital on Roosevelt Island. It was so depressing. We felt so defeated. It was surreal for me joining the cast of *Sesame Street* while this was going on. I remember a psychiatrist yelling at us. I don't remember if it was someone at Bellevue or at one of the other places we were looking at. I just remember that it was a man and I remember what he said. He scolded us for not putting Andy in an institution years before. Saying he should have been institutionalized years ago. I think John and I both wanted to tell him to go fuck himself, that we had done what any parents would for their child, and that it couldn't be a bad thing to do that and that it couldn't be a good thing to give up on a child. But we dared not say anything. We were beholden to everyone. We were walking on egg-shells hoping someone would help our son.

Meanwhile, things got worse for Andy. Bellevue was a terrible place for him. He was pushed around and bullied and his violence got worse. He became more of a danger to himself and others and had to be put in soft ties. And worse. John and I had no idea when we signed that paper that our son was entering a system that could land him on Riker's Island!

We almost didn't find out until it was too late. I came to visit him one morning and was told he'd been transferred to Riker's. I raised hell and in the commotion someone else said that Andy hadn't been taken over there yet and was still at Bellevue's PQ-9 unit.

I told them they couldn't do that to Andy. "You'll kill him!" I said.

No one seemed to be able to tell me anything. They all gave me a collective shrug. I kept asking for who was in charge and finally got led to an office on another floor and an administrator who was a big mucky muck in that hell-hole.

His secretary said he was busy and I told her, "So am I." Then I walked into his office. "Please," I told him. "We just need a little more time. We're trying to find a place for our son. We just need time. He's not a criminal. How can you send him to a prison?"

He wouldn't look up. He was at a file cabinet looking through drawers, pretending he was too busy to see me.

"You can't do that to my son," I said. "You cannot do it. You can't. You will kill him. It's not right."

But he kept acting deaf to my pleas. I said, "Get over here and look at me." I shouted it and I pounded on his desk. "We're talking about a human being."

I shouted at him until he paid attention and finally promised to leave Andy there until we could find something better. But I couldn't get over his insensitivity. To ignore a mother like that. He wouldn't look at me. How could someone like that be in a position of such power? How does someone get so cruel?

I went home sobbing. Sobbing to everyone. Everyone we knew. Sobbing and sobbing, until, finally, my friend, Tresa Hughes, came through for us.

Thank God for Tresa Hughes. The same woman who'd baked marijuana brownies at her party almost ten years ago and gotten her quests sick and freaked out—and who I said I wouldn't trust after that— she had a friend, a psychiatrist who was setting up a pilot program at Bronx State Hospital for adolescents and young adults with developmental disabilities including those with dual diagnoses like Andy, young people who couldn't make it in a school setting or with their families. It sounded like Andy. It sounded like a kind place. A place with a little heart. Not the ideal place—I still had high hopes for my son, something better than an institution one day somehow for my son. But it was a place where he could be safe and be taken care of. Kind, custodial care. That's what they call it—a place to maintain. Better than any of the hell-holes he might have wound up in. Thank God for that!

We called and got an appointment with the psychiatrist in charge of admissions. Dr. Takitomo was a compact man with dark hair, neatly dressed. Quiet. Most of all he was kind. He seemed to understand how difficult it was for us at this time in Andy's life. He was reassuring. That meant so much to us. He let us know right away that there was a place for Andy at Bronx State Hospital. He said that they would work with Andy and keep trying to help him improve but he didn't promise anything. He didn't try to get our hopes up. I appreciated that at least somebody cared.

I remember an afternoon, just a few weeks after Andy moved into Bronx State. I came by to see him and they told me he was in the "seclusion room." He'd hit someone, bitten himself. I felt that dread in my belly. I didn't know what would happen. I was afraid they'd kick him out. But they were so nice to me. They apologized because I'd come all the way to the Bronx on the subway and I couldn't really see him. Then they checked to see if I could at least talk to him for a while. More angels. I wept at their kindness and understanding and their obvious concern for Andy and for me.

Then I saw him through the thick glass window of an iron door. He was all drugged out on Stelazine. I understood that the hospital needed to use medications like that. But it was so depressing to see him like that, worse than any Russian play, if you know what I mean. When I got home I found a little Vermouth. It wasn't hard to find. Then some wine, and had a sip. Then another.

I thought I was handling my drinking all right. I was never drunk as Molly the Letter Carrier on *Sesame Street* or in front of any camera or on any stage. But I knew I was drinking too much. Somehow I'd thought that once we found a place for Andy I'd cut back but that didn't happen. One evening I tried to fix dinner and I was so drunk I chopped my finger up and had to go to the hospital for stitches. I was so ashamed and so fearful in my drunken stupor that I told the ER staff that I was a concert musician so they would be sure to do a good job on my finger.

I told Elsbeth how desperately depressed and anxious I was all the time. She recommended a therapist but after a few months I wasn't feeling any better. A friend of mine recommended another therapist. That one didn't seem to be helping either. Maybe it took more time. Maybe I was impatient but I was going out of my mind—and still drinking to numb the feelings.

One night I was in a taxi on my way to meet John downtown. We were joining another couple to see Pinter's *The Birthday Party*. We were going to all come back to our apartment afterwards for a late supper. I had some filet mignon all seasoned up and had prepared some artichokes. Or had I? As the taxi pulled up to the theater, I realized, in my tipsy state, that I had absolutely no idea what I'd done with those artichokes. Had I left them out uncooked? Had I left them boiling in a pot? Or were they cooked and wrapped up in the fridge? I might have burned down our building. When I got home later, I found those artichokes cooked and wrapped up in the fridge. It scared the crap out of me!

I told my therapist about it. I said, "I think I'm drinking too much." Her response was that I had a choice, that I should drink less if I considered it a problem. But she was wrong. I was powerless.

One night, while John was out of town on a job and Larry was at a friend's house, I got drunk and went to the movies. I was so drunk I couldn't remember the movie. Then I walked down Broadway blasted out of my mind, crying.

Around that time my dear friend, Esther Davidson invited me for lunch. She was a very talented pianist married to a brilliant sculptor. She wanted to know all about the boys and how they were doing. I told her how relieved we were about Andy finally being in a good place but that I still wasn't feeling the relief and I was drinking a lot. I told her about my chopped finger and the artichoke mystery (it turned out I'd cooked them and put them away but the uncertainty had scared the hell out of me).

I can still hear her exact words. "Charlotte," she said, "you've been on a meat hook."

It was exactly how I felt. I asked her how I could get myself off of that meat hook.

She said, "Why don't you go to AA?"

"AA? For alcoholics?" I couldn't believe it. "You don't understand," I said. "I'm not an alcoholic. I'm not that bad. I just need to get it under control."

She said, "They're very nice in AA. Warm." She looked up the number in her white pages directory (remember those?) and wrote it down for me.

I had an appointment with one of my shrinks later that afternoon and I told her about Esther and her suggesting AA. The therapist discouraged me. She said, "You don't need AA to tell you not to drink. You have a choice."

But I didn't feel like I had a choice and I wanted to find out about AA for myself. I felt desperate enough to try just about anything.

That night was the season wrap party for *Sesame Street*. I didn't want to miss that but I was ready to try anything so I found a payphone and called AA and someone told me which meeting would be closest to the restaurant where CTW was having the party, which was at Lexington Avenue and 80th Street. The meeting was in a church, a block away on 81st.

Esther was right. I walked into that hall in that church on 81st and Lex and it was like I had come home. Esther saved me. She was my "Eskimo" as we say in the program. I'm delighted to have become an Eskimo to a few people since then. AA saved me—or helped me save myself.

I started to tell my therapist about the meeting and how much better I felt afterwards and she discouraged me from going back. She said, "It's a cult. Stay away." So I fired her.

Today, I know therapists who won't see a patient with a drinking problem if the person isn't attending AA.

A few months after I joined the program I had a meeting about Andy with Dr. Takitomo and he said, "You know, Mrs. Strauss, something has happened to you. You are different than before. Your gaze. Much more clear. More direct. You seem calm." It was sobriety. Sobriety and the end of my secret shame. I could talk to him or anyone eye to eye.

I've considered not mentioning any of this. After all, it is Alcoholics *Anonymous*. But at this point in my life—after more than forty years of sobriety—I'm ready to tell my story in a more public way. Perhaps one person can be helped by it. I can tell you this much: if not for AA you wouldn't be reading any of this because I wouldn't have lived long enough to write any of it.

# PARTS WEST

The early 1970s were an interesting time to be alive. The social fabric of our country was starting to unravel. The Vietnam War dragged on and some of us marched against it. Some of us campaigned for George McGovern who would have been the most liberal president ever to be elected, and if you lived in New York City you might have believed he had a chance—at least everyone I knew supported him—but of course we were living in a cultural bubble on the island of Manhattan. McGovern lost in a landslide. Nixon's triumphant slogan was "FOUR MORE YEARS," which, of course, proved one of the most ironic phrases of the decade.

1972 was also the year our son Larry had his Bar Mitzvah. He hadn't had any religious training. John was from a non-religious family—like many Jewish people of German decent—and I never wanted to force any of that on Larry. But Larry saw a lot of his friends gearing up for the bar mitzvahs and bat mitzvahs and he asked if he could have one.

My sister, Mimi—somehow, though she lived 1500 miles away from New York City—helped me find a nearby rabbinical student who was willing to forgo teaching Hebrew and give Larry phonetic tutoring so he could sing his *hoftorah*.

The next challenge was to find a synagogue that would give Larry a bar mitzvah. For most of them, a bar mitzvah is the culmination of years of Hebrew lessons and religious training. We had to find a synagogue that didn't have a Hebrew school but was willing to have a bunch of teenagers crowd its aisles for one Saturday morning.

Temple Shaare Zedek, on 93rd between Broadway and Amsterdam answered our prayers. It was in a beautiful old building and the congregation was also beautiful and old. They were delighted to have a bar mitzvah, to see young faces and hear young voices—even if some of those young voices wouldn't shut up when they were supposed to.

It was really quite a sight. All these old orthodox Jewish men and women and our family and Larry's multi-ethnic friends. It was really quite beautiful and when Larry sang like an angel. I'd never really heard him sing before. I mean not since he was a little boy. I couldn't believe what I was hearing. Beverly couldn't get over it either. You have to understand, Larry was one of those thirteen-year-old boys who'd become monosyllabic. Mostly he grunted at us. And here he was now singing like an angel. A choir joined in harmonizing with Larry. We couldn't see where they were. They were somewhere above us and it seemed, for a moment, as if their voices were coming straight from heaven. It was all spontaneous. And it was magical.

Afterwards, we had everyone over to our apartment for a celebration. Nothing fancy. But it was so joyous. With all the heartache of the past few years it was just what our family needed. I felt deep joy.

That year, I got to play Ron Leibman's taxi-driver mother in a heist movie called *The Hot Rock* with Robert Redford. Later that year I did a bunch of Excedrin commercials with Dick Cavitt and Charles Nelson Riley. There were no writers, no script. They asked us to improvise different "Excedrin headaches" and we just ran with the idea, made them up. It was fun! We gave them numbers. Excedrin headache #31—my girdle is killing me! Excedrin headache #8 and #9—we're on a first date and she won't stop talking and he's a bore! Remember those Excedrin headaches? It all started with us improvising in that studio. I was Charlie's wife nagging him about whether or not he got a raise. Dick Cavett was my son who wouldn't get a haircut. I was his dingbat date. Some of ours won Toby Awards as some of the year's best commercial. They were awarded to the ad agency and the agency kept them! We never got anything. But it was fun!

That summer, my agent, Joan Scott urged me to go out to L.A. and try my luck at getting some TV roles. She got me in touch with an L.A. agent and found me a reasonably priced room at the Sportsman's Lodge. I phoned my friend and Excedrin commercial partner, the incomparable Charles Nelson Riley. He had recently moved to L.A.— Beverly Hills, to be exact, on Gloaming Way—and had actually asked me to take over teaching an acting class he'd had to leave behind at the Herbert Berghof studio where Uta Hagen also taught. I went and watched one of his classes and couldn't get over how good he was. He had such good taste and knowledge of plays and insight into character and he knew how to bring out the best in his students. I didn't think I could fill those shoes but I was flattered that he'd asked me. So I called to tell him I'd be in town and he insisted that I stay with him. I didn't want to impose but he was very insistent.

The first morning he served me breakfast in bed. It was the royal treatment. A beautiful tray with bacon and eggs, toast, coffee, and orange juice served on/in fine china and glassware, all of it stolen from the St. Regis hotel in New York. He was proud—of his cooking and his contraband—and his little dog, Rosie.

Charlie was the perfect host. Not only did he make me feel at home. He really showed me around and introduced me to everyone. Seemed like we were at a party or some sort of gathering every night of the week! Next thing I knew I was cast on an episode of *Love American Style*, then I got guest shots on *The Partridge Family* with Shirley Jones who was a most gracious star, then my buddy playwright Oliver Hailey got me on his show, *MacMillan and Wife* with Rock Hudson who was a lovely man, wonderful to work with. My old pal Paul Lynde had a show—*the Paul Lynde Show*—and he got me a guest role on it. I did two episodes with Paul. He was so wildly funny but they had created a dull family show around him. What a waste—and he knew it.

I got to reconnect with a lot of other friends too. Lots of folks I knew from New York and from college who'd all come west and were having success and good fortune. And some L.A. natives I'd known through mutual friends, like Nat Hiken's cousin, Sandi Ruben—former wife of producer Aaron Ruben (*Gomer Pyle, Petticoat Junction*, etc.) Sandi became one of my dearest and oldest friends. And I made some new friends too, including Jean Nidetch, founder of Weight Watchers. She and Charlie had buddied up and he introduced us and we hit it off. Turned out Jean was a big fan of my theater work. We met at her house in Brentwood—on Saltair north of Sunset. We really hit it off. She encouraged me to come back to L.A. soon.

It was a terrific summer for me and though I was glad to get back to John and the boys, I was a little sorry my time on the west coast was over. In a way, L.A. felt like a dream I didn't want to wake up from. New York City had become such a difficult place to live. This wasn't the New York City I visit now and love. I always loved it but the problems were taking their toll. Larry got mugged on his way to school one morning and another time he and his friend were beaten up right on the sidewalk in front of our building. John was robbed at knife-point at the corner coming home from work one night. I can't imagine what it would have been like for us if we hadn't inherited my mother's car and actually had to take the subway to visit Andy at Bronx State Hospital. That car went through more in a few years in New York than it had in its entire life in Milwaukee. Sometimes it took an hour for John to find a place to park it and often it was on some remote strip of Riverside Drive. One morning he found a man sleeping in the back seat. Another time the hood had been crow-barred open and the battery and a fan belt were gone.

It might have all been worth it if my career had been flourishing but there just weren't a lot of interesting offers for me anymore. Or most of my friends, for that matter. The work was sparse. I think all of it—life in the city, the shortage of good acting roles for me—was having an effect on John and me, putting a strain on our marriage. That and his drinking. I'd been in AA a while and I think he felt a little rejected. We used to be drinking buddies but not anymore—in fact, the last few years of my drinking I'd been hiding the bottles from him and he was probably hiding them from me. But I think he took it personally that I'd joined the 12-step program and given up the drink. He never said it but I could feel it.

Then he got a really bad sore throat that wouldn't go away and he was afraid he'd gotten cancer from all the drinking. He went to a doctor who ruled out cancer but told him his liver was way oversized. That doctor told John that if he didn't stop drinking he would die within a few years! He told me about it that night in the living room of our apartment after Larry was asleep. It was terrifying to think I could lose John from alcohol and John wept at the thought of giving up his booze. It was as if he'd lost his best friend.

He quit drinking. He did it cold turkey. The doctor gave him some pills to ease the withdrawals and John never had another drop of alcohol. But he wouldn't go to AA and when I encouraged him to try it he mocked me, said it was a cult religion, said all those homilies on the wall—EASY DOES IT, LET GO AND LET GOD, THIS TOO SHALL PASS—and simplistic "pop psychology" was beneath him. Instead, he attended meetings of Alanon, the 12-step program for the spouses and other family members of alcoholics—and where they use the same "homilies." My sponsor at the time suggested I meet John in a neutral place, a coffee shop, and set some boundaries. I was trembling as I told him that if he wanted to go to Alanon that was fine and that I was going to continue with AA. It was important to me and he needed to stop putting me down about it.

So that's how it was for a while. I was in AA and he was a dry drunk in Alanon unwilling to say he was an alcoholic or needed help. He told me all this later. He said that he would go to Alanon meetings and complain about me and others would tell him to sit down and be quiet and listen. Then someone in Alanon told him he really belonged in AA. Somehow he listened to that person and started attending AA meetings. He didn't like it but he gave it a chance and eventually I think it started to work for him. He got a sponsor and soon he was sponsoring newcomers.

Meanwhile Larry was struggling. His grades hadn't been terrific for a few years and now the administrators at Fieldston were questioning whether he was up to the challenge of their school. He'd been in the Ethical Culture School system since pre-kindergarten and that was the best they could offer—*your son is struggling and that's not our problem.* I understand their point of view. They probably believed they were sparing him the humiliation of failing later on—but he was there on a partial scholarship and I've always wondered if that didn't play a part in how they treated us. I mean, aren't educators supposed to see the potential in their students and do everything in their power to bring it out? Maybe they felt they'd already done that and they just didn't know what else to do to motivate him. Of course, John and I bore a lot of responsibility also. We were preoccupied with Andy and with the struggles of our careers. Larry put up a lot of resistance to his studies and perhaps we didn't work hard enough to push him to overcome that resistance. I felt so awful for him. He'd been in that school for ten years and now they were kicking him out. They didn't really kick him out. They suggested we find a "more appropriate" school for him. But we understood what that meant—and probably so did Larry.

He seemed to take it well. He said he was happy to go to school in the city with more "regular" kids. I think he'd always been a little turned off by the exclusivity of the Ethical Culture School and Fieldston. If you ask him about it today he'll take the full responsibility for not making it at Fieldston. He'll say he should have worked harder. He'll say he squandered a great opportunity. The funny thing, though, is that he's a high school teacher now. He works with some of the poorest, most challenged students in South Los Angeles and he's always the one fighting the administration not to kick a student out. He's the one saying that the student is their responsibility and that if they cannot figure out how to help that student then they need to work harder, use their imaginations and their expertise as educators and get off their asses and do something.

So maybe he wasn't so unscathed when Fieldston suggested he leave.

In the spring of 1973, with John and me still grappling with our new sobriety, I did an off-Broadway show—one of Terrance McNally's early works—about a bunch of drunken TV actors, all named after different brands of booze. It was called *Whisky* and I was Tia Maria. We all eventually burn to death together in a hotel fire. *Whisky* was a strange play but a fun cast to be part of.

After that I played opposite my dear friend Charlie Durning in David Rabe's *In the Boom Boom Room* at Lincoln Center's Vivian Beaumont. It's the story of a young woman who comes to Philadelphia from some small town in hopes of becoming a star and instead becomes a go-go dancer. Her boss wants her to go topless but she refuses, until her sleazy boyfriend slashes her face. Then she doesn't care about herself anymore.

I played her cold-hearted mother who had wanted to abort her. Charlie played my husband, her molesting father. It was a courageous look at the exploitation of women and I was proud to be part of such a ground-breaking show. I think it helped inspire me, a few years later, to keep *The Facts of Life* as real as possible.

Charlie and I met on that show and became friends for life and became L.A. neighbors years later after I sold my house and moved to a condo. He and his lovely wife, Mariane were regulars at my dinner parties—and I was a guest of theirs for dinner.

But *In The Boom Boom Room* was not an easy production, and not an entirely friendly one. We had a legendary producer, Joseph Papp—founder of the Delacorte Theater, and the Public Theater, and who created Shakespeare in the Park—and we had a dynamic director, also a wonderful actress, Julie Bovasso (she was John Travolta's mother in *Saturday Night Fever* and the nurse who wouldn't talk to Paul Newman in *The Verdict*). But she and Joe Papp did not get along.

I love Joe and have great admiration and appreciation for him, but he can be a little dictatorial. That's probably an understatement. He has a very hands-on approach with directors and this did not go over well with Julie Bovasso. She told him to get off the stage. He told her to leave. When I'd done *Romeo and Juliet* in Central Park ten years earlier, Joe had fired the director and took over directing the show, and now he was doing it again. It happened in front of the whole cast and it was ugly.

They were like two bulls in an arena. Joe told her to get out. She refused. They kept attacking each other verbally. None of the rest of us knew quite what to do. One of the actresses in the show was so upset she vomited on the stage. I don't think she really ever got over it and, after the show closed she left the acting profession. Eventually,

Joe wore Julie down and with great defiance she walked out and Joe became our director.

That was the last show I did in New York.

Things had stabilized for Andy. He was in a good place—a good place compared to where he might have been—and John and I were accepting the limitations of his life. If I thought about it too much it was still heartbreaking and terribly depressing. So we tried not to think about it too much. Instead we thought about ways to keep making his life more interesting and satisfying. We always brought him his favorite things to have with him at Bronx State Hospital. Cassette tapes of his favorite Mozart piano concertos and a tape deck to play them on, cheddar cheese wedges, pistachios, mixed nuts, cranapple juice by the gallon. When he was home with us for an overnight, we cooked lobsters and took out Chinese food. We figured out where, in the neighborhood, he could walk by himself so that he could feel a sense of independence and accomplishment—to the stationary store for a popsicle or to Orange Julius or to Blimpies for a footlong roast beef sandwich with everything on it. Our neighborhood kept getting more and more dangerous, but with his long wild hair and medicated expression he looked crazy enough that I don't think anyone ever wanted to bother him.

Things kind of stabilized for Larry also—or so we thought. We got him into a school right in the city that was willing to help him. Baldwin was the name of the school and Larry seemed happy there—he made friends right away and had a busy social life—and so we were happy with the new school. The truth is John and I had no idea what was going on with him. This was before cell phones. In those days your teenager left the house and unless something awful happened you really didn't know what they were doing all day.

Larry was going to school but he was also hanging out in the streets, smoking dope, doing graffiti on subway trains and God knows what else. It was a crazy time in New York and a lot of our friends had teenagers who were acting out. I told Larry he could invite his friends over anytime and sometimes he did bring them home with him to eat. They were a rough-looking crew but I treated them like I would any other friends of my child and I think they appreciated it. One time the superintendent told me Larry and his friend had done some graffiti in the stairwell. I put my foot down and made them clean it off.

One thing I was happy about that year was he had a girlfriend and she was a really nice and really smart girl he'd known at Fieldston. Her name was Dayna and her mother wasn't happy about the relationship because Larry was white. He brought Dayna with him to see *In The Boom Boom Room*. It probably wasn't the most appropriate play for fourteen-year-olds but I don't think they were scarred for life by it. After that matinee performance, I rushed home—between shows—and made dinner for them. Dayna insisted on helping me set the table and clear the dishes. She was really a very sweet girl.

I understood how her mother felt. Larry told me that Mrs. Bowen had said to him that it was nothing personal, that she liked him, but that she'd been mistreated by a lot of white people in her life and just couldn't have her daughter with a white boy. She didn't want them going together. I think Dayna ignored her mother's dictum and she and Larry snuck around together. I was glad. I empathized with Mrs. Bowen but I didn't agree with her.

Early the next year, 1974—out of the blue—I was offered a small part in a play at the Music Center in Los Angeles. Bob Linden who was assistant artistic director of the Ahmanson and Mark Taper theaters at L.A.'s music center knew me from his years in the New York theater and asked me to come play the supporting role of Mrs. McIlhenny, an American tourist in Italy who befriends the lead character in Arthur Laurent's *The Time of the Cuckoo*. It's a drama about middle-aged people falling in love in difficult circumstances—he's in a bad marriage in Venice, Italy, she's a single American on vacation. It had originally opened on Broadway in the 1950s but only had a short run. A screen adaptation called *Summertime* with Kate Hepburn also came out in the mid-50's.

My friends all urged me to go. There were so many more opportunities for me in L.A. But I was torn. It was a great opportunity—better than anything anyone in New York was offering me—and my last trip to LA had been so wonderful but I didn't want to be away from John and the boys. As usual, John urged me to go. He told me he could handle the boys. I appreciated the support but I didn't want to leave it all on him. John worked long—sometimes very long—hours in cutting and sound rooms in midtown Manhattan. So I asked around about someone, a graduate student, who might stay in our extra bedroom and help with Larry. You know, make sure he did his homework on the nights when John was out late.

I was in the waiting room at my doctor's office and got in a conversation with another patient, a middle-aged African-American man and when he told me he was an NYU professor I asked if he knew of any students who might want some free room and board in exchange for keeping an eye on my son.

Vernon Cole—the young man the professor recommended—seemed a little aloof to me when I met him but I thought Larry would like him and I was right. I'm not sure how much homework Vernon Cole made Larry do but I think they had some fun times hanging around together, listening to music, going to the NYU dorms and getting high (I found out years later—right now, in fact, while writing this book with Larry, 7:50 p.m. February 17, 2015). In a strange way I think Vernon was a very positive influence on Larry. I think that getting to know someone who was down to earth but also intellectual helped encourage Larry in that direction. John enjoyed talking about politics with Vernon and Vernon's cousin Umtwalla—who seemed to always be over there—after a long day of work.

Meanwhile, for me, it was long days of rehearsal working with wonderful people. Jean Stapleton was our lead. Most people know her as *All in the Family*'s Edith Bunker but she was so much more—as an actress and as a person. She was one of the most gracious stars anyone could ever meet. We became friends and some years later we flew together to Chicago and roomed together and marched with Phil Donahue and Marlo Thomas and a lot of other people for equal wages for women. Years later, when my sisters were visiting me in L.A., Jean had us all to her beautiful house for lunch.

Being a part of *Time of the Cuckoo* was a special experience for me. I was happy to be doing a wonderful play with wonderful actors and to get some opportunities on some great television shows. The Dean Martin Show wanted me also, but by then I was just too run down and I was also a little preoccupied with a new project: figuring out if it was at all possible—if there was any conceivable way—that we could move to L.A. I'd kind of fallen in love with the place and everyone in the business was telling me I should be there.

And I was running into a lot of my old friends from New York who had already moved to L.A. Like James Prideaux, the playwright who had come out to the west coast and written an episode of the TV mini-series *Lincoln* and went on to write *The Last of Mrs. Lincoln* for Julie Harris and *Mrs. Delafield Wants to Marry* for

Kate Hepburn. He threw a party for me while I was in town and it seemed like everyone was there.

I brought along two of the actors I'd made friends with in *Time of the Cuckoo*; Patty McCormick, a delightful young actress you might know from *The Bad Seed*, *The Sopranos*, and a ton of other things, and a really talented young—and very good-looking actor, Ernest Thompson. We all had a great time and I ran into theater director George Schaeffer who I knew from New York. I introduced them to George and Earnest mentioned that he was also a writer. George asked to read some of his work. Earnest later told me that he sent George some short plays and that George had encouraged Earnest to show him more of his work. Eventually, Earnest sent George a little autobiographical play he'd written called *On Golden Pond*. And the rest, as they say, is history.

When Larry's school was on Spring break, John brought him to L.A. for a week. John fell instantly in love with the city. He'd been there before, of course. During World War II he had done his Army basic training in Central California and had visited L.A. but suddenly a move west just felt right. For both of us. L.A. is a seductive place—the warmth, the light. It happens to a lot of us.

So when John brought up the possibility of moving here, I told him I'd already figured it out. I'd looked into the school system for Larry and the greater challenge was what to do for Andy. He was well cared for at Bronx State Hospital, and though a state hospital had never been our ideal goal for Andy it seemed for now to be the best option. I didn't know where to begin to find a place for him near L.A.

Thank God for my dear dear friend, Sandy Ruben. I'd met her through Kate and Zero Mostel. They'd brought her to our New Year's Day open house while she was visiting New York. It turned out we were both cousins of Nat Hiken—and very proud to be—and Sandi was just a lovely person. Sandy was that rare breed of my generation: a native of Los Angeles. So she knew things about the place and knew a lot of people. She was like a bumble bee, buzzing around everyone and everything and had a great gift for getting people together.

I told her about Andy and when I described him, she said that her artist friend Jay Rivkin had a son similar to Andy. His name was Phillip and he lived at Camarillo State Hospital and Jay was very happy with the place. She set up a lunch for me to meet Jay. It wasn't easy. Jay was in the midst of a divorce at the time but she made it and was so generous with her time. She told me all about the place. Said it was in a rural area, surrounded by vegetable fields and hills and not too far from the ocean. She said that Camarillo Unit 88, where Phillip lived, had a terrific parent group that was really involved with the staff, got together and made sure things were good for their children, and put together holiday parties for them every year and other activities and outings throughout the year.

A few weeks later, Jay took me with her to Camarillo to show me the place. I was very nervous on the drive up. I didn't know what to expect and I was so used to disappointment and rejection when it came to Andy. His violence had made him undesirable to many people. Jay and I talked about our boys and found that we had a lot in common. When I told her about Andy's violence she identified. She said that Phillip had once slammed his head through a window. I felt immediate empathy for my new friend, but there was also an intense relief that maybe Andy wasn't so bad and maybe there were people out here who could understand.

Camarillo State Hospital was just as she'd described it. Beautiful, quiet, lush green trees and grass (this was before the drought); bright, vivid flowers and majestic mountains in every direction. Andy had loved his time at Camphill in Pennsylvania Dutch country and I thought he would like to live in a place like that again, a place where he could walk around outdoors. Jay introduced me to the director of Unit 88 and I told him about Andy. I didn't sugar-coat it. Jay had made me feel confident that I could be truthful about Andy's destructive and self-destructive behaviors and I certainly didn't want Andy moving anywhere under false pretenses. It turned out, Jay was right. The director of the unit—I wish I could remember his name, I'm so grateful to him—said it sounded like Andy would fit in and he promised he would save a place for him.

It was like a miracle. I was so relieved. I'd already found a high school for Larry, Santa Monica High School—Samohi—which was an excellent public school. So when John asked me whether I thought we should move west—and whether we ever *could* move to L.A.—I told him about Camarillo and about Samohi.

I knew it wouldn't be so easy for Larry. Moving would mean leaving all his friends and starting over but John and I both thought it would be a good thing for him in the long run. He was getting into trouble and still wasn't doing great in school. A new place might be just the thing for him.

I returned to New York in the late spring. I almost didn't give up my room at the Sunset Lanai on Sunset Boulevard. I loved the place. It was a real community of actors and writers. Writer/producer Mickey Ross lived there with his wife, Irene. Mickey had helped me with the diet number from my club act back in the late 1940s in New York. Now he and his partner Bernie West were one of the most successful sitcom writing teams in the business. They were head writers for *All in the Family*, creators of *Three's Company*. Mickey and Irene could have afforded a Beverly Hills Mansion or a penthouse somewhere but they lived in a suite at the Lanai. Vinnie Gardenia was there too. And comic Phil Leeds and his wife Toby. And lots of people out from New York would stay there from time to time.

I gave up the room but not really. John and Larry and I were back in a few weeks—once Larry's school ended—and we got a two-bedroom at the Lanai while we figured out the rest of our lives. Audry the manager was a sweetheart and she loved cats, which was a godsend to us with our two New York transplant cats. She took care of a stray cat everyone called Charlie because of the Charlie Chaplin moustache his facial coloring suggested. A few years later—after one of our cats died—I adopted Charlie.

We didn't give notice on our New York apartment that summer or move anything anywhere. We still had to be sure we could make this work. We opened bank accounts and rented cars in L.A. We rented two Ford Pintos. We thought they were great cars. We were New Yorkers. What did we know about cars? We had no clue how dangerous those cars were! The gas tank was in a bad bad place, I read somewhere much later. A five mile-per-hour crash could blow the car up.

One morning I was driving with Larry when we got rear-ended. It felt pretty hard but it must have only been four miles-an-hour because we didn't blow up.

Later that summer, I got to work with Jean Stapleton again. This time on *All in the Family*. It was the opening episode of that season and Carroll O'Conner was holding out for a new contract and a lot more money. While his agents and Norman Lear's lawyers were working all that out, they wrote about Archie Bunker going out of town and disappearing—temporarily, as it turned out—and while he was away Edith threw a Tupperware party. I was Lilian Henderson the Tupperware lady in the first of those episodes. It was called, "Where's Archie."

It was an overwhelming experience for me being on that show, even without Carroll O'Conner. I was in total awe. At the time *All in the Family* was the number one show on television. Everyone watched it. I was so nervous. My heart was palpitating on the set. One day I told Sally Struthers how nervous I was and she looked incredulous. She said, "Charlotte, don't you know how great you are?" I couldn't believe it. That was so sweet of her. So generous. I've never forgotten it. Everyone needs to know they belong—so it never hurts to hear it from someone.

In one of the funniest moments of the show, Edith is giving her opening remarks for the Tupperware party and she is very nervous. She's been rehearsing it all day and then just as she's saying it I (the Tupperware lady) start to pick my nose and then Edith, instead of saying, "I welcome you with open arms," says, "I welcome you with open noses." And guess who told me when and exactly how to pick my nose when we were rehearsing? Norman Lear! I can still remember him sitting there with his finger up his nose demonstrating. It was hilarious.

It really went great and my guest on *All in the Family* led to a guest shot on *Good Times* with John Amos, Esther Rolle and Jimmy "JJ" Walker. I played a social worker, and I think it's fair to say that both of those guest shots put me in Norman's radar and led to *Hot L Baltimore*, *Diff'rent Strokes*, and ultimately to *The Facts of Life*.

John and I both loved the life around the pool at the Sunset Lanai but we had our hearts set on the Westside. I'd made a lot of AA friends who lived around Santa Monica and I'd already looked at the schools there for Larry. So we found a sublet, half a block from Wilshire Boulevard and 25th Street for the summer and we set about the exciting and tedious business of finding a house.

It was crazy. Neither of us had a job—just some money we'd saved up, mostly from a settlement I'd received a few years ago when a taxi I was riding in got hit by another car and my pelvis was fractured.

John and I were two middle-aged people who'd never owned a piece of property. We were like children—didn't know the first thing. We walked through houses trying to imagine ourselves in them. We had no idea what to look for or what to think about. It was a big adventure. We fell in love with a house on Georgina Avenue in Santa Monica. It was a beautiful neighborhood but not nearly exclusive as it is today (these days people like us could never have afforded anything in that area). It was a modest one-story house with a small pool and a beautiful garden. I could see myself in that garden. I felt relaxed just looking at it and thinking about it. John loved it too.

We made an offer and it was accepted. Our realtor got us a loan. We got him through my dear friend Royal Dano, a wonderful actor who I'd met in *Three Wishes for Jamie.* I don't know how that real estate agent found a bank that would set up a home mortgage for an unemployed actress and an unemployed composer. We didn't ask. There was a lot we didn't ask. I knew so little about real estate, the first time someone mentioned escrow I thought they were talking about a salad.

We crossed our fingers and waited for escrow—now that I knew it wasn't a salad—to close so we could move in.

The day escrow closed the realtor had us over to his office to celebrate—and sign over our down payment. He had a bottle of champagne and he popped the cork and poured us some. We were both on AA, of course, so we couldn't drink any, but we celebrated anyway—and signed. We thought we were getting the keys that day but the realtor said we'd have to wait until the bank cleared all the transactions. A few days past. Still no key. The realtor didn't return our calls. Finally we went into his office and he told us there had been a mistake—an oversight—on the title search. There were liens on the house. Mysterious third-party owners. I prayed and prayed that we would get our money back.

Welcome to L.A.

# EARTHQUAKES

Like most new arrivals in L.A., I was a little afraid of those earthquakes we all hear about. The city shakes violently. The earth opens up and swallows all the transplanted New Yorkers. My friend, Jean Nidetch—founder of Weight Watchers—told me what to do, what she planned to do: get to the nearest doorway and eat a chocolate éclair. She said, "If I'm going to go, that's how I want to go."

They didn't turn out to be so frightening—the earthquakes that happened our first few years in California. Felt kind of like a subway train was going beneath us. No, those weren't the earthquakes that would knock me for a loop.

As the summer of 1974 wound down and the long days grew shorter, John and I had to suspend our house hunt and just find a place to live. We found a rental in Santa Monica. The rent was $600 a month. More than double the $250 we were paying for our apartment in New York and neither of us had a job. Just a little faith and a little optimism.

Without faith or optimism I can't imagine how we would have faced the ordeal of packing all our things and moving our family, cats and all, to L.A. I wanted to find a way to keep the New York apartment. We could probably have sublet it but John said no. A clean break. I didn't argue. Who knew the upper west side would be so gentrified—all the way past 106th Street!—and our $250 a month apartment would one day be a million dollar (or almost) condo in a building with a doorman!

We were sad to say goodbye to all our New York friends. Our neighbors and all our theater friends. Natalie Silverstein, who'd watched Andy when I'd gone to the hospital to have Larry, couldn't believe we were moving away. So many other people to say goodbye to. Everyone was happy for us but a lot of them were upset at us for leaving. Eddie Lawrence said, "You're going to Hollywood? Better check your brains at the state line!"

We sold our car to a neighbor, a couple across the street—Larry had baby sat their two little boys. Another neighbor bought our televisions and air-conditioners. Everything else went across the country. We watched moving men empty our apartment and then we hopped a cab to the airport and that was that. It was an emotional experience for me—much more so than leaving Milwaukee to come to New York.

New York had opened its arms to me, taken me in. My memories were joyous and bittersweet. Just about every important milestone in my life had happened between the three rivers that surround the city. It was the only place our two sons had ever known.

Larry started school at Santa Monica High. It was an enormous school—more than 3000 students—and I think that was a shock to him. I asked him how it went the first day and he gave me a typical fifteen-year-old's monosyllabic response: "Fine." I asked him how he liked his teachers: "Okay." I asked him about the other kids. He said, "Blond."

I think he was just being funny because Samohi was a very diverse campus, though a little segregated. Years later he described it to me. How kids of different ethnicities kept to themselves and how hard it was to break through that, though I think he eventually broke through and had a diverse circle of friends like he had in New York.

Andy was still at Bronx State Hospital. No one there could figure out how to get him to Camarillo State Hospital a continent away. I mean, obviously, an airplane was the best mode of transportation but there was no protocol for transferring someone from one institution to another in different states. It was crazy. I guess no one had ever tried to do it before. I kept asking them when Andy could move and they kept saying that they were still figuring out how to process him out to another state. I was praying for a solution. I kept praying and praying and asking God to show me the way. Weeks went by and Andy was still stuck in New York. I couldn't understand what the problem was and the social worker on Andy's unit at Bronx State Hospital couldn't explain it. Finally, I was on the phone with her for the umpteenth time, and I was so anxious and frustrated and I said, "Look, you say it's a big process. I don't know what the process is. I mean, of course, we'll pay for the ticket, but what else do we need to—"

She interrupted me, "Oh," she said, "then there's no problem."

That was it. The whole thing had just been a lack of communication.

We bought Andy a plane ticket and John flew to New York and got him. A thirty-six hour round trip from LAX to JFK, overnight in the airport Howard Johnson, a taxi to Bronx State Hospital, then back to JFK with Andy and on a flight to LAX. Larry and I picked them up at the airport and we drove up the 405 and the 101 to Camarillo State Hospital.

"You like New York City," he kept saying during the trip. Andy never used the first person—always the second. He was a big tease. He knew we wanted him to like his new home so of course he went on and on about the old one. But when we reached the grounds of the place, he got very serious and said, "Nice." He kept looking around at the vast expanse of green—trees and grass.

An institution is never a great place to have to live, but this one had a staff that really cared and enough parent support that the residents, even those who didn't have parents, were well taken care of. There would be time in years to come when Andy would struggle, when he'd have room mates who would torment him—turn lights on in the middle of the night, steal his things, yell at him—and I suppose those roommates might say the same of Andy. But when we left him there that first night he seemed to accept his new surroundings and that gave us a sense of gratitude and peace.

I don't know how long John and I could have survived on unemployment and our savings. Neither of us wanted to find that out—and we certainly didn't want to go through the money we hoped to put down on a house at some point.

But it was tough for a while. For all the encouragement I'd gotten to move to L.A. no one had a job waiting for me. John meanwhile was having problems with the west coast editors union. They wouldn't let him work in L.A. It was infuriating. Unions are supposed to protect workers not discriminate against them. I've always been passionately pro-union and I am loyal to the unions of which I'm still a member, but that crap the L.A. editors union put John through really tested my conviction.

He had to take a New York job—on Elaine May's *Mickey and Nicky*—and spend most of the next year subletting apartments back there. He managed to get some of the post production work moved to L.A. and because it was a New York production the union couldn't harass him, but that was only for a few months out of the year.

Meanwhile, I went on auditions and hoped for the best. I got a TV movie with Maureen Stapleton and Charles Durning. *Queen of the Stardust Ballroom* was a lovely story about two people—a widow and a postman—who find love in a dance hall. What an honor to work with Maureen and Charlie, who I'd worked with on stage in New York just a few years before. Working together again on the west coast solidified our friendship, which lasted a lifetime. My work on *Queen of the Stardust Ballroom* got me an Emmy nomination for best supporting actress.

Then it was back to auditioning. One part I really thought I'd get was the part of Millie, an old lady, on a new sit-com called *Hot L Baltimore*. It was based on a play of the same name by Lanford Wilson. The title refers to the electric sign of an old downtown Baltimore hotel, Hotel Baltimore, but the E in hotel has burned out. They were all really nice; the casting director Jane Murray and writer/producers Rod Parker and Hal Cooper. "We love you, Charlotte," Rod said, "but you're too young."

I told them I could play any age. "Just put on makeup."

Rod said, "This isn't the movies. It's television. You're just too young."

Ironically they ended up casting Gloria LeRoy—who is five years *younger* than me—for the role!

I was awfully disappointed that I didn't get the part. I really wanted some steady work so John and I could relax about money for a while. At an AA meeting I started crying about it and a close friend told me not to worry, that God had something better in store for me. She was right. A week later I got a call that Hal and Rod wanted me for a guest shot as Mrs. Bellotti on the show. It wasn't a recurring role but it was something—a consolation prize, I figured. And I guess you never know. Norman Lear was at the table reading—he was at all of them—and I guess I impressed him. He said I was so funny he was thinking about bringing my character back a few more times. By the time we'd shot that first episode Norman and his team had decided to make me a regular character on the show.

Mrs. Bellotti, for those of you unfortunate enough to have never seen the show, didn't reside at the Hotel Baltimore but she was there every week visiting her son, Moose, who was either eccentric or psychotic, depending on your take on his antics. It was strange playing the mother of an odd-ball son. A little close to home, wouldn't you say? And I appreciated it. I used the joy I'd always tried to savor with Andy amidst the sadness and frustration. Moose never appeared on camera. He lived only through my wild descriptions of him. It was lovely. I would always talk about Moose and always put a positive spin on his antics. Like one day he'd buttered the hallway.

I was the comic relief but the show was a very bold statement about real people and about diversity in our country. Aside from Moose, the Hotel Baltimore's residents included a gay couple, two prostitutes, and a black revolutionary. Norman was so wonderful about how he and his writers handled the gay couple. They were deeply in love and got along much better than the straight couple played by James Cromwell and Conchata Farrell. One of the episodes was about George and Gordon's anniversary celebration and it was beautifully and sensitively rendered. This was in 1975!

Norman Lear was not only a genius and a trailblazer—as if I need to even say that—but he was tireless. I once asked him how he did it—going from one of his shows to the next, observing and taking notes to talk about at the final run-through. He loved it. He thrived on it. He said, "Each time I get on a set it opens up a new bag of energy."

Norman and his producers, Rod Parker and Hal Cooper, were just wonderful. Norman really enjoyed his shows and everyone who made them each week. He showed us all appreciation and I think that kept everyone collegial. I mean no backstabbing or in-fighting.

To this day I remember him laughing at the way I read a line. Something about Moose training circus fleas in his room—I gestured the little whip he was using on those fleas—and Norman fell out of his chair. But that was just Norman. He really appreciated our efforts, enjoyed our work, and that is the greatest appreciation you can show an actor. We loved him for it. He made our comedy mean something.

Toward the end of the season, the writers featured me on an episode—gave Mrs. Belotti a romantic interest. They hired actor, Peter Turgeon to play the part of my beau, and from the first day we did the table reading he was wonderful and so easy and delightful to work with. I was thrilled—and terrified. I was so distracted with nervousness that leaving work the first day I set my script, fresh with revisions, atop my car and got busy talking to a security guard, an older one who I'd become buddies with, and then as I drove off I heard him screaming at me. The pages of the script were blowing all over the parking lot. I stopped and got out of the car and he helped me collect all the pages of my precious script.

Norman was supposed to go to China that week and I asked him please not to go. I told him I wasn't sure how I would do without him being there. He changed his plans for me. That was the kind of TV mogul Norman was.

He once told me that *Hot L* was his favorite of all his shows. Who could blame him? The show was hilarious and it was his strongest personal statement against bigotry. Turned out, though, that the very thing we all loved about the show was the root of its demise. No ABC affiliate in the Bible Belt would run the show. Nor a lot of other stations outside big cities. Advertisers shied away also. The struggle was worth it for Norman—and for all of us. We were all very proud of the work. It was ahead of its time—and got cancelled after thirteen episodes.

Al Burton and Jane Murray wanted me to play Mary's mother on *Mary Hartman, Mary Hartman*. But I appreciatively declined. I'd worked with Louise Lasser and was afraid of the stress. She's brilliant but intense. We had done a commercial together back in New York and she had tried to rewrite all my lines. It was disturbing. I admire her talent but didn't want to deal with her week after week. So instead they got Dody Goodman who endured Louise and was simply terrific in the show.

But I wasn't worried. *Hot L Baltimore* was a great show and a lot of people had seen me on it. I was kind of confident I'd get something else. It was pilot season and impersonator Rich Little was developing a variety show. He needed a supporting cast and his director Ronnie Graham knew me from *New Faces of 1952*—though, of course, I'd ended up leaving that show. Ronnie was such a talented friend and writer and performer. He was Mel Brooks' right hand man with his movies. He wrote "The Inquisition" musical number in *History of the World*—one of the most outrageous pieces of musical satire ever. Anyway, Ronnie suggested me to Rich and the producers of his new show and I guess Ronnie did a pretty good job selling me because the producers called and made an offer.

What a blessing! Not only to work with Rich, who was the gold standard of impressionists, but also Ronnie, who was the best in the business. The writers were original and irreverent and just plain hilarious. Among them were two more of Mel Brooks' guys, Rudy Deluca and Barry Levinson, who went on to become a major Hollywood director and producer.

Rich was adorable and a lot of fun to work with. Always gracious with his guests, who were some of the biggest names in show business—Bob Hope, Glenn Ford, Bing Crosby, Michael Landon, Andy Griffith, Bernadette Peters, Betty White, Mel Torme, Michael Jackson and his brothers. But he was equally kind and gracious with his regulars—Julie McWhirter, Joe Baker, R.G. Brown, and yours truly.

We did a lot of great work together. Not every sketch was a gem—how can you expect that when you've got to churn shows out at nearly one per week?—but most were pretty darned funny. One of my recurring bits was as a desperate woman to Rich Little's annoyed ordinary man. The desperation came easily. It had always been a part of my repertoire—I'd been there so many times over the years with Andy. It is a little strange to play that pain for the world to laugh at. It is also, in a way, healing to turn it into something funny and bring a little joy and escape into people's living rooms.

In the first installment Rich walks into a diner and orders a piece of pecan pie. Turns out to be the last piece. I enter a moment later, a woman obsessed with that very pecan pie, inconsolable that there isn't a piece for me and then homicidal in my desire to have the piece this man was just served. I was a cross between Blanche DuBois and the Glenn Close character in *Fatal Attraction*. Another time I was taking the written test at the DMV and trying to copy answers from ordinary man Rich. He covered his paper and moved away from me and I broke down from the fear of failing the test again and from self-loathing at my own ignorance. The punch-line was that I was a school bus driver. He could hardly keep a straight face doing the scene.

I played Margaret Dumont to Rich Little's Groucho Marx with Michael Jackson entering as a black Groucho with a white moustache. On that same episode I got to sing along with The Jackson Five during the finale. Michael and his brothers could not have been nicer to me and everyone else.

Rich and I were the voices of President Ford and his wife Betty going to bed inside the White House. We were Henry Kissinger and his sister (I don't even know if he had a sister but real or imagined I was her). I was also Bing Crosby's sister—"Ba-ba-ba-ba-ba-ba-ba-BING!"

We did mock commercials for music compilations of all kinds. I impersonated Kate Smith singing, "When the Bird Comes over the Mountain" and Ethel Merman singing "Everything's Coming Up Roses." One week I got to be an opera singer interpreting Elton John songs—"Goodbye Yellow Brick Road," "Crocodile Rock," "Get Back, Honky Cat."

Rich really appreciated what the rest of us brought to the table. We all loved working together. He was hardworking, honest, and reliable. If we rehearsed a scene a particular way, that was how he performed it with the cameras on. You can't always count on performers. Some will change things and throw you off. Not Rich. Never. He was thoughtful, professional, and totally unselfish.

I could have done at least another few seasons on that show. I think all of us were hoping for that. But we got cancelled. I don't know why.

Ratings, I assume. Bad time slot. Variety shows on the decline. There was so much pressure in those days to get good numbers. A lot of shows didn't stand a chance. The only thing you can do is be glad for the thirteen episodes you got to make.

John, meanwhile, was having a hell of a time in his field. He was near the top of the profession—a sought-after music editor and music supervisor—but the editors union still wouldn't budge and let him work on an L.A. production. They had a priority list and because John came from New York he'd been placed at the bottom of the list. Dino De-Laurentiis hired John for his remake of *King Kong* but had to let him go after threats from the union. John was really discouraged but also saw this ordeal as a sign that he should give up the long hours and stress of the movie business and focus on his passion: music.

He'd always been supportive of my following my passions and I wanted to be supportive of him now. He wanted to play and write music. He bought a Fender Rhodes electric piano and joined a jazz workshop to see where it would lead him. Not very far, as it turned out. I think it was hard for him to transition into jazz music. He'd been classically trained. Improvising didn't come naturally to him. But I think the whole experiment was a good release for him. I think he needed a break from the madness of the movie business. He would return to it refreshed and he would do his best and most important work in a few years.

For the time being, we were busy looking for a house. We'd rented awhile and now we were ready to jump back into the ordeal of buying a house. We'd grown weary of realtors with their pressed clothes and happy talk. It was starting to make us hate every house they showed us. Instead we started driving around on the weekends and looking at FOR SALE signs.

One afternoon, we were on our way to a party at Barbara Barry's house. At the time she was playing Barney's wife on *Barney Miller* with Hal Linden; she was and is a wonderful actress, stage and screen. We were speeding toward Sunset Boulevard in Brentwood and saw a FOR SALE sign and decided, what the hell and pulled into the driveway. It was a busy street with a blind curve—kind of like our lives were at the moment and had been for a few years so maybe that just didn't bother us. We liked the house from the outside. It was a nice pink salmon color. We leaned over the side gate and saw orange trees and beautiful bougainvillea, pink and orange. The next day we called the phone number we'd written down and set up a time to see the inside. It was charming and the price was right so we made an offer and the sellers accepted.

We decided to put a pool in the back yard. It seemed like the thing to do. I'd gotten that idea from Bea Daniels, wife of the accomplished Broadway and film choreographer, Danny Daniels. They had a studio in Santa Monica and I'd brushed up on my tap dancing there and got to know them. They invited me to their home in Santa Monica along with their friend Nanette Fabray. They had a beautiful pool, all lit up in the night air. I asked if they'd bought the house with the pool or if they'd had it put in. Bea said, "You're darn right. You don't think a little farm girl from Southern Illinois is gonna come live in California and not have a pool!"

I'm little a farm girl from Wisconsin—well, practically—and I wanted a pool too. We had enough room in the backyard. I thought it would be a wonderful thing for the kids and for ourselves. We got a loan from the bank and spoke to some pool people. We took bids and hired someone. We also had some additional yard work done and converted the garage to an office for John.

Of course, everything ended up costing a lot more than the original estimate and it all took a lot longer.

We moved in with most of the work done—and looked forward to our beautiful backyard pool.

Then a week after we moved in, John woke me up one night. He said we had to talk. It took a minute to gather myself. I really had to fight to stay awake. I asked if it could wait till morning and he said it couldn't. He had recently written his AA fourth step, that's a "searching and fearless moral inventory" of himself and had just presented it to his sponsor who had insisted that he must immediately come clean with me.

He said that he was bisexual. He said that after a brief romance with a boy during his adolescence he'd asked his parents to find him a psychiatrist who could straighten him out. He'd believed it had worked and said I really turned him on when we met. And he assured me that he had been faithful to me until just a few years ago and his infidelities had been few and far between and very brief.

I was devastated. I felt that if only he'd told me all of this twenty-five years ago and let me decide for myself whether I wanted to marry a man with his sexual background. Maybe I would have married him anyway but at least I would have had a choice. You know, there had been times when he'd get very sharp with me and now I couldn't help thinking it was his own frustration, taking out his sexual frustration on me. It wasn't fair not to give me a choice.

Now, he wanted to give me a choice. He thought we should stay together and have an open marriage. He knew people who did that and he said it could work out for both of us and that it might be better for the boys.

I had thought nothing could hurt as much as when that doctor, years before, told me Andy was autistic. But John's confession really got me. First the shock that he'd only recently been with a man, then the loss and the loneliness and the feeling that I'd just wasted twenty-five years of my life. Looking back on it now, I can see where he was coming from. He'd grown up in a different time. He'd lived a life full of his own pain and confusion. I can understand that now but in the moment all I could feel was the hurt and the betrayal.

And then John, having made his confession and his proposal, rolled over and fell into a deep relaxed sleep. I think he was just so relieved to have finally gotten it all out. I got out of bed and nearly lost my balance just trying to get across the room. I stood still to gather myself in the darkness and felt myself starting to faint but somehow I stayed on my feet and got to the phone in the kitchen and braced myself against the counter as I called my friend, Terry Kirgo. It was late and I know I woke her but she could hear the shock in my voice and didn't seem to mind. At least she didn't have the heart to say anything. I couldn't get the words out to tell her what had happened so she told me to come over and talk. I got to my car and drove, in my nightgown, to her house about a mile or two away.

Terry was a dear dear friend of mine from the program and she was so wise. Mostly she listened. Listened to my anguish and my confusion. She'd heard me talk about my marriage in meetings so she knew John and I had had our struggles. Who doesn't? But Terry really got me to see things for what they were and start thinking calmly about my options and about my future.

John and I had much in common. We shared our passion for music and the theater and we'd always collaborated well. He was probably the best damn accompanist I'd ever had. But John was very short tempered with me. "I think his anger comes from his fear, his secret," I said to Terry and then I stopped myself. "Oh, hell, let's not analyze it."

"Listen," Terry said, "it takes two to tango."

She was right. No sense pointing any fingers. Marital problems are usually a joint effort.

"He said I really turned him on when we were dating," I said. Still, the shock.

"I'm sure he meant it," Terry told me.

I kept going on about how we'd been so supportive of each other, always believing in each other.

"None of that has changed," Terry said, "but maybe this is an opportunity for something good. Maybe it's a blessing for both of you. Your chance at freedom. Maybe," she said, "God is opening up the gate."

It sounded crazy but the moment she said it I knew it was true. A clean break. I'd never imagined divorcing John and yet suddenly I was relieved at the thought of it.

I slept late the next morning and awoke to a loud thrashing sound. John was gone and when I opened the bedroom curtains I could see that something else was gone: two of our nicest orange trees! The pool construction guys were chopping up the last of the trunks and carting them away.

I ran outside screaming at them. What the hell were they doing with my beautiful orange trees? When I got out there I realized there was still one orange tree they hadn't touched but I still kept screaming, "What are you doing?"

The contractor stepped out from behind the pile of dead branches and smashed fruit and said, "Too close. The roots are too big. They come through the pool. Make a crack."

"Why didn't you say something?" I demanded. "Why didn't you warn me?"

He just stood there, shrugging. He looked a little scared. I must have been screaming pretty loud. And then I fell to my knees and started weeping uncontrollably. Everything. All of it. The loss, the devastation. Not the orange trees. My marriage. My life.

That poor contractor. He didn't know what to do. I'll bet he never chopped down another fruit tree without checking first.

John moved about two miles away to an apartment on Barrington Avenue. He wanted to be close by for Larry who was sixteen and still in school. We agonized a little about what to tell Andy but that turned out to be the easiest part of it. As soon as Andy saw a bottle of Coca Cola in John's new fridge he was adjusted to the new arrangement.

Things were tense between John and me for a while. Tense but always civil. It was strange being in that house without him after the ordeal of buying and remodeling. Some of his things still sat around in the bedroom and the living room, though he'd moved most of his stuff to his new apartment. And yes, oh yes, there was the mortgage. I didn't know how the hell I was going to pay it every month for the next thirty years when I didn't even have a steady job.

My pal, Sandi Ruben—who'd welcomed me to L.A. and helped us find Camarillo for Andy—got me in touch with her divorce lawyer, the legendary Harry Fain. He was one of the lawyers who created California's groundbreaking no-fault divorce law so people didn't have to fight about who was to blame for a split. Harry was one of the kindest people I'd ever met. He had an office in an old building on Beverly Drive. You could just picture all the Hollywood stars of the 1940s and 50s and 60s in that office handling the legalities of their break-ups. But he wasn't into any of that shit. Just human decency. He understood that people in a divorce are in shock and emotionally vulnerable. He gave me the thing I needed most which was empathy—and he didn't charge me an arm and a leg.

I won't lie. The first months were very difficult. I spent a lot of time crying and talking to my AA sponsor and other women on the program. They proved to be my rock of strength. So were my sisters. Beverly and Mimi were very supportive of me during those awful days. They offered me nothing but sympathy and support. Whatever I needed they'd be there for me. If I needed to come stay with them in Milwaukee or Dallas I could come for as long as I needed to. That meant so much to me. Mimi was especially understanding about John, which I also appreciated. She remained very fond of him and that helped too. No need to condemn the man for being human. She just gave me the gift of her compassion.

It made such a difference to have the support of my family. I wasn't ready to tell a lot of other people. With my sisters' help I began to imagine my future without John and looked forward to it.

John was a good man. He was a hard-working man and a good father and he'd always been very supportive of me, especially when it came to my career. I will always love him for that. But John was also very temperamental and touchy. Maybe he was that way because he had to conceal his secret and maybe he even somehow resented me and what I represented to him. We had lots of good times together and he had a wicked sense of humor which I loved and he was enormously talented in so many ways. But maybe our professional compatibility and admiration for each other had blinded us to other incompatibilities. Not just the one he'd revealed to me but other incompatibilities. I wasn't going to regret our marriage but I was ready to move on. My freedom was a good thing.

The divorce didn't take long. Neither of us contested anything. We didn't own that much and John felt entitled to none of it. Larry was sixteen and I knew John would help with his expenses which weren't that much. John wanted to be there for his sons as much as he could and I'm sure he must have been worried about what the revelation would do to their relationship. I did what I could to make sure they stayed close. Larry spent as much time as he wanted with his father and I never said a single negative thing to him about John.

The truth, though, was that I was terrified about my financial future. I didn't want to lose the house and I didn't know how long I could keep things going with no current visible means of support.

The divorce was finalized on a rainy day in a Santa Monica family court room. John was in New York on a movie he'd gotten and Harry was there representing both of us. I was relieved the whole ordeal was going to be over and really in my heart I'd moved on, but I couldn't help crying a little.

The judge saw my emotional state and asked if I was sure I wanted to go through with it. I was. He asked if I was certain that I didn't want alimony or even a court ordered child support and I said, no, that I didn't want any.

His honor nodded, thinking, looking right at me. Then he leaned forward. He asked, "How will you manage?"

And I said, looking up toward the heavens, "God knows."

And he said, "Well, I know. Mrs. Strauss, you're Charlotte Rae. I recognize you. You're Charlotte Rae, aren't you?" And he leaned over his bench and said: "Well, let me tell you something, Charlotte Rae, I've seen you on television and you are one very funny lady. I think you're going to be a big success. Mark my words." And he pounded his gavel as if he were making a judicial ruling.

I didn't know what to say, other than thanks. I think by then I was standing in a puddle of tears.

I saw the court reporter, still typing. She'd typed his honor's prediction for my career. Somehow that was the most reassuring thing, that it was on the record.

# STROKES OF GOOD FORTUNE

Whatever that judge thought would become of me, I woke up the next morning still unemployed and for the next few years worked sporadically.

Thank God for old friends. I got a week's work on Cloris's show, *Phyllis*, and on Hal Linden's *Barney Miller*. I got a job on Ned Beatty's show, *Szysznyk*. Milos Foreman hired John to be music coordinator for his film adaptation of *Hair* and when John found out about the part of the Pink Lady at the Long Island society party, who sings "My Conviction" and then dances with the hippies, he got me an audition and I got the part.

It was a wonderful song about freedom of appearance sung by an upper class woman who sees past the pretentions of her crowd and appreciates the long hair and flamboyance of the young men who've crashed the fancy wedding of which she's a guest. The song says to all the hippies that they're great and they should just be themselves, be free, just don't hurt anyone.

I rehearsed like a mad woman. I really wanted to do justice to the glorious little number and its wonderful message. It was short but not an easy song. We recorded it at a studio on 7th Avenue with John there in the booth, then filmed it on the back lawn of an estate on Long Island on several chilly November days. I can't remember how many takes they did. I thought I got it right on the first one. Then inside we filmed "I Got Life" where Treat Williams jumps up on a long table, kicking over dishes and candelabras and dancing while he sings and lifting me onto the table to dance with him, then tossing me down to another member of his tribe. What a blast! The crew applauded us when we finished the first take.

I couldn't wait till the movie came out. And then John called me, a few months later. Said he had to tell me something. His voice sounded like it had on that awful night when our marriage ended—though this, it turned out, was trivial by comparison. Rough cuts of the movie were way too long and the cutting had begun. And my song was going to be cut—my song and a lot of other stuff, Milos explained to me. The first act was way too long.

What a disappointment. For both of us. John sounded more depressed about it than I felt—though I was pretty unhappy about it.

He told me he'd fought for the song and I believed him. And poor John was there when they made the edit. I think he felt guilty—like he'd betrayed me again—but I knew that was just show biz. The film was too long and a lot of things had to go. I still don't know why they needed to cut a song that was less than two minutes long but I guess every second counts. I guess someone is always disappointed when things end up on the cutting room floor.

Now I'm an enigma in the film. The pink lady never says a word or sings a word. All you see is that crazy dance on the table with Treat Williams (you can watch it on YouTube if you're interested). And if you listen to the cast album, you can still hear me sing "My Conviction." But who am I to complain? On the film *Mikey and Nicky*, Elaine May hired John, her music editor, to compose the score. It was the opportunity of a lifetime. Film composers are one of the most exclusive clubs in the entertainment industry and he got a membership. He worked his ass off writing that score and then, at the last minute, after he'd led the recording session and laid the theme into the music tracks, Elaine decided the film should begin in silence. She cut his score—all but a few novelty songs he'd written for two bar scenes. Now I knew how he must have felt. I thanked him again for getting me the part. No hard feelings.

And anyway who has time for hard feelings? Life keeps happening. Why miss out on anything? And there was plenty for me to be present for.

Andy was doing well at Camarillo State Hospital. He'd grown accustomed to the place, had routines he seemed to enjoy. He had a job in a sheltered workshop. He punched a time-clock just like anyone else with a job. He seemed to really like that. Mostly he painted windchimes—which I decorated my back patio with. With the money he earned he bought Cokes and cheeseburgers at the token exchange snack bar he could walk to on the grounds of the developmental center.

John and I became active in the parent group and helped make holidays special for everyone on the unit, those with and those without families. We hid Easter eggs and took turns wearing the Easter bunny suit. At Christmas, we bought presents for all the residents and John and I led everyone in singing Christmas carols. I'd start off singing a few but then I always stepped away from the mic so the residents could take their turn. One old man named Raymond sang a pretty good rendition of *Santa Claus is Coming to Town*. A woman with thick glasses always sang *Silent Night*. The lyrics were always a little jumbled and some of the residents weren't exactly on key. But the enthusiasm was so beautiful and inspiring it didn't matter. Even Andy got behind the microphone and sang *White Christmas*. Those were joyful times for all of us. Bittersweet, of course. How could it not be? But always something beautiful amid the sadness. Like the slow movement of a Beethoven symphony. It's the stuff of life.

Andy enjoyed his home visits too. He'd split his time between John and me. John took him to the L.A. Philharmonic. I had a room for him and he loved swimming in my pool and relaxing in the Jacuzzi. "Coozy" he called it. I'd give him money and he'd walk up the hill to the Brentwood Country Mart and buy a roast beef sandwich and a soda. We'd bought a house in the flats of Brentwood precisely so that Andy could walk and it was great having the Brentwood Mart right there for him, about a ten minute walk. I introduced Andy to the man who ran the bookstore and the people at the hamburger place and sometimes I'd call ahead so they'd have his burger ready when he got there with his $10 spot.

He looked forward to home visits, always excited to spend time with us, but he never seemed to dread going back to Camarillo.

In the summer of his second year, Andy's program offered the residents a chance to attend a camp in the mountains. Andy had always loved nature so it was a no-brainer. He came back happy. He really seemed to have a good time and expressed it in his way. "You like camp," he said—meaning that he had liked it. "Andy went to a camp. Go back."

Art, one of the guys on the staff, told me Andy had met a girl there. A girl? I asked Andy about it and he said her name. "Rhonda is a girl. You like Rhonda. Hug and kiss Rhonda."

I asked Art how we might get in contact with her family and he made some calls and got the name of her mother, Edna Brubaker. I called her and she seemed happy to hear from me. "Oh, yeah, Rhonda talks about Andy quite a bit." She said that Rhonda would be in L.A. for a Special Olympics at UCLA. Andy would be there too. Perfect.

What a wonderful event—the Special Olympics. Opportunities for children with challenges to participate in sports and be winners. Andy always required a lot of prompting. He'd take his time "running" the 100 meter race and in a soccer game he'd forget why he was on the field and have to be reminded. "Play like an animal," the staff used to tell Andy and others who easily lost focus, and Andy would repeat the phrase, "Play like an animal!" and he'd run toward the ball and growl and sometimes he'd actually kick it.

After his soccer game, John and Andy and I walked around looking for Rhonda. It didn't take long to find her. Actually, she found us—and ran off the field of her soccer game to give Andy a great big hug. He hugged her back and she shrieked with excitement, then one of her counsellors told her to get back on the field and we watched her play. She was a lot more into her game than Andy had been into his and I could see that she was more high-functioning than he was. We could see that later when her game was over and the two of them got to spend some time together. Rhonda would pull Andy by the hand and tell him to hurry up. She was a little bossy but Andy didn't seem to mind and John and I were just delighted to see this girl so smitten with our son.

They held hands most of the day and had their arms around each other and did a lot of hugging and a little kissing and it seemed a shame that they had so little time together.

I called her Mom again—to tell her how wonderful it had been to see them together and also with the hope that they could see each other again—but it took a while to reach her. This was the 1970s and not everyone had an answering machine. Finally, on Thanksgiving, I reached her.

"*Gobble gobble!*" she answered, in an upbeat voice.

What a beautiful sound—hearing her voice. It had been a pretty depressing Thanksgiving, my first since the split with John. I'd invited an AA friend who didn't have any family, a way to help someone else through the holiday in order to take my mind off my own heartache, and she'd had a sip, gotten drunk, and stood us up. So Edna's voice really picked me up.

We started to chat and it took me a while to get around to asking her about getting Rhonda and Andy together. "Do you think she might like to come visit?" I finally asked.

Edna didn't hesitate. "Sure."

Then I couldn't seem to figure out how to ask my next question: "You know, our children, they've been deprived of so many things in their lives but they do love to hug each other."

"I think you're right, Mrs. Strauss."

"Charlotte. Please call me Charlotte."

"All right, Charlotte." And she asked me where I lived and which freeway got her closest to it.

I told her and then tried, again, to broach the subject of intimacy. "Well," I said, "I'm just wondering, I mean if the kids decide they want to, you know, I mean, sleep together..."

"Sure," she said. Just that simple.

"Oh," I said, surprised at her ease about the whole subject. And then, "I guess we'll have to get Rhonda a pill or something."

"No need for that," she said. "Rhonda was raped a few years ago so they gave her a hysterectomy."

"I'm so sorry," I said. I had so many mixed emotions. The revelation made the intimacy between Andy and Rhonda seem even more precious but I didn't know if I should say that. I didn't know what else to say. Other than, "Happy Thanksgiving."

A week later, Edna was sitting in my kitchen drinking tea with me. Andy and Rhonda were in the living room kissing and cuddling. Rhonda was spending the weekend if she didn't change her mind and want to go back to Arroyo Grande with her mom.

"You have a nice home," Edna said. Then she asked me what I did.

I told her I was an actress. She nodded and said, "I thought you looked familiar." Then she added, "I work for Bird's Eye. Strawberries and string beans. Get 'em ready for freezing."

I nodded.

We could hear Rhonda's voice, bossing Andy around. Then loud music came out of the guest room. The Archies: "Sugar... Aw, Honey Honey..."

"Turn it off," Andy said. Then he said, "Too loud!"

I stood up to resolve whatever was going on but then decided to leave them be and let them figure it out. The music got softer and so did Andy's voice. Then the guest room door closed. Edna and I looked at each other and nodded at each other. I think I started to cry—to know that our children could have this, could have something that most people have, it was a beautiful thing.

Edna and I became fast friends. Good friends. And Edna would still be my friend if she hadn't passed away. I named Mrs. Garrett after her. Mrs. G didn't have a first name until the network spun her off of *Diff'rent Strokes* and onto *The Facts of Life*. Then the writers got together with me to develop her character. I wanted her to be warm, caring, and wise and I kept thinking of women I'd known who were like that and no one was more like that than Rhonda's mother, Edna. So I told them I wanted Mrs. Garrett's first name to be Edna. Edna

Garrett. When I told the real Edna she couldn't get over it. She was so proud.

I almost didn't play Mrs. Garrett on *Diff'rent Strokes*. At the time it was offered to me, I was under contract to CBS who were looking for a series for me. I'd signed with them after *The Rich Little Show* got cancelled. At the time, CBS was doing an adaptation of the classic British comedy show *Are You Being Served?* They called it *The Beans of Boston* and I played Mrs. Slocombe, the woman with purple hair. The show was hilarious—just like the original but without the accents. We thought it was a sure thing. But the wife of the head of CBS at the time didn't like it and so it never got picked up. Can you believe it?

After that CBS put me together with Al Rogers, one of the writer/producers from *The Rich Little Show*. He was working on a pilot for a show about a woman Sheriff. It was the 1970s, anything with a woman doing something she didn't used to do was supposed to be revolutionary, but this show didn't resonate with me at all. It just didn't feel right for me. They were all so nice I hated to reject their show—not to mention the fact that I needed a job.

Then my agents got a call from Norman Lear about a new show he was doing on NBC. They'd already done a test pilot with Conrad Bain and two African-American boys—Gary Coleman and Todd Bridges—and the network ordered a season. They were interested in me for the part of the housekeeper.

When I got the call I was shooting an *Eddie Capra Mysteries* episode at Universal. I drove over to Norman Lear's company, Tandem Productions in Hollywood, on my lunch break. I met with Jane Murray, the casting agent, and executive producer Budd Grossman and I assumed I was going to have to read for the part but they didn't ask me to read or anything.

They just asked me a bunch of questions—about being a house keeper. "What do you think are the qualities this household would need?" I told them the character would have to be very loving and really care about all three of the children, including Mr. Drummond's daughter. None of the three kids had a mom so they all might look to the housekeeper for some mothering. She'd need to be lighthearted and understanding and generous with the TLC but also strict with the children. They'd need structure and discipline along with warmth and joy.

I guess that was what they wanted to hear. I got the part.
Nothing like that had ever happened to me before—getting hired like that off a casual conversation!

The problem was that I was still under contract to CBS. The deal allowed me to work on other networks Work on another network but not to have a regular role on a series for another network. No getting around that. I was so worried that they wouldn't let me out of that contract. I called Norman Lear to see what he could do. I called him on a Sunday and he picked up and he listened. No hurry. Just listened and then he told me not to worry. "I've done a few favors for Bud Grant," he said. "I'll bet you a nickel I can get you out of that contract." I almost cried, to know that he was willing to call in a favor for me, that he wanted me for the show that badly. I knew he'd get it done—and he did.

It was my third series since we'd come west and I was hoping that three would be the charm. Seemed like a sure thing with Gary Coleman who was a sudden sensation.

It was a fun show. Everyone was very nice to work with. Conrad Bain was absolutely gracious and professional. The boys, Gary and Todd, were adorable. Dana Plato was a sweetheart too. I'd say the three kids were all great, especially considering their parents who were all a little problematic.

Dana was adopted, I found out, and her mother, who was as sweet as could be, seemed not to understand how to raise her. She and Dana's adopted father had divorced and I don't think he was around much. Dana seemed very hungry for a father. She was always trying to get attention from the men on the set.

Todd Bridges' parents ran a talent agency for children. They had split because the father had an affair with his assistant. He and Todd's mother both seemed very self-involved.

As for Gary's parents, there's been enough said about them and the battles Gary fought with them about money over the years. All I remember was that they worked him like crazy. I remember that as summer was approaching Gary wanted to go home to Zion, Illinois and be with his grandparents and his friends during his vacation, but he'd been offered a TV movie and his parents wouldn't let him turn it down.

You can't just fault the parents for that. All those producers and agents and executives—they suck up to the parents and get them to buy in. And people start believing all that gravy train nonsense. They've got to cash in on their kid while he's hot and they forget they're trying to raise a child. Gary was an overnight sensation and no one knew how long he would last. Or how long poor little Gary would last. He was on dialysis. They had the machine right there in his dressing room. I remember going to see him during a dinner break between shows on tape day and discovering that his mother was also his dialysis nurse.

All I could think of was how brave he was. Trying to be a kid with all the pressure of a sit-com and his illness.

Our director, Herbert Kenwith, was a pleasure to work with. Conrad wasn't crazy about him but I never understood why. Herb was the one who named my character Mrs. Garrett. He said he'd had a housekeeper by that name. She didn't have a first name—I mean my character, at that point; I'm sure Herb's old housekeeper had one.

You'd think I would have enjoyed my time on that show but I can't say that I did—at least not as much as I should have. I was so darn insecure, always worried about how I was doing. The writers and producers didn't give me much feedback. I guess I should have taken their silence as a sign that I was doing fine but I didn't trust it. Norman was always good about letting us know we were meeting his expectations, but he wasn't around much.

Some weeks I hardly had anything to do and I started to take that as a message from the writers and producers. One show, at the reading, I counted only twelve lines for Mrs. Garrett. I figured they were going to get rid of me. I had such dread about it, such apprehensions. I called an old pal from AA. Let's call him Tom. He'd always been good at giving me moral support and he was good looking and a lot of fun. He came over on his motorcycle—I called him Captain Marvel on that big bike with his leather jacket on.

Well, as soon as Dana Plato saw him she moved in. Poor Dana was so needy. I introduced her to Tom and she jumped on his lap. Just hopped on like they'd known each other for years. She sat there and put her arms around him and, come to think of it, I never got any moral support from Tom.

A few days later we taped the episode. We always taped one in the later afternoon, then got notes over dinner for the later taping with a fresh audience. We'd get some new lines or at least some new blocking or business. Of course, with only a few lines there were no notes for me. I thought they must be phasing out my character. And afterwards, the producers pulled me aside. I was sure they were going to let me go.

They probably had no idea what I was going through. They spoke to me with no emotion, no sense of affection or camaraderie. They said that Fred Silverman, now the head of NBC, wanted to spin me off onto a different series, my own series. Their tone was so detached, so businesslike that I almost missed what they were saying:

"Something about a boarding school for girls. You're to be the house mother at a girls' school."

# COLD HARD FACTS

Of course I was thrilled that NBC and Tandem Productions wanted to build a show around Mrs. Garrett. And when I heard the premise I thought it had promise. I also thought it was suspiciously familiar—a writer friend of mine had pitched it, more or less, to a Tandem executive two years before. It wasn't identical. Rowland Barber's idea was that I was in charge of co-eds in a university dorm and dealt with their personal and interpersonal problems each week. Not exactly the same as an all-girls' boarding school. But it made me uneasy. The Tandem exec Rowland had pitched to before, Al Burton, was the creator of my new show.

Rowland was one of the nicest people I've ever known. And one of the most talented. He co-wrote Harpo Marx's classic memoir, *Harpo Speaks*, still in print after decades, and a sequel, *Harpo Speaks About New York*. He co-wrote boxer Rocky Graziano's autobiography, *Somebody Up There Likes Me* and wrote the screenplay for the film adaptation of that book. He had an eclectic and very impressive list of credits but he was a relative newcomer to television. He wasn't part of the club and he got robbed.

I didn't know what exactly to do. I certainly didn't want to refuse my own series on moral grounds but a part of me thought maybe I should.

I had to at least tell Rowland—and he was so gracious about it I wanted to cry. He told me I would be crazy to make a fuss about it. I had too much at stake to worry about him. I told him if he wanted to sue I'd back him up. He said he wasn't going to do that; it would just make him a pariah in the business and he couldn't afford that.

I really don't think he expected me to do anything on his behalf but I felt I had to stand up for him in some way. I went to Al Burton and suggested to him that he'd stolen the idea for the show from Rowland. Al, of course, denied it. Said he didn't remember Rowland or his pitch—but he knew, I'm sure of it, and he hired Rowland to write an episode of the first season and another pilot on salary.

It was exciting and there was lots of work to do. The writers needed to create Mrs. Garrett's background, her history. We met at the production office and I told them I wanted her first name to be Edna. I didn't say why. It was my private tribute to the Edna I knew. We talked about growing up in the Midwest—what we used to call "the Middle West"—and how down-to-earth people are and we wound up making Edna Garrett from Appleton, Wisconsin in honor of my home state. I don't remember why we decided on Appleton. Probably the name. Appleton. Sounded like apple pie and you can't get more Middle America than that. We wanted to make her a liberated woman, wise and courageous, and I thought it was important that she not be from New York or some other big city on the east or west coast.

The focus would be on the struggles and triumphs of these teenage girls coming of age during turbulent times. We wanted everything to do with the girls and their school experiences to be authentic. So we did a little research on a visit to one of the exclusive private schools in L.A. Al Burton's daughter was a graduate of the prestigious Westlake School (it has since merged with the Harvard school for boys and is now Harvard-Westlake) so Al set up a tour of the school and got the school to arrange for a group of their students to sit in a room with us and talk to us about their lives and their goals and challenges and how they felt about things.

It was all very interesting and inspiring. Pretty much all of these girls had big goals. They pretty much all wanted to be professional women. The one girl who wanted to have children and be a housewife sounded almost confessional about it and slightly ashamed that she wanted to do something so old-fashioned.

We listened and took notes. One of the girls in the group was this adorable slightly chubby Jewish girl. She was very bright and very funny. I kept asking her questions to hear what she had to say and to hear her funny little voice and after a while I started thinking we should have someone like her as one of the girls on the show. I mean, we had this lovely little Texas Christian girl and an adorable little African-American girl and all these other cute skinny little girls and they were all darling but it occurred to me that the show would be much richer to add a girl like this one.

I brought it up later to the producers and not only did they obey my suggestion, they hired the girl from Westlake. Her name was Mindy Cohn.

Mindy really was a natural. I have great admiration for all the girls on the show. It can't be easy going through the ordeal of series television at their ages and they all seemed to do it with such a great attitude, such positive energy. But I really have to take my hat off to Mindy.

The rest of the girls were already professional actresses. Mindy joined our cast with no prior experience at all! One day she was a student at Westlake, then suddenly she had to perform on a network television show that would be seen all over the world. And she pulled it off. I mean, more than that. She was terrific.

All the girls were terrific. They were talented, funny, and they seemed so relaxed about it all. Meanwhile, I was a nervous wreck! This was my third television series since moving to L.A. but it was the first time I was the central character. It's what we all want but it's also a lot of pressure. And for me the fear of failing was a constant. It started almost immediately after they offered me the show. I worried that we'd flop and I'd be out of a job and wouldn't be able to keep my house. My managers—Harold Cohen and Jerry Levy—put in my contract that if *The Facts of Life* didn't succeed I could go back to *Diff'rent Strokes*. And it almost happened.

One of the first things I did to try to ensure that *The Facts of Life* would succeed as a show was to bring in John Bowab to be one of our directors. My dear friend Geoffrey Barr—the manager who represented Nancy Walker, Jean Simmons, and so many others—recommended John, who had produced and directed on and off-Broadway. I called John, who was interested in breaking into television and was already observing another director who'd done some episodes of *The Mary Tyler Moore Show*.

I can still remember just before the first season meeting with John at the Movietown Denny's on Sunset Boulevard down the street from the Studios where we were shooting.

John's New York theater background really impressed me and I wanted to do whatever I could to bring him onboard. A sit-com always runs the risk of veering off into silliness and shallow humor. Staying grounded was what would work for us and I told the producers that John would help us create and sustain that.

John proved me right and then some. He knew exactly what the girls and I needed to work with in order to maintain the integrity of our characters through all the changes—graduation from the Eastland School, opening Edna's Edibles, the fire, etc. He made it all so much more endurable for me and he really knew how to work with the girls. I think he is one of the main reasons *The Facts of Life* was such a long-term success. He was so good at script and character. Not surprisingly, he went on to do a season of *The Cosby Show* and lots of other successful quality television shows.

Those first episodes of that first season of *The Facts of Life* were chaotic and nerve-racking. I wasn't the only one who was nervous that we
wouldn't succeed. The producers and the network executives were too.
Fred Silverman had made ABC into the #1 network and now he was
running NBC which was at the bottom of the ratings and needed a
strong comedy to compete with all the hits on ABC and CBS.

That desperation seemed to permeate our show that first season.
There was a lot of grasping—for something that would hook an audience. We wanted to be relevant. We wanted to touch on important
themes—we were, after all, a Norman Lear show.

In the first episode, Cindy the tomboy (Julie Anne Haddock's character) got ridiculed for expressing affection toward other girls. Mrs.
Garrett had to put her at ease, let her know that she had nothing to
be ashamed of.

We also needed to be funny. That wasn't hard with all those talented
girls. Lisa and Mindy and Kim along with Molly, the two Julies (Haddock and Piekarski), and Lee. I can understand why we had such an
unwieldy cast that first season. Imagine the auditions—it would have
been hard to choose, they were all so sharp and funny and adorable.

I think some of the network guys seemed to think our greatest asset
as a show was all those cute little girls. They had the girls bouncing
around in these cute little outfits and sometimes they seemed to be
blocking scenes so that the cameras would show a lot of legs and butts
and breasts.

We did some good work that first season. Chaotic and stressful as
it was, we worked really hard at our characters and made them come
alive. This was much more challenging for me than *Hot L Baltimore*.
As Mrs. Belotti—on *Hot L*—I was scattered and a little loopy with
my eccentric off-camera son. Mrs. Garrett had to be real. I didn't want
her to just be this one-dimensional all-knowing purveyor of advice.
She had to be sure of herself with the girls but beneath it I wanted her
to be vulnerable and not always so sure of herself. That's the way it is
for parents and anyone to offer guidance to teenagers. It's the hardest
thing for many parents, believe me, and it's understandable. What do
we have to guide us to guide them? Our own experience? The problem
is that a lot of us go through adolescence semi-conscious, in a state of
turmoil and crisis, so our memories don't always give us the wisdom
we might like to call upon.

I worked from my own uncertainty—and I had plenty of it. Uncertainty about the show, uncertainty about my life—as a single woman

in middle-age and in general—and my uncertainty, the uncertainty I would always feel, about my son, Andy. Was there more we could do for him? Was there more we could have done? I don't think there was but we loved him so much that those questions still haunted us.

A saving grace for me that first crazy season of *The Facts of Life* was that as busy and stressed as I was I could still have Andy home a few weekends a month. Thank God we taped the show on Tuesday night. It meant that Wednesdays were the table-reading of the new script. Then Thursday we'd get script changes and Friday we'd try out the new scenes. But the late days—the endless grueling maddeningly stressful days were camera day on Monday and the taping every Tuesday. So I got off work on Friday afternoon in time to drive to Camarillo and get Andy for the weekend. Thank God for that.

Mostly John and I split those weekends with Andy. I'd pick him up and he'd sleep over at my house on Friday night, then he'd sleep at John's on Saturday night and John would usually take him back to Camarillo on Sunday evening. Sometimes Larry would take Andy to the movies or dinner or something. Sometimes he'd do one of the drives up or back.

Andy loved to eat so we always tried to make it special. Steak and seafood—usually at the Sizzler and for special occasions something a little fancier. Chinese food. Burgers. He always knew what he wanted wherever we took him. He'd blurt out his order and wolf down his meal. Sometimes I'd cook for him at the house. Leg of lamb and roasted potatoes with mushrooms, onions, and mint jelly. Usually it became a family meal. Andy always managed to bring us together.

He still loved classical music. "Mozart," he always called it, even if it was a different composer, though Mozart was his favorite. We listened to piano concertos in the car and it seemed to soothe him to the core. Sometimes John would take Andy to see the L.A. Philharmonic at the Dorothy Chandler Pavilion. Andy called it Lincoln Center because John had taken him to Avery Fisher Hall to see the New York Philharmonic before we moved. I always thought it was funny that he still said Lincoln Center. If you've been to both places you know what he means—they aren't identical but they were built in a similar style. It was almost like he knew and was alluding to the architectural likeness. That was the thing about Andy, he always seemed to be smarter than he was letting on. He always kept me wondering if there couldn't be more to life for him.

We did a lot for him—John and me, and Larry too. Time and money and effort and patience. But I have to say that I think he did a lot for us. I know he did for me. Those weekend home visits for him kept me grounded during that first season of *Facts*. All the tensions of a new show with an uncertain future got put into perspective when I pulled into the state hospital and walked down the long hallway of Andy's unit and saw all the other residents, some of them without family support, always desperate for a handshake or a hug and a few words with a familiar person.

That first season of *Facts* was stressful but it was also very exciting. Some nights were booked with promotion—interviews and appearances—lots of flash bulbs and questions and a lot of folks making a fuss. Seeing Andy and talking to Andy on the phone all the time, hearing his simple needs—which he was always happy to repeat over and over and over... and over and over—kept me from taking any of that attention too seriously.

You know, it's funny—I'd spent most of my life craving the spotlight, wanting to be a star to somehow validate myself. Now, here I was, the star of a TV series and all I wanted was to do good work, to give a really powerful and satisfying and true performance.

Sometimes that was a real challenge. Not because there was anything wrong with the writing. The writers gave us good scripts and for the most part they listened to my feedback. The big challenge was making Mrs. G complex, giving her emotional depth when most of the stories were driven by the emotional lives of the girls. They were teenagers full of turmoil and conflict. I was the wise adult and wise adults like Mrs. Garrett have emotional lives too but they don't usually confide much of it in teenagers who have enough of their own problems to worry about. So I had to create the emotional depth and find ways to let it come through indirectly, subtly. I think it paid off.

In a way our worst fears came true—the show was in 74th place and didn't break the top 50 until late season when a lot of viewers would watch their second or third choice because their favorite shows were in reruns. Ironically, though, we survived anyway because NBC was so low in the ratings that we were among their top shows!

I think that just goes to show you what a little patience will do for any show. If ABC had been more patient with *Hot L Baltimore*, it could have been a huge hit. Same with CBS and *The Rich Little Show*.

Same with a lot of Broadway shows. I understand how it is. There's always a lot of money at stake and no one likes to lose more money than they have to. But why put a show on the air or on a stage if you have such little faith in it in the first place? Give the actors and writers and everyone a chance and make it work. Give the audience a chance to discover the show. When I think of all the shows pulled before they were really given a chance—all the time and effort, the creative energy and passion, and all the money—it's just really sad.

*The Facts of Life* proved that it takes time and that it's worth waiting a little. Of course, don't tell that to Molly Ringwald or Julie Piekarski or Julie Anne Haddock or Felice Schachter. They were all wonderful, hard-working, talented, funny and they all got let go at the end of the first season.

It was nothing personal, of course. It never is. The network thought there were too many girls. They were probably right. I think it was difficult for the writers to keep building all those characters and developing all the relationships. A thirty minute sit-com is really about twenty-two minutes per episode. Success often requires simplicity. I have no idea how anyone decided which characters/actresses to cut from the show. I think they kept Mindy and Kim and Lisa because they stood out from the rest. Their characters were the most distinctive. But all those actresses were top notch. Some of them came back on the show in later seasons and were always very professional and gracious and a lot of fun, and good. Of course, Molly Ringwald went on to become a very successful movie actress as part of the "brat pack."

But I'm sure it didn't feel good for any of them to get cut. I've been there and it never felt good to me. You have to move on. You try not to take it too personally and try not to let it discourage you, but it's not pleasant and I really felt for those girls. I was relieved as hell and happy that *The Facts of Life* was going to get another season. I couldn't believe my good fortune. But it was bittersweet for me knowing that it wasn't going to be another season for everyone.

# ONWARD AND UPWARD

Having worked for so many years in the theater, I never got over my fear of forgetting lines. Maybe it was silly of me. The girls were all very relaxed about it. They'd make a mistake and the director would yell CUT and they'd laugh it off and re-shoot. But my stage actor's experience wouldn't let me. I'd started out in the theater and was used to delivering lines and not fidgeting around with them. Professionalism or perfectionism? Whatever it was I wish I'd been a little easier on myself. After all, I was playing the role of a woman who was always telling the girls she looked after to be more loving of themselves—what they looked like, their talents and shortcomings—stop worrying about pleasing everyone else and find contentment within themselves. The girls seemed to be having a blast and I was the one who was a nervous wreck. I mean, this wasn't the theater. The writers were changing our lines all week, revising the script on the fly. We'd tape one show, then get new lines while we were eating dinner and have to deliver them for the second taping. No one expected anyone to be perfect—except for lil old perfectionist from the theater. Even Carroll O'Conner blooped from time to time.

I guess our producer, Jack Elinson, must have noticed how nervous I was. He pulled me aside one day and told me to relax. He said, "I know you want to get it right, Charlotte, but don't worry. This is television. We can re-tape." Somehow, coming from him, it did relax me. A little. Jack was such a talented and thoughtful man. And so unpretentious. I mean no phony airs whatsoever, though he was extremely successful in the business. His producing and writing credits went all the way back to *Make Room for Daddy* and included *That Girl, Good Times*, and *One Day at a Time.*

There were lots of bright moments those first few years of the show—amidst all the pressures. Too many bright moments to even remember, much less recount. I loved being introduced to the audience before each taping and then introducing my co-stars and our guest stars for that week.

It was a joy to see the girls grow up in front of me. Even week to week I sometimes noticed it. A lot of my actor friends would ask me how I could stand being the only adult on the show with all those teenage girls and I have to admit that at times it could be very lonely.

Blair and Tootie and Natalie and Jo would confide in Mrs. G but Lisa and Kim and Mindy and Nancy were politely distant from me.

Only recently have I discovered why. Actually it was Nancy who told me. She had me on her new show, *Can't Hurry Love*—a few years after the end of *The Facts of Life*—and she confided in me that because I was the star of the show, because I'd been a part of the show since its conception and had participated in its development, she and the other girls had all assumed I was part of management, allied with the networks and the producers. I certainly was not, but I understand—from their points of view. Loyalty and trust aren't always a sure thing in the theater or in television but I'd always been so fortunate, for the most part, with my fellow actors. Even on *Diff'rent Strokes*, I had a warm and friendly relationship with the kids on that show. It never occurred to me that the girls on *Facts* might think of me more as a boss than a colleague.

Of course, I had the occasional adult guest star, which was extra fun for me. I think my favorite was Molly Picon, who played Natalie's grandmother. Molly, of course, was a legend from Yiddish theater and vaudeville. She appeared in many films starting in the silent era and worked in television from its inception.

I knew Molly from our days on *Car 54 Where Are You?* She'd played the part of a woman who refused to vacate her apartment despite an eminent domain order. Every time the cops came over to evict her she fed them sponge cake and a cup of tea and they couldn't bring themselves to put her out. She was hilarious. Always hilarious. A comic genius. By the time she appeared on our show she was in her eighties and not too quick on her feet. She had her sister Helen with her to help her around. I had such respect and affection for Molly that I gave her my dressing room every time she guested on our show so she wouldn't have to climb stairs or have so far to walk.

The last time she came on the show she really struggled to remember her lines. She was such a professional about it though and, like me, a theater actress at heart, so instead of stopping when she drew a blank she'd adlib. She would go way off script. None of us wanted to embarrass her so we'd improvise along with her until someone in the booth would stop us and say there was a sound problem or something. It was very sweet. It made me proud to be part of the show.

When the writers had her die, I was really sad. Mrs. Garrett was already sad for Natalie, who'd had to go through a divorce and relied on her grandmother for emotional support. I was sad that we wouldn't have Molly guest on the show anymore.

We dealt with a lot of important issues on the show. It wasn't exactly ripped from the headlines but it was from the heart—from the angst and anguish of teenagers coming of age in challenging times (which, I guess, is any time, come to think of it). Of course, we tackled disability with Blair's cousin played by the amazing and talented Geri Jewell. We addressed the sensitive issues of bullying and date rape and body image. We dealt with that one on the show and we dealt with it on the set. As the girls matured physically and their bodies began to naturally fill out, the network execs and the producers put pressure on them to lose weight. It was ugly. I think most of the pressure was on Lisa because her character was that of "the pretty one." The producers had a scale on the set and made her weigh in every week. She had never talked to me about it at the time but told me recently that she would get on the scale and ignore what it said and ignore the irresponsible adults telling her to lose weight.

I think that if anything that pressure just made the girls eat more. Not that all of us didn't already have enough pressure on us. No sense glamorizing it, a TV series is hard work. It's a grueling, often tense, other times tedious business. A show a week. New script every Thursday. Memorizing lines and blocking. Then getting new lines last minute. Not to mention all the work it takes to deliver a performance knowing the world will ultimately be watching—or whatever share of the world we might have that week. Actually our ratings did improve significantly after NBC and Embassy Television retooled the show and brought in Nancy McKeon for that second season. But it wasn't easy. It never is.

One thing I didn't want to let happen to me was the nervous eating. There was always a great spread on the set and plenty of time to raid it but having a hit show gave me the opportunity to finally really focus on health and weight control. And to do it in a comprehensive and sane and smart way. I wanted to be able to really enjoy my success. I mean for a while. I knew that good times were ahead and I knew my Father had died from that heart attack in his fifties and there was cancer on my mother's side of the family. So I wanted to shape up and get healthy.

During summer hiatus between the first and second seasons, I hired a nutritionist. She was recommended to me by my friend, Bonnie Franklin (star of *One Day at a Time*). Kathleen Villela had also worked with Linda Lavin (star of *Alice*). I called her and we met and right away we hit it off. What a lovely person. So patient. So understanding. That was what I needed after a life of poor eating habits and the diet mentality. Kathleen got me on a food program of healthy, nutritious and satisfying meals. She also got me on an exercise program—she'd work me out three times a week and whenever I'd see her we'd check in about the food.

Within a few weeks I felt the difference. Less tired. More alert. Soon after I could see the difference. I went from a size 13 or 14 to a size 5 or 6! I looked better than I had since my twenties—and I was now in my fifties. I loved my new body and it made life as a single woman a lot more fun.

But more than that, Kathleen influenced the way I have lived and eaten ever since. Nothing militant. Just lots of fresh fruits and veggies, lean meats and in the right combinations. Desserts and all the other fun foods occasionally and in moderation. I don't have to go into detail. It's what hundreds of magazine articles and books advise. But she made it accessible for me. She helped me make the transition.

I was blessed to have Kathleen and I know also that I was blessed to be able to afford to buy really delicious fresh food. I don't take that for granted, and I hope we can find a way to make good health available and affordable to everyone. I know we're a long way from being there but it ought to be a priority. As I write this I'm looking forward to my 89th birthday. I cannot imagine I would be here right now if Kathleen hadn't taught me how to be healthier.

When I returned to *Facts* for our second season, I had Kathleen come to the set three times a week to keep working with me on nutrition and exercise. I insisted that the producers upgrade the food they made available on the set during rehearsals. I didn't mind if they wanted to keep the bagels and cream cheese and pretzels but I got them to add fresh fruits and vegetables. They were more than happy to accommodate and I think that made a difference for all of us, cast and crew.

With a hit show came a bigger paycheck and with that the responsibility of having more money. For most of my adult life I'd been living the uncertain life of an artist. When the show closes, when the movie wraps, you start calculating how long you can make do with the unemployment checks. Now, the big worry was investing so that the money would last—even if the show didn't.

It was a strange feeling. Wonderful but also strange and a little frightening. I'd grown up in the Great Depression. My parents had come from virtually nothing. Just to own a house and put their children through college was a monumental accomplishment. Now I was making more money in a few weeks than my father used to make in a year. Of course, that was before taxes, agents and managers, not to mention paying the business manager who was supposed to be making sure the money would last.

My Daddy had always told me that real estate was the best investment, so I bought an apartment building. Nothing too big. Five units at the edge of Hancock Park. I spent a lot of money fixing it up. The tenants were all so nice. When the exterminators had to tent the place and I offered to pay for everyone to be out of their apartments for a few nights, they all said not to worry, that they had places they could go. I wanted all my tenants to be happy. I never wanted to raise their rent, especially the old woman in apartment 2. They appreciated it and were so nice and warm toward me. When I had my hysterectomy, they all got together and sent me flowers!

After a while I was losing a lot of money and my business manager advised me to sell it. Eventually I gave in and put it on the market, but when I got an offer I made the buyer put in the contract that he wouldn't raise the old woman's rent.

I was very careful about choosing who was going to manage my money. You hear stories about shady business managers who lose or steal their clients' money, but I made good choices. I think I must have learned that from my father. He was always very careful, never believed in anything that seemed too good to be true. I never wanted to become filthy rich. That never interested me in the slightest. I just wanted to make the money last so my family and I would be comfortable. I didn't care about an extravagant life. I wanted to be able to do the work I wanted to do and not have to make career decisions based on money.

I enjoyed being able to support organizations that were doing good work, helping people, and being generous with my children. I gave a lot of money to Andy's unit for holiday parties and other activities. And it felt good to make things nice for all the other residents as well—especially the ones who didn't have supportive families. One year, when John was on location in Prague with *Amadeus*, Andy and I spent Thanksgiving at the home of one of the hospital administrators. He lived just outside Camarillo with his wife and children, and during dinner he told me about his plan to create a garden and train some of the residents to tend it. I was so excited. It seemed the perfect thing for Andy. So I got out my checkbook after dinner and wrote him a check for $10,000. It never happened. I don't think they planted a single seed but I didn't mind. They did plenty for Andy and I think everything John and I did for the unit encouraged them to really look after Andy and to be more patient with him when he wasn't at his best.

Being the star of a TV show also meant fame. I was used to being recognized by strangers—some of the time. But now I was Mrs. G and people weren't ever shy about reminding me. I have to admit I enjoyed the attention—some of the time. I remember during one hiatus I was visiting my dear friend, Jane Cecil, in New York. Jane lived on East 65th between Lex and 3rd, right around the corner from a school. One afternoon I unwittingly walked out just as school was letting out and it was a mob scene. But that was about as crazy as it ever got. This was in the days before the paparazzi and celebrity journalism became an industry—and I'm not sure they would have hunted me down anyway. But fans of the show loved to let me know how much they enjoyed the show and that was always nice to hear.

It's still nice to hear whenever it still happens. Just a few years ago in New York City I was coming out of the 72nd Street subway station and a tall good-looking young man looked at me and shrieked. Then we both hugged and went on our own way. I loved it. I'll take a hug over just about anything any day.

I've also enjoyed the perks of celebrity. I don't mean all that red carpet business. I mean all the things people want to do for you when they recognize your face. Let me just say that it's completely unfair but let me also say that it's nice to only have to wait so long for a table in a crowded restaurant and it's nice to get seated at a really nice table. And sometimes celebrity has really saved me. Like when I was on vacation with my dear friend, Sandy Ruben. We were traveling through the South of France with a ton of luggage. We were getting off a train and didn't know how we would manage. It was a small town and there didn't seem to be any porters. Sandi used her semi-French to ask a group of young women. They ignored her, ignored us. We were two foolish Americans with a bunch of luggage and it wasn't their problem. Until one of the young women noticed me. "Mrs. Garrett!" she squealed in her French accent. "Ooo la la!" The rest of them recognized me. Suddenly they were climbing over each other to help us.

It still amazes me some of the lengths fans will go to in order to show appreciation. One night I was in line for a movie—back in the days when people used to line up to see a new movie. One of the ushers walked next to the line to make sure no one was cutting in or jostling for position. He recognized me and wouldn't let me wait on the line, which was bad enough, but then he wouldn't let me buy my ticket. He wanted to let my friend and me in for nothing. That just killed me. I mean, if you're going to give away movie tickets, don't give them to a celebrity. Give them to a homeless person or anyone who maybe can't afford to buy one. Be an angel in someone's life.

I've had so many angels in my life. So many I'm sure I've forgotten to mention some—but one I could never overlook is Sister Johanna.

She was at the Mary and Joseph Retreat Center on the Palos Verdes peninsula. My AA friends and I used to drive down there for weekends sometimes to hear Sister Johanna. She would interpret the psalms in terms of living day to day, finding a spiritual path and maintaining an attitude of gratitude.

She told me so many important things. She used to say over and over again, "Be good to yourself," and I always thought it sounded selfish until I realized that if we aren't good to ourselves then we aren't of much use to others. Kindness and love start from within. What a beautiful lesson.

And she used to tell us to stay with our "castle friends." She'd say, "Don't waste your time on people in the basement, the ones always complaining about everything." She urged us to go with the joy. "Life is short," she'd tell us. "Life is beautiful." Who could ever argue with that in such a beautiful place?

One time she sent us off to make a list of what we thought would be the good qualities of a best friend. We came back and she wrote them all down together. Humor, loving, honesty, supportive, etc. She wrote them on the blackboard and said that God was infinitely more. And it was easy to understand her message in that beautiful retreat in the hills with all that green and all those flowers.

I am so fortunate that she was a part of my life—and I a part of hers. I even went on a trip with her to Sister Johanna's birth place in Ireland. We had tour guides but Sister Johanna was the best guide anyone could have. We toured the ring and saw the Irish countryside. Sister Johanna told us all about the poverty of her homeland and how the

English took all the good farming land and left the barren areas for the Irish with far too many rocks where no food could grow.

We went to see Sister Johanna's niece, a doctor at the famous Trinity College and also saw plays in Dublin and saw the homes and neighborhoods of Joyce and other great Irish writers. That trip was really a highlight and Sister Johanna will always be one of the angels in my life.

I did a lot of traveling those years and had so many wonderful experiences. Like going to Rome with my dear friend, Sandy Ruben and staying with her old friend, Amy DiSica—daughter of legendary Italian director, Vittorio De Sica (*The Bicycle Thief* and many others). Amy was the best host. She had a driver named Peppino for many years and an elegant Mercedes but for trips around the neighborhood we'd pile into her little Fiat. We'd drop into the butcher or the green grocer and everyone was so friendly and warm, we got the feel of Rome and had a kind of authentic experience. That was really a highlight for me.

Every day she would cook lunch for Peppino and her housekeeper, Maria. If Sandy and I were around we'd join them. Lamb chops sautéed in olive oil or something simple and delicious.

Peppino was too old for long trips so we hired a driver and drove with Amy and her daughter to Pasitano and it was incredibly beautiful. Still brings tears to my eyes to remember how exquisite it was. Angela Lansbury had been there just a little while before us with her kids. Her daughter, who's now a friend of mine, met her husband on that trip. They have that fabulous restaurant in Brentwood now, Enzo and Angela.

My favorite trip will always be the time I spent with my sisters in Paris when Tandem and NBC sent our show there to film *The Facts of Life Goes to Paris*. I'm so glad that we got that chance to get closer before Beverly passed away.

There had been a lot of competitiveness and some mistrust between us but most of it had already faded as we'd gotten older. I think that the end of my marriage brought the three of us much closer. Mimi and Beverly were so supportive when I really needed it. Suddenly the old sibling jealousies seemed so silly to us. I wasn't the only one who'd been through hardships. Bev and Mimi had faced their own challenges. Raising kids. The ups and downs of marriage. We'd grown up taking each other for granted and maybe being a little too competitive. Now we really appreciated each other.

So when The Facts of Life went to Paris, I took Beverly and Mimi with me. We were filming in the summer of 1982—between the third and fourth seasons of the show. My dear managers, Jerry and Harold, got me two first class tickets from L.A. to Paris. I cashed one in and got a pair of coach seats for Beverly and Mimi to join me.

They were extras in one of the opening scenes of the movie, when the girls and I are walking from the gate at Charles de Gualle Airport in Paris. The two women walking right behind us, talking up a storm, are Beverly and Mimi. Probably making plans to shop because that was just about all Beverly wanted to do—shop and eat and get her hair done.

And after she got the French salon treatment, she wouldn't let us open the windows, though it was hot and our rented car had no AC. We nearly suffocated in that cozy little car. I had about five days off from filming so we tootled around outside of Paris.

We did do a lot of shopping and it was great fun to spend time with Beverly doing what she loved more than anything. Mimi wanted to soak up the culture and that was fine by me. Beverly wasn't as enthusiastic about art as she was about commerce but she went along and endured it. For Mimi and me, though, the museums and galleries were a highlight. Those were special moments to share with my sisters. I also wanted to see some of the natural beauty around Paris, like the Luxembourg Gardens and the walks along the Seine River. Beverly wanted no part of that. She was so funny. "Charlotte, dear," she said, very soberly and tenderly, after a few hours of sightseeing, "you've always liked nature. Sometimes it even makes you cry. But I like to get somewhere and do something."

The one thing we could all agree on was food. The meals were exquisite. The restaurants, well, I don't have to tell anyone what Paris has to offer. And, oh, by the way, we were shooting a TV movie. Actually, that's what the girls and I were doing most of the time, though we did get our share of free time for sightseeing and what-not. Nancy and her father were real connoisseurs of the French cuisine. The rest of the girls were having their "mac attacks" and always on the lookout for a McDonalds.

Meanwhile, our poor director, Asaad Kalada, was tearing his hair out because the French crew refused to be rushed. They worked at their own pace and they wouldn't let some American director push them around. On a shoot in the U.S. it's not uncommon to get a thirty-minute lunch break. In France nothing less than two hours was acceptable.

And if that meant more free time for my sisters and me then that was a blessing.

I understood, even at the time, how special those days were for us. And at no moment was that more true than one afternoon—during one of those two-hour lunch breaks—sitting between my two sisters under a studio tent on the banks of the Seine, right across the river from Notre Dame and eating a beautiful, simple lunch. Fresh bread and butter. Veal cooked just right. Cheese and pastries for dessert. And each other's company. I kept thinking that the Lubotsky sisters had come a long long way. What a great moment for us. A peak experience in my life. One I will never forget.

# HEART OF THE MATTER

As soon as we all returned from Paris to L.A., we were back to work. Three shows in three weeks, then one week off. It still amazes me how many people do it. I mean, of course, it is the dream of many actors to have a series but the reality of it is exhausting. At least it was for me. Maybe not so much for other people. I remember watching Doris Roberts on *Everybody Loves Raymond* and thinking that she seemed perfectly relaxed and at ease and well-rested, and I wondered if she was just stronger than me. I know Doris. I knew her late husband, the great novelist, Bill Goyen, and to me Doris always seemed very strong, but I don't know.

I'd been feeling light-headed, spacy, since arriving back from Paris. Maybe it started while I was over there—or even before that. Maybe it had been gradual and I just hadn't noticed. I guess I'd always been a little spacy, at least at times, so who knows? Maybe I had always suffered from irregular slow heartbeats. Sometimes they were too fast. Other times too slow.

By late August it was getting pretty bad. NBC had booked me on *The Merv Griffin Show* and I almost forgot about it and during the interview with Merv I felt lightheaded and kept wanting to say things—about Paris, the bread and what it was like for the girls being there for the first time—and I couldn't think of the right words. Felt like eighty percent of my vocabulary had gone out the window!

I probably should have seen my cardiologist weeks before but I didn't trust him. I'm not going to say his name and I'm sure he's a fine physician. What I didn't like about him was that when I'd told him about the stress of the show and how I thought it had been affecting my health—I'd been feeling that for a few years—he'd said not to think that way. He'd said that he wanted his patients out in the world doing things, accomplishing things. That was the best medicine. I didn't disagree. I understood all that. I loved the work and I knew how lucky I was to have the success I was having. But the stress was real and it wasn't subsiding and something was wrong with my heart from it.

Now, when I needed to see a doctor, I didn't want to see that one. I didn't think he'd take me seriously. So I found a new cardiologist at UCLA medical center. I didn't know him and he didn't know me—and he couldn't find my pulse. He tried my chest, my wrist, my neck.

Nothing. He pushed his hand into my groin. I thought I was being assaulted! He said I did have a pulse. He said it was around 35. Then, matter-of-factly, he added, "You'll need a pacemaker."

As if it was nothing. Like I needed a cavity filled or a splint on my finger!

Sick sinus syndrome was what I had. The sinus node that was supposed to regulate my heartbeat wasn't working. Without it my heart rate could drop dangerously low and I could lose consciousness. I needed a battery operated replacement implanted in my chest—a pacemaker.

Now, my head was spinning. It was too much. I went from being a little spacy, forgetful, to thinking I was going to die! A pacemaker? Sounded like a last resort for a very old person. I was fifty-six years old. I thought I was in the prime of my life. And, thanks to Kathleen Villela, I was in the best shape I'd been since college. I'd been eating right and exercising religiously. It seemed so unfair!

But whoever said life was fair?

Not me. Not anyone I know. It is what it is.

The doctor told me to think of it as an insurance policy—since I lived alone and might pass out with no one there to call for help—and so I got it done as soon as I could. About a week later. Labor Day weekend, 1982. You'd think the tabloid reporters might be on vacation like everyone else but someone must have seen me checking into the hospital and gotten the word out. I was approached in the hallway. What was I there for. I said, "No comment," but a week later it hit the tabloid newsstands: *Mrs. Garrett gets pacemaker.*

It shouldn't have bothered me. It was the truth and I was so fortunate that I would be all right and that with the help of my new pacemaker I could live a long time. But I didn't want everyone to know. I used to hand a note to the security people at the airport letting them know that I had a pacemaker and that they'd have to hand search me because the pacemaker would set off their metal detectors—and most of the time they'd scream out: "Hey, got a pacemaker here, need a hand search!"

As for the surgery itself, it really was pretty routine. The surgeon did a fantastic job. Hardly left a scar. I was home in a few days, back at work in a few more. And feeling so much better. Dr. Rudnick introduced me to a woman my age who also had a pacemaker and she convinced me that it didn't cramp her style in the least and that helped me have a positive attitude about the whole thing.

Everyone on the show gave me a warm and enthusiastic welcome when I returned. I cried right there on the set. The girls were darling. They had a WELCOME BACK sign and balloons and they'd had a plaque made honoring me for being nominated for an EMMY that year. I still have it hanging in my guest bathroom. It was just the sweetest thing. It says:

CONGRATULATIONS
ON YOUR EMMY NOMINATION
FOR BEST ACTRESS
SEPTEMBER 1982
"CREAM ALWAYS RISES TO THE TOP"
AND THAT IS ONE OF
"THE FACTS OF LIFE"
WE LOVE YOU
LISA – KIM
MINDY – NANCY

What a miracle! Spend a weekend in the hospital and get another forty years (so far) of life! And I guess I've had a lot of miracles in my life—I don't think you live to be as old as I am without a lot of them. Some people call it God. Other people call it a higher power, a spiritual force. Doesn't matter what word you use. I've been blessed and I know it and I'm just profoundly grateful.

But, you know, in my program—in Alcoholics Anonymous—we say the Serenity Prayer at every meeting:

*God grant me the serenity*
*To accept the things I cannot change*
*The courage to change the things I can*
*And the wisdom to know the difference*

In other words, I appreciate the miracles in my life but I've also got to do my part. I had a heart condition that was probably genetic and I was on a television show which was a lot of pressure. At least it was for me. I didn't know how long I could do it or wanted to do it. I didn't want to die on the set—and have the writers scramble to write my death into the show. Dying on stage or set or in the wings might sound romantic—and I guess it could be if you're 90 or 95 years old—

but I was fifty-six. I thought I had a lot more life in me. My father, God rest his soul, had died at fifty-eight of a coronary.

I'd gotten used to being on first year shows and worrying about getting cancelled. Now here I was, finally, at last, a show with some legs. But I think I was starting to get a little bored, restless. I wasn't used to playing the same part for years and years. I was starting to hunger for something else. I used to complain to the writers about how uninteresting Mrs. Garrett's character had become but I don't think it was really their fault. Blair and Jo and Tootie and Natalie were growing up and growing up is a transformation that's easy to put on screen. Mrs. Garrett was their rock, their stability and that made her kind of static. No dark side of her character. No deep inner conflict or anguished backstory. I always tried to give her complexity and layers but there was often very little to work with on the page.

Meanwhile, as they grew up, the girls were more independent—the actresses and their characters. They worked things out themselves much of the time and needed less and less from Mrs. G. It was a natural progression though I think the writers could have created some interesting storylines for my character. But that just wasn't the direction they chose to go in. Can't please everybody and I really never stopped being thankful for having a show but I have to admit I was getting pretty restless.

I told Brandon Tartikoff, president of NBC, how I was feeling and he sweet-talked me about it. He said that yes, a lot of the storylines were about the girls but that I was the centerpiece of the show. Without Mrs. Garrett, he said, there was no *Facts of Life*.

I appreciated the sentiment but I still wanted to do a little more as an actress. I asked my agents and managers to please find me some interesting roles to do when I was on hiatus but there just weren't a lot of interesting roles out there for me. My managers negotiated me a development deal from NBC and Tandem Productions, money to buy scripts for me and try to get them produced. I hired a development person and rented an office in the studio where they shot *Facts of Life*. It was exciting for a while and we did find some interesting projects—some for me, others that I just thought would make good movies—but nothing that NBC wanted to make. The closest we came was a project about a woman who was deaf and blind. NBC VP Ethel Wynette was on-board but the network still said no. I thought NBC's vision was so narrow, so safe!

The television industry has changed since then. A lot. Much more risk-taking. Probably by necessity. Three networks used to represent the entire creative world. Now there are so many more options for viewers—on their televisions, computers, phones. Or, like always, they can always just turn all of it off and read a book, which is what my dear friend Mickey Ross—creator of *Three's Company*—used to say. He always had a pile of books with him at the Sunset Lanai pool and he'd say that more people should hit the off switch on their televisions and read something.

Well, there are more important things than producing television movies. Like the milestones of our children. In 1983, Larry married a beautiful woman from Guyana (formerly British Guiana). We threw the wedding for Larry and Angell Gravesande in my backyard on a spectacular August afternoon. It was a special moment for all of us. My sisters were there with their families. Mimi and Don and their kids, Keri, Myra, and Dennis. Beverly and Jules and their son Bruce and his wife, Inez, and their other son, Ron and his wife, Sheri (Bev's daughter, Ellen was too pregnant—with their third child—to make it).

John was there with his partner. At the time, John was working on Amadeus with producer Saul Zaentz and director Milos Foreman and even they managed to find time to honor John and be there. Along with so many friends. My dear friend, Terry and her husband, George Kirgo. And Jane Cecil from New York along with her sister Glad and her husband Bill. A baroque trio played while the setting sun lit the sky over the flowers floating in my swimming pool. The food was catered by my friend Leona Van Scoyk and her food was glorious.

A few years later came my first grandchild, Carly Erica. She was big and healthy and was born with a huge head of black curly hair. It was so wonderful for me to be around and be a part of her life growing up. I got to babysit her and have sleepovers and take her to the movies and sometimes pick her up from school. A TV series keeps you busy but every three weeks or so you get a week off and when I wasn't completely exhausted I got to have some really special time with family.

By the fifth season of *Facts*, I dreaded going to work. I cried in the summer when it was time to start up another season.

But I didn't want to leave the show until I was sure the girls could succeed without me. Maybe they were ready after the fifth or sixth season, but I wasn't sure and I didn't want to be selfish about it. Meanwhile, we managed always to do some good work. I worked with whatever the writers and producers gave me. Always. Tried to get the most out of every moment. I tried to make every line, every beat, every reaction specific and meaningful. You know what they say: there are no small parts. How ironic for the star of the show to be reciting that.

I'm glad I stuck around to work with the girls a little longer. It wasn't always easy—and sometimes I found myself feeling like a patient old horse—but it was worth it. Years later, Nancy McKeon told me she didn't know how I put up with her and the other girls. She said she really appreciates how patient and understanding I was with them.

Honestly, though, it wasn't that hard. Yes, they were teenagers but so much of the time they were very sweet and thoughtful. They always seemed mindful of respecting me, as an elder and as an experienced actress. And as a person. At the time, I was still smoking cigarettes. I'd cut down to only four or six cigarettes a day but the pressure of the show had kept me from quitting altogether. But that didn't stop the girls from trying to get me to quit. I mean I couldn't smoke in front of them! If any of them saw me with a Kent 100 in my mouth, they'd yank it out and crumple it into the trash. It was a little annoying sometimes but I appreciated the sentiment and now I'm definitely glad they did it.

Those last few years also gave me the opportunity to form a lasting friendship with our wonderful director John Bowab. John and I became pals and had lots of laughs. Like when Zsa Zsa came on the show as a countess with a line of cosmetics Blair was selling, using Natalie as her model. Zsa Zsa, of course, was perfect in that role. And charming—*chah-ming, chah-ming*—all week. You never know how that's going to go. She'd been a big star and now she was a guest on our show—and I'd been making fun of her and her sisters in my comedy routine for more than thirty years!

But she really was the consummate professional. A real darling. With me, the girls, and with John and the crew.

Then, after the second taping had wrapped, my personal assistant, who I'd just hired a few weeks earlier, gave me notice. She said she was going to work for Zsa Zsa.

John and I had a good laugh about that. We wondered if Zsa Zsa would really keep the woman as her assistant. It seemed like such an obvious gesture aimed at me. But who knows. Maybe it really did work out between them. I don't know. What I do know is that John Bowab and I are still good friends today. We see each other often and always look forward to working together. He is such a generous soul. For my eightieth birthday, he threw me a big party for friends and my family who flew in from around the country. I'll always be grateful for that. And then recently, for my fortieth AA birthday, he helped put together a big celebration for me and my dear friend, Jessica, who was also celebrating forty years of sobriety. What a mench John Bowab is!

My last few years on *Facts* I did manage to get some other things. *Words by Heart* was a PBS movie, based on a wonderful book, about a courageous African-American family who move north in 1910 only to find more bigotry. I played a self-made wealthy woman who gives the family an opportunity—the man and woman jobs, their daughter an education. What an honor it was to work with Robert Hooks and Alfre Woodard. They were fabulous and generous actors. Fran Robinson, the daughter, was terrific too. Not to mention my old pal, Rance Howard, a terrific actor—and a great father. He and his talented wife—also an actress, Jean Speegle Howard—can be proud of their son, Ron Howard, not only a fine actor and accomplished director but one of the nicest people you could ever meet.

Mary Chism, the character I played on *Words by Heart*, was a liberated woman, which meant she drove her own car, a revolutionary act in the Midwest at that time. It was a revolutionary act for me too because it meant having to learn how to drive a stick shift and operate one on a replica of an old roadster.

The next summer I got to do another fun project, *The Worst Witch*, for British TV and HBO with Diana Rigg and Tim Curry. It was based on a book series about a school for witches and the struggles of one young witch to keep up and fit in. We shot it in England and what a joy it was to work with such a great cast and crew. You know, life is good when someone is paying you to fly to England and romp around playing a witch and in your free time see all the great shows in the West End.

But I really felt that I had to make this my last season. I needed to do other things, other work and travel and more time to just sit and enjoy life, more time in my beautiful back yard with the orange blossoms and the birds and Andy's wind chimes.

By then I knew the girls could carry the show themselves. I really had become expendable. I don't mean that in a bad way. I was proud of the girls. They had really emerged. We were an ensemble cast now. The Network and the producers, however, did not believe in my expendability—and I guess they assumed I was holding out for a big payday. That's what they offered me. A lot of money to stay.

It was tempting. I won't lie about that. My friend, writer Everett Greenbaum—who wrote everything from the old *Mr. Peepers* (with Wally Cox) and *How to Marry a Millionaire* to *The Andy Griffith Show* and *Love Boat*—urged me to stay with the show. He said, "Get every nickel out of it." And I understood what he meant. Most of us only have one chance to make the big money. But I'd already made enough—more than I ever thought I would, more than I'd ever thought I needed. For me, it was never about getting rich. I just wanted to be able to keep my house and afford to plant new flowers every spring and get around in a decent car and travel a little and leave something for Andy and for Larry and his family.

I had all that. And no amount of money was worth the pressure and anxiety of a network series. Not anymore. Not at sixty years old with so much left to do in my life.

# AFTER THE FACTS

People who recognized me from *The Facts of Life* used to stop me in the street—or wherever—and almost always asked me what I was doing. It is a funny question to be asked by a stranger but I understand it. I was in their living rooms, in their bedrooms sometimes. It's an intimate experience, watching a program between your feet while you're lying in bed. And now I was gone or hardly ever showed up. Like a friend who'd dropped them. I think that most people must understand the absurdity of this relationship but the emotions are basic. They are strong. So the question arises. I used to want to reassure them that I hadn't died, that while I might have been missing from their television sets that I was not missing from my own life.

We go on living—even after the show is over or we are no longer on it. We keep living. In some ways we start living.

That is kind of how it felt for me. A new and exciting life.

I've tried to make the most of what I was blessed with in my work, in my family life and social life, and I've tried to make a contribution to make the world a little better. And I've tried to balance all that. That was one of the reasons I'd wanted to move on from the series. Too much focus on the work, not enough balance.

As an actress, these past thirty plus years, I've tried to challenge myself. I've tried to take on a variety of different kinds of roles. And I've tried to lend myself to projects that meant something to me, plays and movies and shows I felt some passion about, though sometimes it's good just to work, to stay active in the business, or to have some fun on something silly. And help pay some bills.

I thought I might just take some time off after *Facts* and do some traveling. Well, I ended up doing some traveling but without taking much time off. I joined the touring company of Sondheim's *Into the Woods* for the Fort Lauderdale and L.A. runs. I played the part of Jack's mother (Jack from Jack and the Beanstalk, if you're unfamiliar with the show or the recent film adaptation). I had originally auditioned for the role of the Witch. They ended up going with the great Cleo Lane instead but wanted me in the show so they offered me the role of Jack's mother.

*Into the Woods* was an innovative show by one of the all-time greats of the American theater. Fearless and imaginative and brilliant. Working with Sondheim was one of the highlights of my career. James Lapine, who'd written the brilliant book, was our director and our inspiration. Soft-spoken and sensitive, he brought out all the emotional and psychological dimensions—not to mention the great humor and humanity of the work. It is always a great experience to work with a director who listens and understands, who works collaboratively with actors. James and I had a personal connection of sorts also. He told me, the first day of rehearsals, that he'd been a fellow at the MacDowell Colony in New Hampshire at the same time my husband, John had—back in the early 70s.

But there were so many terrifically talented people in that touring company of *Into the Woods*. Including Ray Gill, who played the baker, a wonderful actor who'd done a lot of theater. He'd also been in the film, *Next Stop, Greenwich Village* and done some TV guest shots. We became dear friends and when Larry and his daughter, my granddaughter, Carly, came to visit me in Florida, Ray was two year old Carly's Uncle Ray. Carly watched the show from a seat toward the rear of the orchestra—close enough to the exit in case she got frightened by the voice of the giant or by some other larger-than-life element in the show. But she never got scared. Instead, the first time she saw me on stage—make-up and costume and all—she blurted, "Granny!" and started down the aisle and Larry had to chase after her and swoop her up to keep her off the stage.

It was nice being back on a stage. I enjoyed the rhythm of the theater. Rehearsals can get intense but once the run begins it can be relaxing. Having most days off. I got to spend time with my son and granddaughter in Fort Lauderdale. We went to SeaWorld and watched dolphins do tricks and I got to hang out with my beautiful sweet little granddaughter in my hotel suite and read to her and sing with her.

From Fort Lauderdale it was onto Palm Beach, then back to L.A. for a run at the Ahmanson Theater downtown. That was wonderful—being part of such a great show for all my friends and colleagues. Everyone came to see it and just about everyone loved the show. What's not to love about it? Great music, a brilliant book, terrific choreography, and a really poignant message about life and how we sometimes miss what's in front of us because we're too damn focused on some idea of what it should be. I really like what I recently heard Rob Marshall say during a Q&A about his film version of *Into the Woods*. I can't remember his exact words but it was something like this: In the first act, everyone gets what they want in life and in the second act shit happens, life happens, and it's not the way they thought it would be but people come together and there's a feeling of community, people helping one another to get through it.

From L.A. the show went on to Pittsburgh, Dallas, Boston, Schenectady, then back to Florida—Melbourne and Sarasota—then Houston and Philadelphia. Sounds like bad geography but touring companies are booked on the local theater schedules, not the convenience of the cast or crew. After the run in L.A., I let another actress have her turn at playing Jack's mother and I went on to my next big adventure. I stayed in touch with a few of my fellow cast members, especially Ray Gill. He'd revealed to me that he was fighting AIDS. I couldn't believe it. He was so alive, so robust. He managed to finish out the tour and kept working on stage and screen until almost the end. He died in 1992 and I will never forget him. His optimism and the way he faced his mortality. It was a real lesson for me and, I'm sure, for everyone else who knew him. He was so warm, so supportive, so talented and so much fun to be around.

It was great to be back on the stage and to have all the wonderful opportunities that I would have now because of the series, but just as wonderful were all the family times. Having a grandchild, well, if you're a grandparent I don't have to explain the joys of grandparenting.

Carly and I had so many fun times together. Arts and crafts and singing and dancing together. Peek-a-boo when she was little, hide-and-seek when she got older. We had sleepovers at my house, jammy parties, sometimes with one of her friends. After raising two boys it was extra special having a girl for a grandchild.

A few years after I left *Facts of Life* I was invited to be a celebrity guest at Disney's MGM Studios Amusement Park in Orlando. I got to bring my family along and that was really something. Carly was the perfect age. She loved Mickey Mouse and Minnie and all the other Disney characters and as my guest she got special access to the whole experience. It was like a dream come true. Every day they had me as the Grand Marshall of their parade and Carly was right there with me.

My next big theater adventure was playing one of my roles in one of my favorite plays, *Driving Miss Daisy*. It's the story of Daisy Werthan, a southern widow who happened to be of the Jewish faith, and her African-American driver, Hoke. It's about humanity transcending race and class but also about the subtle ways that bigotry can infect human relationships. It's a very complex and poignant play. I'd seen Vanessa Redgrave and James Earl Jones do it brilliantly on Broadway. Jessica Tandy and Morgan Freeman really brought it to life on screen.

I was offered the part of Daisy at the Briar Street Theatre in Chicago. I replaced Dorothy Loudon. Ellen Burstyn and Sada Thompson played Daisy before us. So I was in good company. Bruce Young played Hoke, the driver. He was a wonderfully strong, sensitive actor. It was such a relief to return to the theater, exploring a role, able to really take the time to get inside my character and serve a great piece of art. The play is only about ninety minutes long but it is profound.

It was great being in Chicago. The Goodman is such a great theater. It felt, in so many ways, like I was back home. Not only back on the stage but to be in Chicago where I'd gone to college. I could still remember going down to Chicago to go to the Jazz Limited and hear the incomparable Sidney Bichet playing his soprano saxophone or spending an afternoon at the art museum. I felt a little nostalgic about the place—the beautiful buildings and the hustle and bustle of it all. But most of all it was just wonderful to play Daisy in such a great play. I would do that play again and again.

Being in Chicago also meant being just 100 miles from Milwaukee, a chance to visit family and friends from the old days and visit with them when they all made the trek to see the show. I have a lot of cousins—since Mother and Father each had nine siblings—and most of them still live around Milwaukee. It was great to see so many of them and remember the old days and count our blessings. Most important, I got to spend quality time with my dear big sister, Beverly and her dear husband, Jules.

In middle age, Bev and I could get past all the bullshit and be real with each other. We could talk about how we really felt—about everything, including each other. And what it was like for each of us growing up together. Those were special moments for me. Very special—even more so because this was just a little while before Beverly's cancer.

It was pancreatic cancer. Just like our mother twenty years before. Beverly faced it with great courage. She fought like hell and Jules, who knew pretty much every doctor in the state, made damn sure she survived for as long as was humanly possible. I know that she suffered terribly. But she did it with such courage. I think she really wanted to stick around, no matter how bad it got. She didn't want to miss out on anything she didn't have to. If she could have a little more time to see her grandchildren grow up, a little more time with her husband of more than fifty years, a few more laughs with Mimi and me, she wasn't going. She had two wigs and got a kick out of wearing them—she had names for them. One was "Susie." I can't remember the other one's name but she was so funny about it. And she loved all the elegant new clothes she could wear when she lost weight. That was our sister—finding something positive.

She actually, for a while, went into remission. A gift from God, even if it didn't last. At the time I was performing in *Solid Gold Cadillac* at the New Theater in Kansas City. Beverly and her husband Jules and Mimi arranged to come see me and I arranged for the three of us to perform after the show that night, as a curtain call. The theater's public relations guy, Pat Patton, what a wonderful man to make it happen for us. He got an electric keyboard and synthesizer for Mimi to play and after the cast of the show and I took our final bows I came out in front of the curtain, as an encore, and introduced my two sisters who joined me on stage. Mimi played and the three of us sang together but really it was Beverly's show. Her voice was as beautiful as always and she hit some high notes and brought the house down. Afterwards she thanked me for making it all happen and, most of all, for letting her be the diva that night. Pat filmed the whole thing and made DVDs for all of us. Beverly and Jules watched it together and played it for all the nurses.

We're all mortal. Who knows that better than an actress? Sometimes we even have to die on stage (sometimes, especially in comedy, we die unintentionally). Beverly lived about as long as a person with pancreatic cancer could. Her courage inspired me in many ways.

Dame Peggy Ashcroft, the renowned English actress, once said that Samuel Beckett's *Happy Days*—that 64 page virtual monologue—is to the actress what Hamlet is to the actor.

*Happy Days*—no, not the TV show with Richie and the Fonz—is a stunningly brilliant and touching play by the playwright who most famously wrote *Waiting for Godot* and *End Game*. In *Happy Days*, Winnie, who I played, is submerged, waist-deep, in a mound of what looks like dirt, while she goes through her daily rituals. Her man is somewhere, she cannot quite see him, lying around, reading the newspaper and saying things of not much interest. Winnie seems aware that she is stuck but she knows and she perseveres anyway and makes the best of things, the most of every day. A noble soul. She has a loaded gun in her possession, an escape valve in case life gets too unbearable, but she never uses it, not even during the second act when the mound goes up to her neck. It is all strange and symbolic and brilliant. What an honor to be among the many actresses who've lent their interpretations to this work.

I had a sensational young director working with me. Carey Purloff really understood Beckett, the existential darkness but also the irony and humor. And she really let me go—let me find my way to my own specificity with each moment of this exquisite work. I also had extraordinary help from my dear friends, actress Judith Jordan and her significant other, director Genaro Montanino. So when I wasn't at the theater rehearsing with Carey I was at home with Judith and Gene working out more details about Winnie, more layers and nuances of her emotional life and surfaces throughout the piece.

We all got high praise from the critics—Carey and I by name, Judith and Gene in spirit. Here's what Silvie Drake wrote in the L.A. Times:

When Charlotte Rae as Winnie is cheerful and breezy, it is impossible not to laugh. Is this woman for real? Is this meant to be funny? Oh, yes. Gradually we listen and learn. Gradually we begin to really hear the play. Winnie, even when performed by Rae—*especially* when performed by Rae?—is the defiance of the species. Grace under pressure. Quiet resistance. Winnie against the dying world.

Because of her association with TV sitcom, casting Rae in the role was risky, but it was a brilliant stroke. Yes, there were isolated pockets of people at Friday's performance who still thought that anything that came out of Rae's mouth had to be just plain hilarious, but fewer and fewer as the play progressed.

Her cracking voice, her almost foolish matronly squeal occasionally slicing the air, the very *ordinariness* of this Winnie—nobody grand at all here, nobody messianic—endows the performance a creeping and ultimately gripping stature.

Director Carey Perloff wisely lets Rae be Rae, and by the time this play is over, you know this Winnie is as frail and conquerable as the rest of us. But much, much braver. The hush that fell on the house in the second half, when all that is left of Winnie is her head, above the sand—her frightened eyes, her endless concatenation of words, her unfathomable dignity—was no accident.

Rae had earned it. Bravely.

Carey and I reprised it that fall at the CSC Rep Theater in New York where it was similarly received. It was terribly gratifying to meet the challenge of that role and get a little recognition for it. A high point really. Fame can be fun, but respect is so much more meaningful. And the most meaningful of all is just knowing that I took on the challenge and delivered. It's something no one can ever take away from you. During the run, a woman approached me in a department store. She said, "I really didn't like that play. But I loved Winnie. I felt for you in it."

It was wonderful to have such freedom as an actress. I mean, that I could take the jobs I wanted to do and say no thanks to everything else. I've been so blessed professionally. I said yes to *St. Elsewhere* and *Murder, She Wrote* and started doing voice over work on cartoon movies and TV shows. *Tom and Jerry, The Itsy Bitsy Spider, 101 Dalmatians*. My good friends, Ron Cowan and Dan Lipman, gave me a part as John Whistig's (Garrett Brown's) home care nurse when he was dying of Alzheimer's for three episodes of their show, Sisters. I got to work with Phil Sterling, a wonderful actor. I also played a confused woman for four episodes of *ER*. On *Michael Hayes*, David Caruso's short lived show between *NYPD Blue* and *CSI Miami*, I played a concentration camp survivor Michael (David) talks to as part of an investigation. He was so nice to me. Such a gentleman. So gracious.

Actually, almost without exception, everyone I've worked with for the past thirty-plus years has always been nice to me. Kevin James and Leah Remini—and, of course, my old pal, the wonderfully talented and funny and friendly Jerry Stiller—on *The King of Queens*. Adam Sandler when I worked with him on *You Don't Mess with the Zohan*. If you haven't seen it, I had a really raunchy part. Adam played Zohan, an Israeli spy with a weakness for much older women. His cover is a hairdresser and he wants to please his clients, whatever that takes. And I was one of his clients. I mean, it was really raunchy. And it was a lot of fun. What a gentleman Adam was and what fun to work on that set.

Recently, I had the opportunity to play Meryl Streep's former mother-in-law in *Ricki and the Flash*, directed by Jonathan Demme, a really great director. He made *Philadelphia* with Tom Hanks, a courageous and transformative film. And many other wonderful movies. Not to mention that he's a great human being, a regular guy, modest and very down to earth. I met his wife and kids when they came to the set one night. Great warmth—and we became friends.

Aside from his sensitive direction, Jonathan's spirit is so uplifting with everybody in the film and all the members, cast and crew, and his loving joyful spirit trickles down to everyone involved so that he creates a hard-working joyful company. It was a great honor to work with Jonathan and to be in a scene with Meryl, and yet the greater honor was how Meryl and Jonathan honored me.

I have to admit I was nervous working with Meryl Streep but she went out of her way to put me at ease. She said so many nice things to me. I mean, I was a little in awe of her and she just wouldn't have it. Whenever I told her how great she was she told me I was too. And Kevin Klein, her co-star, he was so much fun to work with. A consummate professional. And so witty! I got to be part of his on-set birthday party. Our producer, Marc Platt, got a big cake and we watched Kevin blow out the candles.

Everyone was so nice to me. I mean, extra nice. I got a chance to talk to Audra McDonald on the set. A brilliant actress and singer. I'd seen her on Broadway as Billie Holiday in *Lady Day*. She was incredible. I mean there were moments when I really forgot I was seeing a play. I asked her how she did it, and her answer was simple and honest and it was the answer I already knew: hard work. She also told me that she'd gotten help from the late Maya Angelou who had known Billie Holiday. Audra has won six Tony Awards, including at least one in each of the four categories for an actress.

I think the highlight of my experience on that movie was my last night. We'd spent a long day in the cold shooting all the wedding scenes. I'd been dancing for hours and when we wrapped, Jonathan said, "Some of us will be leaving after tonight and we want to thank them for their work..." Then he said my name and the whole cast stood and applauded me. It was overwhelming. You know, I've been nominated for Tonys and Emmys but this little special tribute on the set of that movie, I felt so warmed by it, I can't imagine anything making me feel more appreciated.

Show business can be a rough business. I've known that first hand. There are a lot of self-interests colliding with each other all the time. Feelings get hurt. They get pulverized. I've been on the receiving end of that—especially when I was starting out. So it's an extra pleasure for me that after all these years in the business, I've finally been able to enjoy what every actor deserves: a little kindness.

Isn't that what everyone—actor or anyone else—wants from this world? Is it so difficult to provide it for them? It shouldn't be. Not at all. It's actually pretty easy to treat people with courtesy and kindness. Nations and their leaders need to learn those lessons. They could save a lot of lives.

It's one of the reasons why I joined The Friendship Force. It's an organization, started by then outgoing President Jimmy Carter and his wife Rosalynn. We traveled to other countries and met people as ambassadors of our country and of peace. It was a little like being an exchange student as an adult. My friend, Rhonda Furgatch, and I stayed with lovely families across Europe and met with others. At one gathering, President and Rosalynn Carter were there along with people from all over the world, getting to know each other, bridging language and cultural barriers. I saw men in keffiyehs embracing men in yarmulkes. It was very moving to witness and be a part of it.

It's easy to be cynical about something so idealistic as cultural harmony or world peace, but cynicism doesn't help anyone. We should all at least try to do something to make the world a better place.

No small kindness or gesture should ever be discounted. Actually, I think that in the long run that's the only way we're going to save ourselves. Small acts of kindness, understanding, and love with everyone pitching in. I have a friend whose husband always talked to people he didn't know on the elevator. So his wife asked why he did that. He answered, "Well, everyone can always use a little love." I'm with him on that—and as a matter of fact I sometimes talk to people I don't know in elevators. It makes people smile and I love to make people smile whether it's talking to them in an elevator or singing for them in a cabaret. Makes me feel like I'm one of God's little sunbeams.

I've been blessed to be able to see a lot of this world and there is so much more I wished I'd seen. Not that I'm done, but there are some places I just don't think I can manage anymore, not at my age.

Being an actress has meant traveling. Sometimes that's a burden. When the boys were young I hated being away, but years later traveling for work was a bonus.

One of my favorite jobs was being on a Theater Guild Cruise to the Mediterranean. I went with Patricia Neal and another college buddy, Helen Horton. Eli Wallach and his wife Ann Jackson were on there with us. So were Jane Powell and her partner Dickie Moore and Larry Kert and his partner. It was really a star-studded cruise. I got to know

Colleen Dewhurst and we became good friends. And what a wonderful woman. Colleen gave the absolute best performance I—and a lot of other people—have ever seen as Mary Tyrone in *Long Day's Journey into Night* and also gave a hell of a performance in *Moon for the Misbegotten*.

We'd sightsee all day in various cities and ports and at night all the very talented people onboard would perform scenes and give readings of poems. I introduced them all.

It was a Mediterranean cruise on the Norwegian Vistafjord ship. One class only—and it was pretty much first class for everyone. All the performers sat together at meals and told funny stories from our experiences in the theater. It was wonderful for all of us, sharing the experience with so many special people.

Armina Marshall was with us. Armina Marshall—who'd helped run the Theater Guild for forty years and brought seven of Eugene O'Neill's plays to the stage—was now in her nineties and I couldn't believe how she managed to get around. In Egypt, the public rest room toilets were built into the floor and you had to squat over them. Not much privacy either—and at her age Armina seemed to have no problem.

Our cruise docked near Jerusalem and that was very special for me. I'd never been there before but I was deeply moved, remembering how much it meant to my father when Israel became the Jewish state. I kept thinking of him being there and it made me think about his life as a boy growing up in a shtetl in poverty, a Jew and being marginalized for it and now seeing his nomadic people with a homeland. I've always understood that the state of Israel is a controversial place and I haven't always agreed with the actions of their leaders, but I know that the pride my father felt was real and that it was profound and being there now I felt it too. I didn't get a chance to make it to the city of Hadera to see the tire factory my father helped build there but I did get there on another trip and felt so proud of what my father had helped accomplish.

At the Golden Domes, Jane Powell burst into tears they were so beautiful. I'd already been crying just being there.

At the Church of the Nativity in Bethlehem, Larry Kert—who, of course, was the original Tony in *West Side Story*—spontaneously began to sing "Silent Night." Patricia Neal joined in. Then Coleen Dewhurst. Then all of us. We all sang it together. It was a very special moment.

Outside on the street, some Israelis recognized me from *Facts*. One of them invited me to come with him on a dig. Of course, I couldn't stray too far from our ship. He said to come back one day and go on a dig. I asked him where. He said anywhere. The history of human civilization was always beneath our feet.

But the highlight of the cruise was just sitting around that dinner table each evening talking to all my wonderful colleagues, sharing stories, all the wonderful and funny things that had happened to all of us. It was a special group. We all felt so comfortable together.

One night, I even asked Jane Powell if she and her significant other, Dickie Moore, were ever going to get married. They'd been together for a while and seemed like such a great couple. I don't know what got into me but I asked.

They didn't seem to mind. Dickie had been a child actor, most notably in the *Our Gang* shorts in which he was known by his real name. He was also in a Shirley Temple movie and gave her one of her first on-screen kisses. Now he ran a public relations firm.

Jane, of course, had a long and very successful career in movies and television. *Seven Brides for Seven Brothers, Royal Wedding*, and on and on and on. A much-deserved, very successful career. She was a terrific and a darling woman. At the time she was also working on a one-woman show about her stage mother and how much she'd driven Jane.

Anyway, Jane and Dickie didn't seem to mind my interrogation. They both answered the question and their answer was No. Jane said that all his marriages had failed and he didn't want to ruin things with Jane. But a few years later they did get married and today they're still happily married!

I'm so honored and fortunate to have known and worked with so many great actors in my career. So many. Not just the famous ones either. There are so many great actors and actresses. And then, on the other hand, there are a few not so great ones.

By that I don't mean untalented—I've never been much of a critic in that way. I mean actors who are mean-spirited, who are selfish and unwilling to simply serve the play. As Shakespeare's Hamlet said, "The play's the thing." It's a competitive business and that can bring out the worst in people. But it just doesn't take that much to be a little generous to a fellow actor when it's his or her moment. I'm not going to mention anyone by name—though I guess I have already mentioned a few—but they surely know who they are. Well, maybe not. Maybe that's the problem. I only bring it up to underscore my gratitude for the many many gracious professionals I've had the good fortune to work with. Not just gracious on stage or on the set but also loving and supportive when the lights and cameras are off. Colleagues who are fun to work with, fun to know and be friends doing the thing we do best.

We all have our struggles and we need the support of others to get through those difficult times. I've been so blessed to have so many wonderful friends—in and out of the business—and so many close comrades in Alcoholics Anonymous—I don't know what I would have done without my AA pals, especially my sisters in the program— and such a wonderful family. I've already tried to be there as much as possible for others, especially the people I'm close to. My friends, comrades, and family were certainly there for me through my rough times—the divorce, and the challenges of illness and major surgeries, and of course all the struggles with Andy.

John and I always remained cordial. We shared a commitment to our two sons—and both remained involved with Andy's well-being—but more than that. Our love and respect for each other was bigger than our marriage, bigger than what ended it. When John became involved in a relationship and moved in with his new partner, he wanted me to meet him. Meeting my former husband's new boyfriend wasn't something I was tremendously excited about but I did think it was nice that it mattered to him, that he wanted it to matter to me.

So we met at the Fromin's Deli on Wilshire Boulevard in Santa Monica and I met Lionel Freidman. We ate and drank coffee and talked and I won't say that it wasn't awkward but I will say that I'm glad we did it. Three human beings—three middle-aged people— breaking bread together, talking, breaking the ice. Life. Not perfect but beautiful somehow in its own way.

Later, on the phone, John asked me what I thought—about Lionel.

I didn't hesitate. "What's to think?" I said. "Congratulations. You've got yourself a nice Jewish guy!"

We never gave up hope for Andy—to improve or, at least, to have a better life. By "we" I mean John, our other son Larry, and me. We did what we could to help take the edge off his life in that institution— home visits, dinners out, classical concerts at the Dorothy Chandler Pavillion, and a hefty supply of all his favorite treats for him in the Unit 88 kitchen.

We pitched in with the Christmas carols and Easter egg hunt and with the Special Olympics. Every summer I had everyone over to my house—residents, staff, and their families—for a picnic and a swim or a Jacuzzi. We always chipped money for activities, including the dances they put on for the residents. Andy loved to dance and his dance card was always full. Mostly another resident named Jennifer. One time, when I was in the supermarket with him getting Cokes and all his favorite snacks, he asked me to dance with him.

"Right here?" I asked him.

"Mommy dance," he said, and I figured what the hell—I'd learned to cherish any direct interaction with my developmentally disabled son, so we danced in the soda aisle of Albertson's in the town of Camarillo.

Andy's relationship with Rhonda was beautiful but only lasted a few years and he never really had anything like it after that. Some of the more sophisticated residents at Camarillo found ways to be intimate with each other but Andy never could figure that out on his own.

Sexual frustration always seemed to be a part of his tendency still to be violent and self-injurious and at one point I found a sex therapist willing to work with him. Even just to help him figure out how to masturbate and relieve some of the stress. I drove him out to the therapist out in the West San Fernando Valley, a rustic house on a wooded street. The therapist was a lovely woman and she worked with Andy for about a month. I don't know all the details of what went on during their sessions but in the end it didn't help as much as I'd hoped.

After the last session, Andy seemed a little agitated. When I got him in the car he said, "Don't want to masticate!"

It was sad—to know how physically pent up he was and to know that something was preventing him from relieving himself. But eventually I did manage to laugh when he repeated the statement. I don't know where he got the word "masticate" or if it was just a coincidental mispronunciation, a kind of autistic malapropism. Andy certainly did like to *masticate*. Steak and lobster, salad with blue cheese dressing, burgers and onion rings, oysters on the half shell. He could masticate it all.

It was moments like these that always made us wonder about him—if there was some place in his mind that understood more than the rest of his mind would let on. He used to mix up the words "seizure" and "Caesar" so that he would recount the time during his childhood when he'd had a "Caesar" at the Central Park Zoo and the ambulance came for him; and then in a restaurant he'd ask for a "seizure salad."

For the most part he seemed content with his life at Camarillo Developmental Center. Most of the staff was very good with him and he seemed to get along with most of the other residents. Most of the time the doors were unlocked so he could go in and out and walk the beautiful grounds if he felt like it. He liked his job in a sheltered workshop, punching the clock and getting paid and after more than twenty years my backyard wind-chime collection had grown quite big. Some of them fell victim to the occasional strong wind but mostly they played a symphony. Andy's symphony.

We never really got over the sadness of his condition and all the limitations of his life. But somehow we always tried to make the best of his situation and find the joy and help him to find it. Sometimes he didn't need any help. Sometimes he would just suddenly burst into a smile and laugh with abandon and sing. One night in the car with me and his brother, Andy looked up through the rear windshield at the moon and sang a verse from, "Fly Me to the Moon." Where had he ever even heard that song? Moments like that we almost always found ourselves looking for some deep meaning, some possibility that Andy could be and do much more.

One of Andy's favorite places was always the zoo. As a child, he could spend hours there, mostly looking at the elephants. He was enamored with those enormous mammals. Their presence, their beings and the powerful motion of their bodies seemed somehow to soothe his soul. When I'd been off *The Facts of Life* for a few years I got Larry to help me take Andy on an overnight to the San Diego zoo. It was a special time for us with Andy. We spent hours there, though he never liked to walk much and was exhausted after a short while. San Diego's elephants habitat is big and imposing and I didn't think we would ever pull him away from it. He just stood before them in a hypnotic stare at those elephants. He didn't want to leave. Not even to go have lunch—and Andy was always ready to eat. He finally agreed to go get a burger with us but only because we promised that he could return to the elephants afterward.

Another time we took him to my friend's house in Lake Tahoe to see snow. He called it "Lake Taco" and for years afterwards talked about being there in the woods with that spectacular lake.

A few years after that, I thought it would be a treat to take Andy back to New York City. It was a very memorable trip. Larry came with us and I splurged and bought first class tickets. By then Andy was pretty overweight and I didn't want him to be uncomfortable in a coach seat.

It was a very memorable trip. From the moment we landed, he had a twinkle in his eye. The sounds and smells of the airport were the sounds and smells of New York. From the car window, driving across the Queensboro Bridge, Andy was mesmerized by the night lights of the tall buildings stretching across the island that used to be our home. He leaned back and laughed and, with his usual wicked sense of humor, reminded us all of so many traumatic moments:

"Had a seizure at the Central Park Zoo," he said. As usual he pronounced "seizure" as "Caesar," like a Caesar salad. Then, "Bellevue hospital, PQ-5, broke the television," and on and on. Always a little inspiring to see how easily he let go of the awful moments of life. How he could so easily recall them and laugh. It always helped me to laugh about it.

We stayed in a midtown hotel, just a few blocks from Central Park. We walked to the zoo. It was so different than when he was a little boy but he still smiled at all the trees, the stone walls, everything that was still familiar, though the seals were gone—replaced by penguins. Andy remembered the seals and asked me to imitate them for him the way I used to when he was little. He laughed just as he always had.

We went to Rockefeller Center. It was June and Andy kidded about the Christmas tree and the Rockefeller Center ice skating rink, pointing to where it would be and insisting that it was there. We rode the subway and the Staten Island Ferry and we walked through Grand Central Station. We took him to visit my cousin Marcella who still lived in our old building on West 96th Street. Poor Marcella had heart problems and was in bed. Andy not only remembered her after all those years but he was so sweet, so sympathetic. He sat next to her and held her hand and told her to feel better.

We met up with my cousin's son, Nich Haber and his wife, Lynn, and they came with us to visit our other old building on West 106th Street. Andy and his brother, Larry posed in front of their old building with their sunglasses on. They looked like The Blues Brothers. We went to Riverside Park and sat on the benches and breathed the familiar upper west side air—though I think it's a lot cleaner than when we lived there. Andy was still a little jittery when the pigeons came near but not so much. Not nearly so much. More of a reflex now. A reflex of a memory.

We took Andy for New York pizza and submarine sandwiches and bought him hot dogs and pretzels from the street vendors. He asked for roasted chestnuts and laughed because it was June and he knew they were a winter treat. We took him for a lobster dinner and a concert at Lincoln Center and at intermission gave him money to go get himself a cola with cherries that he sipped and looked at and savored.

Simple pleasures. In a nice restaurant he ordered leg of lamb and asked for mint jelly. That's my Andy. He always knew what to order—and said it like he was the king of a great empire. He knew how to enjoy himself and we always enjoyed ourselves helping him to enjoy himself.

He asked to go to Bellevue Hospital, and at first we assumed he was teasing but he kept asking until we figured what the hell—it was his trip and if that was where he wanted to go then we would take him. So we went to Bellevue where Andy first found hope with Elsbeth Pfeiffer—and where years later, by coincidence—and after he'd become a danger to himself and to us—he was locked up in a psych ward.

Of course, Bellevue Hospital is now a gigantic medical complex that has nothing to do with Andy's childhood. But the old building we'd known was still there on 30th Street. It had been turned into a homeless shelter and homeless people were everywhere. What a strange few minutes we spent in that place. Andy grew somber and so did we. I got all teary seeing those sad men around us. I'm not sure why. I guess because they were all little boys once and someone had given up on them and we'd been told to give up on Andy. I don't know. There were so many feelings going through me in those moments.

For me the highlight of the trip was visiting Mrs. Pfeiffer. She had an apartment downtown near Washington Square and she invited us up. When we rang the buzzer she opened the door and opened her arms—as she had thirty years earlier—for Andy and me. Andy couldn't get over her. Older, of course, but she hadn't changed that much. Same loving, upbeat Germanic voice. Same intense eyes. Same warmth. Their love for each other was beautiful. And my love for her. Elsbeth Pfeiffer had saved my life. She'd given me back my self-esteem. She had helped me understand my son. Doctors always wanted to hang labels on him and none of it quite made sense. She'd told me that all the labels—autism, retardation, schizophrenia, epilepsy—were true and none of them were true. Andy was Andy and we had to listen to him and learn from him and love him. And Elsbeth had told me over and over and over again that it wasn't my fault, it wasn't my fault, it wasn't my fault. She'd told me never to listen to those voices that were blaming me for Andy's condition. Not the voices in my mind or the ones in my ears. I'd been so immobilized with despair and guilt and frustration that I don't know if I could have accomplished anything in my life without her encouragement and understanding.

Now, all these years later, Mrs. Pfeiffer told me that she had watched The Facts of Life along with her niece. "You ver vonderful!" she declared.

"No," I had to say. "You're wonderful." Then I told her that if not for her there would have been no Charlotte Rae, no Mrs. G, no *Facts of Life*.

It was a wonderful trip, a great time for Andy and for Larry and me. It was always so wonderful to be able to give to Andy. Giving to Andy was always a way for John and Larry and me to give something to ourselves—seeing Andy's joy always became our joy. Andy gave us many gifts. He kept us all full of gratitude and helped us to appreciate the small beauties. What a gift.

Meanwhile, Larry had inherited the family struggle as an artist. He'd published three novels and one was optioned by Sony Pictures but never got made. He'd written scripts for animated shows and been hired to write a screenplay that didn't get produced, but he was still plugging away and now he was teaching English and coaching basketball at an alternative high school in South Los Angeles. He told me that growing up with Andy gave him the patience and understanding and empathy that his students now appreciated.

I don't think any of us were ready when the state of California decided to close Camarillo State Hospital and Developmental Center. The very thing that made that place so livable—the place was spacious and uncrowded—was its undoing. The state calculated how it could move everyone elsewhere and the state wanted to turn the facility—the land and some of the buildings—into a university (what is now California State University Channel Islands).

It was devastating news for us. I mean, who can be against building a state university? But where was Andy supposed to go? Some of the residents were assigned to facilities hundreds of miles—hours and hours of travel time—away. Andy was moved to Fairview Developmental Center in Costa Mesa.

Andy's first few weeks there were traumatic. He hardly knew anyone and the staff didn't know him. They didn't know our family. They put him in a more restrictive unit and that agitated him. Doctors increased the medications that were supposed to calm him. One of those meds caused him to gain a lot of weight. He literally blew up. I begged the doctors and the staff to get him to exercise and to check his heart but they ignored me.

Meanwhile, we tried to get him out of that place. Our only alternative was to get him completely out of the institutional setting. It meant he would have to live with one of us and have professional supervision. Larry and his new wife, Eleanor volunteered to have Andy live with them. What a beautiful gesture. I was so touched, especially that my new daughter-in-law, without hesitation, was open to the idea. In fact, Larry told me, she had suggested it!

They were expecting a baby—my grandson, Sean—and were looking for a bigger house. They would find one with a guest house or garage apartment for Andy and a possible caretaker. They found one. But the Westside Regional Center, which oversaw Andy's placement, balked at the plan because of a recent increase in violent behavior.

Ironic, huh? He was living in a place that was making him act out and because he was acting out they wouldn't let him leave. Andy still came home every few weeks for an overnight visit and never got aggressive or self-injurious. That should have proven that he would be fine living outside of that institution.

Soon Andy's weight ballooned to over 300 pounds and a doctor warned us that his body fat to weight ratio was severe and that he could suffocate in his sleep. We took him to a private doctor but we couldn't even get Andy to hold his breath long enough to take a chest X-ray. The doctor agreed that Andy should lose weight.

Finally, after nearly a year, the Westside Regional Center approved Andy's placement "in the community."

"Want to live in the meuw-nity," Andy would say incessantly.

And now, finally, it was going to happen! He spent a weekend at Larry's house with a caregiver from the regional center. A practice run for the rest of his life. Then he went back to Fairview Developmental Center and two nights later he died of a massive heart attack. December 9th 1999, nineteen days from his forty-fourth birthday.

I was working on my Christmas cards, sitting at my kitchen table with the TV on and the cable box tuned to some classical music. It was about 9:00 p.m. and the phone rang. I picked it up.

"Mrs. Strauss?"

"Yes."

"This is…" It was a doctor but I don't remember the name. What I do remember was, "…from Costa Mesa Developmental Center."

I said, "Is Andy okay?"

He didn't answer. He said, "Let me connect you to the nurse's station."

"Hello?"

Another voice. "Mrs. Strauss?"

"Yes? What is it? Is Andy all right?"

"We're so sorry, Mrs. Strauss, Andy just passed."

"What???"

"He was in his bed. He had a heart attack."


We were devastated. All of us. It was so sad. To have been so close to making a new life for Andy and then to lose him so suddenly.

Andy had always had a morbid sense of humor. Once when we were at Coney Island, he pointed to a white-haired old man on a bench and said, "Moldy." At Bronx State Hospital he would sometimes point at the bars on the windows and say, "Like monkeys in the zoo." Ever since John's father died—in 1968, when Andy was thirteen—he'd remind everyone: "Go visit Grandpa? No, Grandpa died." When a man in his unit at Camarillo died, it was, "Talk to Alvin? No, Alvin died." And so on. Maybe it was how he understood mortality. What happens to us and what it means.


John and I put together a memorial for Andy and had so many of our friends and family come to support us. So many people who'd known Andy over the years. We played Andy's music and remembered things about him. I danced the way I used to dance with him—like the time he had asked me to dance in the supermarket.

I think the whole ordeal took a big toll on John. Six months later he was in a nursing home. He lived there with his long-time partner, Lionel Friedman, who'd developed Parkinson's Disease. I visited the two of them regularly and brought them things. The three of us still shared holidays with Larry and his family. After Lionel died in 2003 I made more frequent visits to John to help him take the edge off his loneliness. Eventually he developed Parkinson's Disease also and became almost completely non-communicative with everyone. But I kept visiting. I used to sing to him sometimes and one time, out of nowhere, he mumbled, "You still have a beautiful voice." I still cry thinking about it. Such a sweet gesture from someone who can barely move. John passed away on Valentine's Day 2011, a few months from his ninety-first birthday.

Getting older means saying goodbye, celebrating people's lives after they're gone. And cherishing our friends who are still with us.

A few years ago my dear friend Joanne Worley and I got together and organized a luncheon with some of our contemporaries. Ann Jeffreys, Nancy Dussault, Karen Morrow, Miriam Nelson, Jane Kean, and Dee Stratton. We met at Cravings, a restaurant on the Sunset Strip with lots of disabled parking spaces. We had such a great time together that it became a regular thing. Once a month, the ladies who lunch meet for lunch. We're all at least sixty-plus and some are in their nineties. We talk about what's going on and tell funny stories, mostly from our experiences in the theater, and laugh our heads off. It's all very informal, casual, and it's always lovely to connect.

We've grown a bit, added a few other women, though we always try to keep our lunches to no more than twelve. We still meet at Cravings. It's a good location for everyone and not only do they have lots of parking for us old gals, they'll always do separate checks—a must!

I have so many blessings and so much that I'm proud of. Most of all, my children and grandchildren.

Andy, despite everything, touched many people. He got the most he could out of life. He did love and he did have joy and I'm so grateful for that.

Larry has made me so proud. He's the father of three. Carly, Sean, and Nora, who is his step-daughter but he thinks of her as his daughter. That's just how he is. His students are his children also. He became godfather to a young man whose parents wouldn't accept him being gay and that young man also calls him Dad. Larry works so hard but has always made sure he's there for his children.

He teaches at a high school in South Los Angeles where many of his students live below the poverty line and he helps them become the first in their family to graduate high school and go to college. He really cares about his students and does so many extra things for them. He brings food for the ones who don't get enough to eat at home and sometimes if they stay at school late he drives them home so they won't have to walk through the dangerous streets of their neighborhoods. He writes dozens of college recommendation letters and helps dozens of students write their personal statements for college and even helped a few of them pay for college.

He's also a very talented writer. He's written for television—including one episode of *The Facts of Life*—and he's been hired to write scripts and several of his novels were optioned for movies, though none of them were made. Not yet. He wrote a really beautiful story many years ago that I optioned when I had that development deal with Tandem and NBC and everyone liked it—except for the executive who made the final decision. It was called *Heartstrings* and it was about an unlikely love story caused by a heart transplant. One of the characters was an old Jewish song writer. His songs were corny but beautiful and around that time, for my birthday, Larry had his songwriter character, Sam, write this one for me:

> There is a lady with a very nice face
> You've seen it on TV but don't remember what place
> Simple things she likes, snobbery she ain't got a trace
> Good manners has she, to get an autograph she needn't chase
> Charlotte's a person to talk to
> She's a lady to trust
> Charlotte likes men as friends
> But don't think she's out of lust
> She worries a lot about little things
> And meditates until the telephone rings

Carly is also a teacher and also works with disadvantaged students. And she's so creative. She's a painter with such an original style and she makes things. She likes to recycle things into art or jewelry or clothes. But what I'm most proud of is the person she's become. Kind and conscientious and supportive of her friends and hard-working. It's not easy for young people these days. Not like when I came to New York and apartments were cheap. But Carly is out there living the life of the artist and making her art. I'm so proud of her—Larry and his former wife did a good job and I'm proud of them. I still get together with Angell sometimes. She's remarried to a terrific guy and they live in Torrance.

Sean is a teenager now. I can't believe it. I remember when my grandson was a bald-headed little fat baby. Now he's a lean six-footer who makes films, scores them with his own original music, plays drums and golf and skateboards through the city—carefully, I pray! And he's a good person. He really cares about people and about important things. He's got a lot of humanity, especially for a teenager.

I guess that comes from their parents. Larry and his beautiful wife, Eleanor. She's an anthropology professor but she's more than that. She really works hard for her students and helps them become better students. She was a high school teacher for many years and so she knows that not all students come to a class prepared and a lot of them are too timid to ask for help. When she's giving a long test, she bakes cookies for her class and helps them through it. And, let me tell you, she makes a hell of a batch of cookies. In one of her on-line classes, she had a student who had been deployed to Iraq and was in a pretty dangerous place. Somehow he managed to keep up with the class but one time he sent her an Email saying that his company had been taking hostile fire and an assignment might be late. She excused him, of course, and then sent him a batch of cookies. Most important, though, she's been a great mother to Sean and it shows. He's a really happy camper.

So is his sister, Eleanor's daughter, Nora. She lives with her wife in Boston and just got her MBA. Nora has worked for non-profit theaters since college. She's a talented actress in her own right but chose the business side of things and has been committed to the theater. Her wife, Katrina, works for an organization that helps underprivileged high school students apply for college and then helps them through college. They got married a few years ago and we all went to Boston for the wedding and what a beautiful time it was. Two beautiful young women tying the knot and I was so honored to be a part of Nora's gigantic modern family. We all had such a great time together and we all danced up a storm. Including little old me!

# STILL HERE

Where do all the years go? If you live long enough that question is hard to avoid. Sometimes I can't believe I'm still here. It's been a while now since I stopped dying my hair red. It happened one day when my hairdresser, Lucy, told me, "Oh, my golly, you've got a lot of gray in your hair." I told her to lose the red and see what happens. We washed out the color and it was a beautiful white, like a platinum blond. Like Jean Harlow. And why not? I'm grateful to be an old lady so I might as well be what I am.

But a still-*working* old lady. As long as I'm still getting offers, why not? I do voice-overs and play readings and small parts in movies and on TV shows. Mostly I get to play old ladies in hospital rooms. I'm still available for singing gigs with my one-woman show or bits and pieces of it. I did it a few years ago at the Plush Room in San Francisco. And I always try to make myself available for performing benefits, especially for The Actor's Fund.

I've always thought it was a miracle that I was able to make a living as an actress being so short. So many of the actors I've admired are so tall. I feel like a midget amidst them. Of course, now that I play old ladies—and am an old lady—it doesn't matter so much how tall I am.

What does matter is that I have the best agents I ever had. Todd Justice and Rodney Ponder in L.A. and Paul Hilepo in New York. They are all terrific. Always looking for work for me. They work really hard even if it's just to get me small parts—like the one I just played in *Ricky and the Flash* with Meryl Streep directed by Jonathan Demme. They are the absolute best in the business.

I still attend my AA meetings and try to help myself by helping others with their sobriety. I say the serenity prayer all the time. I say a lot of prayers. For the people I love, including my fellow alcoholics, and sometimes for the whole world. We live in frightening times. I guess we always have. And sometimes I ask others to pray for me.

Like when I had open heart surgery to replace my mitral valve. The doctors saved my life but they had to crack open my chest to do it (now, of course, they can do that surgery laparoscopically). The doctor recommended a pig or cow valve. He said it's what he would want for his own mother. But my old friend, actor Robby Benson, warned me.

He'd had the surgery and said the animal valve had been a disaster for him and he'd had to replace it with a mechanical one. So I insisted on a mechanical valve. It's still working.

I take blood thinning medicine now. During the mitral valve surgery, doctors cleaned out my left carotid artery, that's the one that delivers blood to the brain. The doctor said it was 90% clogged but they got in there in time and I'm still here. They also added a defibrillator to my pacemaker.

There's been plenty of drama over the years with my pacemaker. Don't get me wrong, I love my little electric jump-starter—and defibrillator they added on. But it runs on a battery and I'm glad to say I've outlived a few of those batteries.

I'm an eternally grateful cancer survivor. What a miracle. Returning to my hometown as a celebrity to talk about pancreatic cancer. I was asked by a group of Milwaukee oncologists and surgeons and PanCan—the Pancreatic Cancer Action Network. They knew that my mother and sister had died of pancreatic cancer in Milwaukee. So I went there to go on radio and television and make a personal appearance to talk about the importance of early screening—annually—especially for those who come from a family that has lost people to pancreatic cancer. I asked them if my sister, Mimi, and I could get the screening test—endoscopic ultrasound—while we were there and they thought that was a great idea and set it up for us at one of the hospitals.

Mimi got a clean bill of pancreatic health. I was told I had two cysts. I asked to have them examined and a few days later they did another endoscopic ultrasound and took out samples of the tumors and concluded that they were benign. They said to have them looked at again in six months. I scheduled a follow-up in L.A. six months later but foolishly cancelled it because I didn't like the doctor and waited another six months until I returned to Milwaukee to promote pancreatic cancer awareness again. By then I had a stage three malignant tumor in the tail of my pancreas.

I immediately flew back to L.A. and my son, Larry took me to see what could be done and it was a miracle. The same diagnosis that had overwhelmed Mother and Beverly was now—years later—caught early enough to be diagnosable and treatable. "Operable," my doctor said. A surgeon could remove the cancer. Chemotherapy could blast away any chance of cancer spreading to any other part of my body.

I asked my dear friend Jackie, who had miraculously survived her own cancer of the esophagus, to stand by me with her strong faith in God. I had my own strong faith and I wanted to hold onto her faith as well. I needed all the support I could get. I asked my dear friend, Tyne Daly if there was any way I could talk to her friend, the great opera singer Marilyn Horne, who was also a pancreatic cancer survivor. Tyne didn't hesitate to give me Marilyn's number and tell her that I would call.

We had a lovely conversation and Marilyn was so helpful. I told her how terrified I was. My exact words were, "I'm scared shitless about the surgery."

She said, "I know what you mean." Then she told me she'd gone to a hypnotherapist to help her overcome that fear. She gave me the name and contact info and urged me to contact her. What a wonderful piece of advice that turned out to be. Cheryl O'Neil was her name and she was just what I needed. She helped me with positive imagery. She gave me a CD to use on my own and helped me tremendously to feel secure and calm and positive when I went in for the surgery.

Now Marilyn and I are friends and I have such admiration for her. She's a great artist and an even better human being.

My surgeon, Dr. Howard Reber, was the best. So was the anesthesiologist and everyone else at UCLA Medical Center. Jackie and I stayed close through the surgery and the next six months of the chemo sessions. My hair began falling out so I had Lucy shave it off. She made me a really beautiful white wig. I took pills for digestion and the imagery was enormously helpful too. My oncologist sent me to a nutritionist who helped me with my diet post-surgery and to help me figure out the best way to eat at this time in my life.

Jackie and her husband, Dean, came with me for my first post-surgery visit to the oncologist, Dr. Isacoff. They took notes and reassured me that I was going to pull through. My last chemo was on April 22nd, 2010, my eighty-fourth birthday. I was cancer free!

Since then I've tried to do my share for others trying to survive pancreatic cancer, making personal monetary contributions and helping to raise money for pancreatic cancer research. Along with the Actor's Fund, PanCan is my passion. Every June I go along with PanCan members from all fifty states (more than five-hundred of us all together) to the Capitol building in Washington D.C. for three days and speak to our senators and congressional reps and lobby them for additional research funds. Our nation spends more than three billion dollars a year on breast cancer research and almost one and-a-half billion on prostate cancer research and I'm all for that—but we spend but a tiny fraction of that amount on finding prevention and cure for pancreatic cancer and we intend to help improve that figure.

Cancer is a terrible disease but it isn't always a fatal diagnosis, and it doesn't have to always be. So many of us who've survived it are determined not only to defeat it in our own bodies but in people all over the world.

I don't know what the future holds in store for me. Just recently, I blacked out and fell on the floor of my kitchen. I banged up my nose and my left temple but somehow managed not to break any bones. I got up light-headed and thought it was from vertigo, which I'd had a month before but just in case I made an appointment with my ENT guy, Dr. Finnerman, for first thing Monday morning.

He checked me out. No, it wasn't vertigo. He told me it was circulatory. Fortunately, my cardiologist, Dr. Chaikin, was down the hall from Dr. Finnerman. Dr. Chaikin was remarkable. He diagnosed the problem immediately—the lead wire in my pacemaker.

I got right on the phone and called Bill Barnett from Medronic and I told him what was happening. Bill has been with me ever since my first pacemaker. He's a great guy and I really trust him and I wanted him to be in on what was happening.

Then I drove to the clinic. They tested the pacemaker and said it was okay. I told them I didn't feel right. They told me to dance around a little. I did—and the pacemaker died. The lead—the wire from the device to my heart—had stopped carrying the electric charge. My heart was making 35 beats per minute and there was no pacemaker to help it.

It was my worst fear. Doctors were baffled about what to do next. They'd gone in and replaced and modified things so many times they didn't think they could attach any new leads in that pacemaker and they didn't think I'd be able to have another surgery to fix anything.

Thank God that's not how it turned out.

The doctors did an X-ray to be sure there wasn't any bleeding in my brain from when I fell and then rushed me into surgery. They didn't even bother removing the non-functioning pacemaker on my left side. They just plunged into the right side of my chest and installed a new one.

The pacemakers, it turned out, had become much better—smaller and less invasive and more efficient.

A miracle! That one doctor was just down the hall from the other doctor, who was also in his office and could see me right away, and then called the pacemaker clinic and got the specialist, who was also available and could get me right onto an operating table in a busy hospital.

My dear friend, Betty Winslow was there with me through it all and Larry joined us as soon as he could get there. It's so important to have people with you to look out for you in those situations, angels in your life when you need them. And I have to say that finding such a close friend as Betty so late in life, that's something really special. All my friends are special to me. Betty and Ruthie now, but all my friends throughout my life.

I guess I really am a survivor. Cancer and now I've outlived my own pacemaker, survived long enough to get a new and improved pacemaker. Within a few hours I was in the hospital and the surgical team had been assembled. Next thing I knew I was out cold, then I woke up. A new person filled with joy and laughter and profound gratitude.

The doctors told me later that my first words as I came to were, "I'm alive!" Then I thanked them and told them, "I love you all. God bless you!" That's how I always wake up from surgery. At least that's what all the doctors have told me.

It's how I want to wake up to each day. Full of gratitude and love.

And wherever I go after my last day—whenever that is, hopefully not too soon—I hope I go there with the same outlook, a spirit of joy and wonder, gratitude and love.

# Charlotte Rae – Career Highlights

**Television:**
US Steel Hour (1954)
Armstrong Circle Theater (1954)
NBC Opera (1955)
Philco-Goodyear Television Playhouse (1955)
DuPont Show of the Month: Harvey (1958)
The Phil Silvers Show (1955-58)
Play of the Week: The World of Sholom Alechem (1959)
Car 54, Where Are You? (1961-63)
Girl Talk (1963-67)
DuPont Show of the Week: Hold-Up! (1963)
New York Television Theater: The Immovable Gordons (1966)
New York Television Theater: Apple Pie (1968)
Sesame Street (1971-72)
The Partridge Family (1972)
McMillan and Wife (1972)
Love American Style (1972)
The Paul Lynde Show (1972)
All in the Family (1974)
Good Times (1974)
Queen of the Stardust Ballroom (1975) Emmy nomination
Hot L Baltimore (1975)
Phyllis (1976)
Barney Miller (1976)
The Rich Little Show (1976)
All's Fair (1976)
Szysznyk (1978)
Family (1978)
The Eddie Capra Mysteries (1978)
Diff'rent Strokes (1978-79)
Hello Larry (1978-79)
The Facts of Life (1979-1986) Emmy nomination
The Love Boat (1982-85)
The New Hollywood Squares (1986-89)
St. Elsewhere (1987)
Murder, She Wrote (1987)
227 (1989)

Baby Talk (1991)
Thunder in Paradise (1994)
Sisters (1994-95)
The Secret World of Alex Mack (1995)
Can't Hurry Love (1995)
101 Dalmations: The Series (1997-98)
Diagnosis Murder (2000)
Strong Medicine (2004)
The King of Queens (2005)
ER (2008)
Life (2009)
Pretty Little Liars (2011)
Girl Meets World (2014)

**Film:**
Jenny (1970)
Bananas (1971)
The Hot Rock (1972)
Sidewinder 1 (1977)
Hair (1979)
You Don't Mess with the Zohan (2008)
Thomas Kinkade's Christmas Cottege (2008)
Love Sick Love (2012)
Ricki and the Flash (2015)

**Broadway:**
Three Wishes for Jamie (1952)
Three Penny Opera (1954)
The Golden Apple (1954)
The Littlest Revue (1956)
Li'l Abner (1956)
The Beauty Part (1962)
Pickwick (1965) *Tony nomination*
Morning, Noon and Night (1969) *Tony nomination*
The Chinese and Dr. Fish (1970)
In the Boom Boom Room (1973)

**Off-Broadway:**
Happy Days (Beckett)
70, Girl, 70

Vagina Monologues

**Regional and Touring Companies:**
Into the Woods
Solid Gold Cadillac
Driving Miss Daisy

**Shakespeare in the Park:**
Henry IV, Part 1 and 2 (with Stacy Keach and Sam Waterston)
Romeo and Juliet (with Martin Sheen)

**Record Albums:**
Rogers and Hart Revisited
Songs I Taught My Mother

# Acknowledgements

There are so many people to thank, I don't know where to begin. Thanks, of course, to my son, Larry Strauss for all his hard work helping to get my memories and thoughts down on paper and thanks to our agent, Jennifer DeChiara, for believing in this book and working so hard to make it happen. Thank you to Ben Ohmart and Bearmanor Media for their enthusiasm and patience.

Of course, I have to thank my dear younger sister, Mimi—so talented and loving and supportive—and with a terrific memory for our childhood and other things I relied on writing this book. And her son, my nephew, Dennis Guten who helped me with some of the family photographs. Thanks, also, to my cousin, Daniel Ottenstein, who also helped with family photos, and James Dybas who helped with theatrical photos. And my dear friends, Betty Winslow and Jim Brochu and to Jennifer Hanson—for lending their eyes and insights to the process of writing this book. And thanks always to my dear, hard-working personal assistant, Diane Sweet.

But it doesn't stop there. So many people have supported me throughout my life and throughout this process with inspiration, love, and kindness.

Miss Bubeck, my social studies teacher who inspired me to want to do something to make the world better and made me realize the value in writing.

My college acting teacher—who also directed me in NU productions of *Twelfth Night* and *Three Penny Opera*—Margaret Webster. My voice teacher, Amelia Haas. My trainer and nutritionist, Kathleen Villela.

My sponsors in Alcoholics Anonymous, Marjorie P. and Ruth K. And all the members of AA.

And my former husband, John Strauss, may he rest in peace. Always my biggest supporter—before, during, and after our marriage—and the best accompanist I ever had.

Nancy, Lisa, Kim, and Mindy and all the other wonderful actors with whom I've had the honor of working over the years. And Norman Lear and all the terrific writers on his shows—and all the other terrific writers. What do we have to say without the writers?

And my theatrical agents, the best agents I've ever had. Todd Justice, Rodney Ponder and Paul Hilepo.

My doctors, of course—I wouldn't be here without them. Dr. Chai-kin, Dr. Shehata, Dr, Reber. And Bill Barnett, the technician from Medtronic (the pacemaker company). He keeps me ticking.

My lifelong dear friends in the business and beyond—always there for me: Jane Cecil, Faith Strong, Jerry Stiller, Ann Meara, Charles Durning, Alan Mandell, Jack Rollins, John Bowab, Patricia Morrison, Carl Reiner, Sheldon Harnick, Dan Lipman and Ron Cowan, Barbara Jansen, Bruce Vilanch, Larry Pressman, David Galligan, Ted Snowden, his partner, Duffy, Ted Seifman, Al Frantz, Barry Moss and David Staller.

And all my new friends and fellow cancer survivors who've been so supportive to me and appreciative of my support of them, especially Jackie Stolber, her husband Dean Stolber and the great singer Marilyn Horne; Kitty Swink and her husband, Roberta Luna and her husband, Vic, Ralph Cheney and his wife, Marian; fellow actor, Armin Shimerman, and everyone else I've gotten to know through the Pancreatic Action Network (www.pancan.org).

And here's to you—reader, fan, audience, fellow traveler on this crazy adventure called life.

## About the Author

Larry Strauss is the author of four novels, most recently *Now's the Time*, as well as numerous works of non-fiction on a wide range of subjects. He and his wife have two adult daughters, one in Los Angeles, the other in Boston, and a teenage son with whom they live in Los Angeles, just a few miles from granny Charlotte (Rae).

CPSIA information can be obtained
at www.ICGtesting.com
Printed in the USA
LVHW081932180420
653966LV00028B/433

9 781593 938529